FORMULA ONE
CIRCUITS FROM ABOVE

First published in 2014
Second Edition 2016

Carlton Books
Carlton Publishing Group
20 Mortimer Street
London W1T 3JW

Managing Editor: Martin Corteel
Design Manager: Luke Griffin
Production Manager: Lisa Cook

A CIP catalogue for this book is available from the British Library.

ISBN 978-1-78097-839-0

Printed and bound in China

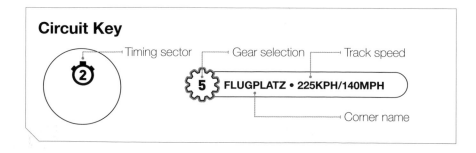

Circuit Key

Timing sector — Gear selection — Track speed

2

5 FLUGPLATZ • 225KPH/140MPH

Corner name

FORMULA ONE
CIRCUITS FROM ABOVE

SECOND EDITION

BRUCE JONES

CARLTON
BOOKS

Designed with

Google Earth

Contents

Page 3: The Autodromo Hermanos Rodriguez in Mexico City made a welcome return to the World Championship in 2015

Opposite: Sepang's 15 spectacular corners and 5.5km (3.4-mile) track never fails to provide drivers, and spectators, with a nail-biting Malaysian Grand Prix.

McLaren's Jenson Button dives into Turn 3 at Marina Bay Circuit in the 2013 Singapore Grand Prix.

Introduction

Any fan of motor racing is sure to have a favourite racing circuit. It might be Monza, Monaco or Spa-Francorchamps, favoured because of a mighty corner, a sequence of bends, their special ambience, because their favourite driver or team won there or simply because that was where they first saw and heard a Formula One car being driven at full tilt. The beauty of this is that these and 27 other circuits featured in this book are the greatest circuits raced on since the World Championship began in 1950 and they are all so different, all with very much a character of their own.

In all, the World Championship has held grands prix at 71 circuits across 30 countries through its 66-year history, but the 28 circuits chosen for this book – spread across the planet from Argentina to France, Mexico to the United States of America – represent the cream of the crop. Silverstone, Monaco, Spa-Francorchamps and Monza have stood the test of time from that inaugural World Championship, so it's intriguing to look at how they compare with the very latest additions to the roster in Bahrain, Singapore, Abu Dhabi and the United States. Their histories could not be more different, as the long-standing circuits have been raced on by all of the sport's top names, from Juan Manuel Fangio to Jim Clark and Ayrton Senna to Michael Schumacher, each adding their own layer of history, while the newer circuits have been the domain thus far of Sebastian Vettel, Fernando Alonso and Lewis Hamilton.

Working in conjunction with Google's amazing Google Earth photography, this book shows these circuits as never before, with its pin-sharp satellite photography picking out the details that are seldom or never seen on television, showing clearly from above not only every twist and turn of the circuit but how each circuit sits in its landscape or weaves through a town, as with Adelaide, Monaco and Singapore. You can pick out the F1 pitlane and paddock, the control tower and grandstands and, by adding corner names, gears and speeds, you will have a fantastic viewing guide for when the World Championship next visits, hopefully adding to your enjoyment of the world's fastest moving and most cosmopolitan sport. To give you an even better understanding of what it must be like for the drivers, I've highlighted the eight key corners from each of the selected circuits and explained the particular challenge that each of them provides. The Becketts sweeper at Silverstone stands out, as does Parabolica at Monza, the first two corners at Sepang and the esses at the Circuit of the Americas.

For a number of the circuits, I've also picked out a quartet of the great races held there and highlighted the four drivers who have reaped the greatest results there across the decades. With a record 91 wins to his name, Michael Schumacher has, as you would imagine, an entry alongside many of the circuits.

The passage of the decades, but more importantly the continual progress in building ever faster cars, has led to circuits being modified to ensure the safety of the spectators as well as the drivers, with straw bales being replaced by crash barriers and debris fencing, chicanes being inserted and gravel traps or asphalt run-off areas added over the years. Corners have been altered too or the circuit cut and reshaped, as happened so comprehensively at Hockenheim when its forest loop was truncated in 2002. To show the march of time and safety standards, it was awarded the German GP full time back in 1977 after Niki Lauda's near-fatal accident on the 23km (14-mile), 176-corner Nordschleife to convince the championship organizers that driver safety really ought to be considered, and the German GP passed to Hockenheim. To some die-hard fans, this was seen as removing F1's character, but the fact that drivers stopped perishing every month was a definite bonus. New for this edition is another safer version of what went before it: the Red Bull Ring.

This book highlights how the World Championship has reversed its heavily European bias that lasted until the 1980s, as marked by the arrival of grands prix in Malaysia, China, South Korea, Bahrain, Singapore and Abu Dhabi. It also charts the odyssey to find a true home for the US GP after long-time base Watkins Glen was outmoded and an infield circuit at the Indianapolis Motor Speedway failed to hit the target; the race reached its 10th venue in 2012, the wonderful, tailor-made Circuit of the Americas.

Bruce Jones,
March 2016

Below: The spectacular Circuit of the Americas is the latest home of the United States GP.

Spectators on luxury motor yachts and balconies line the track at Tabac during the 2013 Monaco GP.

Chapter 1
Europe

Spa-Francorchamps

This amazing road circuit, rising and falling through the hills of the Ardennes forests, has been part of the World Championship since its inauguration in 1950 and continues to provide one of the sternest challenges that the drivers face all year.

> " I've had lots of great times at Spa. It's been the place virtually every highlight of my career took place: my first race, my first win and my seventh world title. "
>
> *Michael Schumacher*

There can be no escaping the fact that Spa-Francorchamps is a proper circuit, one that has a character of its own, shaped by the landscape rather than by a circuit designer's hand. It is very much part of the hills and forests that it bisects, a hugely challenging stretch of blacktop that offers one of the most distinctive settings visited by the World Championship each year. Add to that its rich and occasionally tragic history, and it has a character very much of its own; even today it is a place that needs to be shown respect.

Two-time World Champion Jim Clark was a driver who appeared to have the measure of every track that he raced on, but he would famously fear and hate the place, something that was reinforced on his first outing there by the death of compatriot Archie Scott-Brown in a sportscar race they were contesting in 1958. This was Clark's first brush with death and it affected him deeply.

The circuit started life in 1921, when a triangular course laid out to the south of the village of Francorchamps was used for the first time in a race for motorbikes. The riders had to race over the hill into the next valley to Malmedy before travelling along the valley floor, then turn right near Stavelot and start the climb back to complete the 15km (9.2 mile) lap at what is now the La Source hairpin. A year later, car racers had their first crack at it and, with long straights and many sections threaded through the forest, it was no place for the timid because there were no barriers to contain the cars. Making matters all the more potentially dangerous, rain would often sweep in, with the added difficulty that it would frequently hit only one part of this spread-out circuit so that the track might be bone dry around the pits but soaking wet over by the fearsome Masta Kink, where drivers had to stay as hard on the throttle as they dared while the track flicked left, then right between some houses.

Over the years, little changed other than the reprofiling of some of the corners to make them less severe. What made the place all the more awesome was the hugely high speeds that were maintained around much of the lap, with BRM driver Pedro Rodriguez's winning average speed in the 1970 Belgian GP being a fraction under 240kph (150mph). Worried by this, the organizers relocated the grand prix to Nivelles and then Zolder, both bland but infinitely safer circuits.

The only way back for Spa-Francorchamps was to cut its lap length, axing the entire section in the next valley and to join the outward leg with the inward one via a new section of circuit that turned right at Les Combes and then dropped down the hill to rejoin the original course again before Blanchimont.

That was in 1979, with the lap being reduced to 6.9km (4.3 miles), and the grand prix returned in 1983. The changes reduced Alain Prost's winning average lap speed in his Renault to 191kph (119mph). Since then, there have been some tweaks to the circuit, most frequently at the Bus Stop chicane at the end of the lap, but the essence of Spa remains the same. Speeds have crept up again and Sebastian Vettel's winning average for Red Bull in 2013 was 220kph (137mph).

The stand-out corners are the sharply rising and twisting Eau Rouge, the long straight for slipstreaming that follows it up to Les Combes, then the downhill, double-apex Pouhon and the flat-out uphill lefthander on the return leg called Blanchimont. It's a circuit that offers a fabulous flow for the drivers, with enough width for them to attempt to overtake.

Spa-Francorchamps is vital for its place in F1's long and varied history, as one of only four circuits used in that first World Championship in 1950 and still on F1's calendar today, along with Silverstone, Monaco and Monza. However, it's also vital to F1 because it proves that modern F1 cars can still go racing, and race well, on a circuit that was not designed on a computer. For photographers, of course, with its spectacular, natural backdrops, it's also a rare joy. ∎

Opposite: Spa-Francorchamps' majestic descent from La Source past the old pits and then into the compression at Eau Rouge.

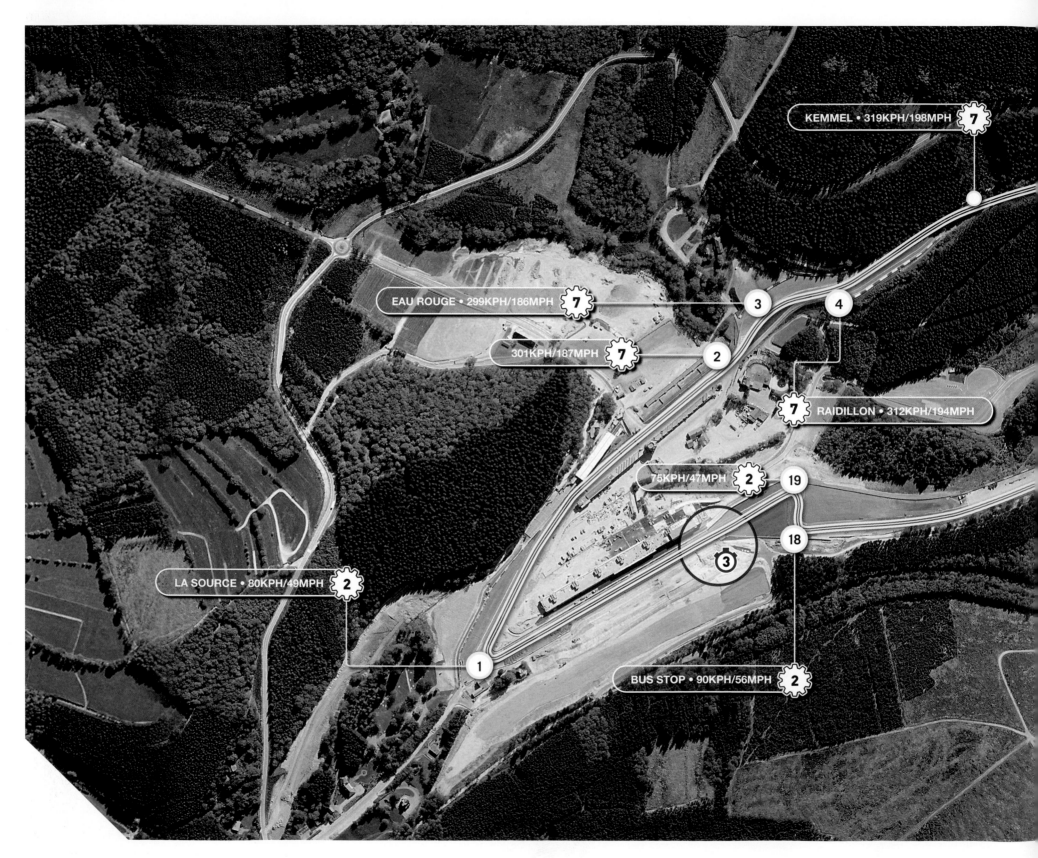

KEMMEL • 319KPH/198MPH **7**

EAU ROUGE • 299KPH/186MPH **7** **3** **4**

301KPH/187MPH **7** **2**

7 RAIDILLON • 312KPH/194MPH

75KPH/47MPH **2** **19**

18

3

LA SOURCE • 80KPH/49MPH **2**

1

BUS STOP • 90KPH/56MPH **2**

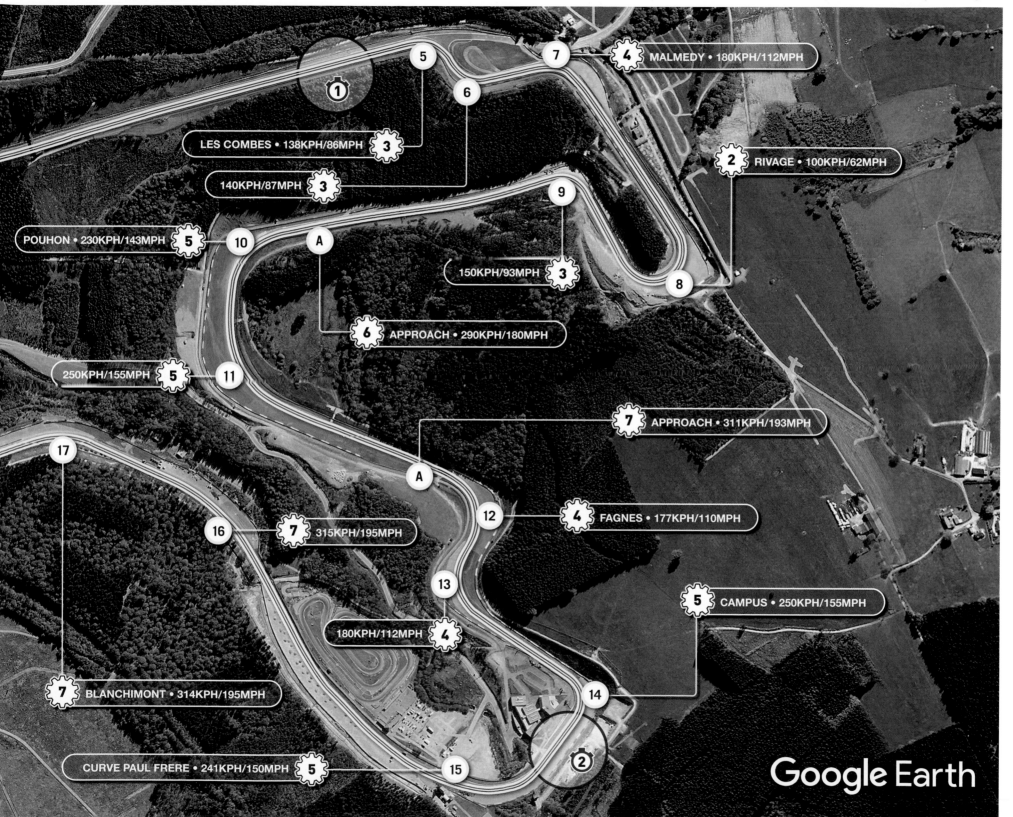

MALMEDY • 180KPH/112MPH

RIVAGE • 100KPH/62MPH

LES COMBES • 138KPH/86MPH

140KPH/87MPH

POUHON • 230KPH/143MPH

150KPH/93MPH

APPROACH • 290KPH/180MPH

250KPH/155MPH

APPROACH • 311KPH/193MPH

FAGNES • 177KPH/110MPH

315KPH/195MPH

CAMPUS • 250KPH/155MPH

180KPH/112MPH

BLANCHIMONT • 314KPH/195MPH

CURVE PAUL FRERE • 241KPH/150MPH

Google Earth

Image © 2014 Aerodata International Surveys © Google 2014

Circuit Guide

Belgium's Spa-Francorchamps is a wonderfully organic mix of everything that a racing circuit needs. It has high-speed corners, medium-speed corners and tight ones. It has incline, camber and long straights for trying to pull off a passing move, all with a beautiful backdrop.

Turn 1 • La Source
Gear: **2**
Speed: **80kph (49mph)**

Having a hairpin as the opening corner of the lap, which has been the case since 1984, when it was moved there from its original position on the downhill slope to Eau Rouge, means that Spa-Francorchamps has had its share of incident over the years. After the short sprint to reach it from the starting grid, drivers have to decide whether to be fast in on the inside line or go in wide and be fast out for the blast towards Eau Rouge. There's an escape road straight ahead.

Turn 2/3 • Eau Rouge
Gear: **7**
Speed: **299kph (186mph)**

This right/left flick is renowned throughout the racing world because it's made a corner to reckon with by its dipping approach being followed immediately by the steepest of inclines, compressing the cars' suspension. Once fabled as a turn that only the brave would take flat-out, it's now less of a challenge due to superior aerodynamics and levels of grip, but it remains a tough corner because it's taken in seventh and momentum out of here is magnified up the long straight that follows.

Turn 5 • Les Combes
Gear: **3**
Speed: **138kph (86mph)**

This is the point at which the circuit was made to turn right when it was almost halved in length in 1979. It now marks the end of a long uphill straight from Raidillon and drivers can attempt a passing manoeuvre here if they can get a good enough tow up the hill. Braking hard from almost 320kph (200mph), the drivers then have to get their car into the righthander and position it almost immediately for a sharp left that follows on the brow of the hillside.

Turn 8 • Rivage
Gear: **2**
Speed: **100kph (62mph)**

The circuit dips gently from Les Combes towards the righthander called Malmedy and then the slope steepens noticeably as it tips the cars down the hill towards Rivage. This is a second-gear, double-apex righthander with trees running down its outer flank on the way in and a steep earth bank on the inside. Drivers have to balance their cars on the way in so that they can accelerate as soon as possible and continue their descent through the faster left flick that follows.

Opposite: Juan Pablo Montoya noses his Williams inside Michael Schumacher's Ferrari at the Bus Stop in 2004. ***Above left:*** Schumacher leads Jarno Trulli's Renault and Felipe Massa's Sauber out of La Source, also in 2004.
Above right: A view down through the trees to the pitlane, with the La Source hairpin visible in the background.

Turn 10 • **Pouhon**
Gear: **6**
Speed: **230kph (143mph)**

Continuing down the slope from Rivage, the drivers gain a feeling of space down this wide stretch of track as they look back towards the control tower above the pits that lie straight ahead to the north. What they can see in front of them is the first part of a two-part corner, and it's a great place to see an Formula one car and its driver really put to work as they attempt to carry their speed through its broad, double-apex format.

Turn 15 • **Curve Paul Frere**
Gear: **5**
Speed: **241kph (150mph)**

This righthander marks the lowest point of the lap and it's the point at which the infield loop inserted in 1979 feeds the cars back on to what was previously the long, flat-out blast from Stavelot to the completion of the lap. The turn is taken in fifth gear after the short dash from Campus, and it's essential that drivers don't scrub off any of this speed because they will be able to carry any momentum up the hill. The corner is named after 1950s racer journalist Paul Frere.

Turn 17 • **Blanchimont**
Gear: **7**
Speed: **314kph (195mph)**

Most of the flat-out straights which F1 drivers fly along these days are wide open in nature. Not so this uphill stretch of track. It has a bank of trees on the slope rising behind the barriers on the drivers' left and just thin air beyond the barriers to the right as the ground drops away towards the river that runs down the valley. Pushing on at 314kph (195mph) through this lefthand kink, drivers know that they have to balance their turn-in, or they might run wide with horrible consequences.

Turn 18/19 • **Bus Stop**
Gear: **2**
Speed: **90kph (56mph)**

Introduced in 1980 to slow the cars before they complete their flat-out blast back up the hill to the La Source hairpin, this strangely named corner has generally been a sequence of lefts and rights, and drivers bouncing across the kerbs of these has been the norm. Most recently, it has been simplified into a one-part corner, with just a tight right followed by a left whereas it was for years a left/right followed by a short straight and then a right/left.

Great Drivers & Great Moments

Spa-Francorchamps is a circuit that has always been a considerable challenge to both man and machine. Throw in the added difficulty of the often unpredictable weather, and you have a recipe for thrills, spills and excitement. It's a place that yields only to the very best drivers and seldom fails to add a twist to the tail.

Great Drivers

Michael **Schumacher**
Spa wins – 6

Schumacher's record number of wins at Spa-Francorchamps started with his first grand prix victory. This was in 1992, one year precisely after his F1 debut and he read changing conditions best to win for Benetton. He then added three wins in a row from 1995, the first with Benetton, then the next two for Ferrari before crashing into the rear of David Coulthard's McLaren in atrociously wet conditions in 1998 when way in the lead. Two more wins for Ferrari, in 2001 and 2002, complete his haul.

Ayrton **Senna**
Spa wins – 5

Delayed by a broken-up track in 1985, the Belgian grand prix was run later in the year and Ayrton Senna won for Lotus on a drying track. It then became a very happy hunting ground for the Brazilian: he won at Spa four years in succession for McLaren from 1988. This run could have been longer still because he'd been taken out of the lead by a clash with Nigel Mansell in 1987, then gambled wrongly on staying on slicks in the rain in 1992.

Jim **Clark**
Spa wins – 4

The most remarkable thing about the Scot's four wins here is that he loathed the place, considering it to be unacceptably dangerous, as proved by the 1960 Belgian GP when two drivers were injured in practice and two killed in the race. However, Jim Clark put his fears aside to win four years in a row for Lotus from 1962 to 1965. He would have won again in 1967, but it was only the second race for the new Ford DFV and he had to pit because the spark plugs needed changing.

Kimi **Raikkonen**
Spa wins – 4

History relates that only the very best drivers win at Spa-Francorchamps and Kimi's record of four victories bears this out. The Finn first won here for McLaren in 2004 in a chaotic race of six leaders and three safety car periods and then added another the following year, by almost 30 seconds. He then changed teams to Ferrari yet kept on winning on F1's next visit in 2007. His final win, also for Ferrari, came in 2009, but only by less than 1 second from Giancarlo Fisichella's Force India.

Great Moments

1952 Alberto **Ascari** starts a nine-race winning run

Alberto Ascari missed the opening round of the 1952 World Championship because he was preparing for the Indianapolis 500. However, he made his first outing in Ferrari's new F2-based challenger count and, after getting past Jean Behra's fast-starting Gordini on the opening lap, led all the way in heavy rain. He then won the next eight grands prix in a sequence that included the five remaining races of the 1952 season and the first three of the next to net him both drivers' titles.

1998 David **Coulthard** triggers a first lap pile-up

Every driver racing at Spa knows that the first corner can spell trouble, as there's only a short blast from the grid to La Source. In 1998, on a wet track, the drivers managed not to collide going into the hairpin, but David Coulthard lost traction on the wide exit, his McLaren spearing to its right and setting off a chain reaction involving 13 cars, which forced the race to be restarted. Damage was so heavy that four cars were unable to take the second start.

2008 Felipe **Massa** given win as **Hamilton** disqualified

Lewis Hamilton held a six-point lead over Ferrari's Felipe Massa, then drove a blinder at Spa, coming out on top of a frantic battle with Kimi Raikkonen in the other Ferrari, until the Finn spun off. However, the stewards then penalized the McLaren driver 25 seconds for cutting the Bus Stop chicane when fighting for the lead. Although he immediately relinquished the position to Raikkonen, he outbraked the Ferrari into the next corner and this is what earned him the penalty and handed victory to Massa.

2015 Teenager **Verstappen** causes intake of breath

Tyre failures were the talk of the paddock in 2015 and the record books show that Lewis Hamilton led home Nico Rosberg for a Mercedes one–two. However, in years to come, what F1 fans will remember most is Max Verstappen's incredibly brave move to pass Marcus Ericsson's Sauber at Blanchimont. This is a corner taken at nigh on 190mph, but the Dutch rookie simply pointed his Toro Rosso around the outside and went for it. His natural flare belied the fact that he had yet to turn 18.

▌▌Magny-Cours

This is a circuit that deserves a far better reputation than it enjoys and the reality is that its disappearance from the World Championship calendar and France's grand prix with it, was mainly down to the fact that it was located in the middle of nowhere, too rural to be loved.

❝ Magny-Cours can be quite a challenging track to set up for because its characteristics change a lot, probably more so than at most other circuits. ❞
Kimi Raikkonen

When Magny-Cours opened in 1961, no one would have imagined that it would become France's premier racing circuit, the home to the French GP. However, this is what happened due, largely, to politics.

Built outside the town of Nevers some 240km (150 miles) south of Paris, it's safe to say that it was a venue destined for nothing more than hosting club racing and, at best, rounds of France's national racing championships as well as becoming home to the Winfield Racing School that was the starting point for almost all of the stars of the future. Its only real link to the World Championship was that it was called the Circuit Jean Behra, named after France's mercurial but fated star of the 1950s.

In 1968, Magny-Cours also became the base for Martini Racing Cars, which used the track as a handy testing venue for its latest single-seaters that were so popular in the junior French championships. Indeed, this is how the circuit operated, even after 1971, when its lap was all but doubled in length at the suggestion of the local mayor. This was achieved by the addition of a long, thin loop that made the track turn left where it had doubled back on itself at a hairpin and then fed the cars through a very long righthander onto a lengthy back straight up a gentle slope to the distant Adelaide hairpin. Not that it was called that then, as the corner names that include Estoril, Nürburgring and Imola were added in the

late 1980s, when the circuit gained international aspirations. The return leg of this new loop returned the cars to the original circuit at the exit of the hairpin from which it had been rerouted.

What happened next was a matter of political expediency. President Mitterand put his weight behind developing the extremely rural Nevers region ahead of a national election and allocated considerable resources for the development of Magny-Cours, allowing the rebuilding of the circuit, with the old pit and paddock complex on the infield of the circuit on the descent from Château d'Eau being demolished and a new one built on the outside of the circuit after the next corner, Lycée. To help boost local employment opportunities, an industrial estate was built outside the circuit gates to operate as a hub for the French motor sport industry and its associated suppliers, with the jewel in its crown being the fact that this development attracted France's only F1 team of the time, Ligier, to move there.

The final piece in its transformation came in 1991, when it took over the hosting of the French GP from the Paul Ricard circuit in the south of the country. The teams and drivers were impressed by its super-smooth surface and its mixture of corner types, although some felt that there weren't enough fast corners. What Magny-Cours did have, though, was a fail-safe overtaking spot, with drivers able to line

up slipstreaming moves into the Adelaide hairpin, so the racing was almost inevitably exciting, at that part of the lap at least. In fact, it was considered by many to be the circuit's only overtaking spot.

What F1 insiders didn't like, though, was the circuit's isolation, which meant that hotels were few and far between, meaning that many team personnel had undesirably lengthy commutes to the circuits. This rural location also limited the number of spectators, something that was perhaps a matter for which those present had reason to be thankful, as access to the circuit itself was through just one gate.

Nigel Mansell won Magny-Cours' inaugural grand prix for Williams, a feat that he repeated in 1992 before Alain Prost took his ride for 1993 and gave the crowd a home winner.

The French GP remained at Magny-Cours until 2008, when Ferrari's Felipe Massa was the final winner in what has remained the country's final grand prix. There is talk of the French GP being revived and perhaps returning to the modernized Paul Ricard, leaving Magny-Cours back once more with its original diet of club and national racing series. ■

Opposite: Kimi Raikkonen punches the air with delight after powering out of the final corner to win for Ferrari in 2007.

LYCEE PIN • 89KPH/55MPH **2**

APPROACH • 286KPH/178MPH **6**

A

13

14

APPROACH • 290KPH/180MPH **6**

IMOLA • 230KPH/143MPH **6**

CHATEAU D'EAU • 80KPH/50MPH **2**

11

10

A

12

2

ADELAIDE • 72KPH/45MPH **2**

5

A

1

APPROACH • 306KPH/190MPH **7**

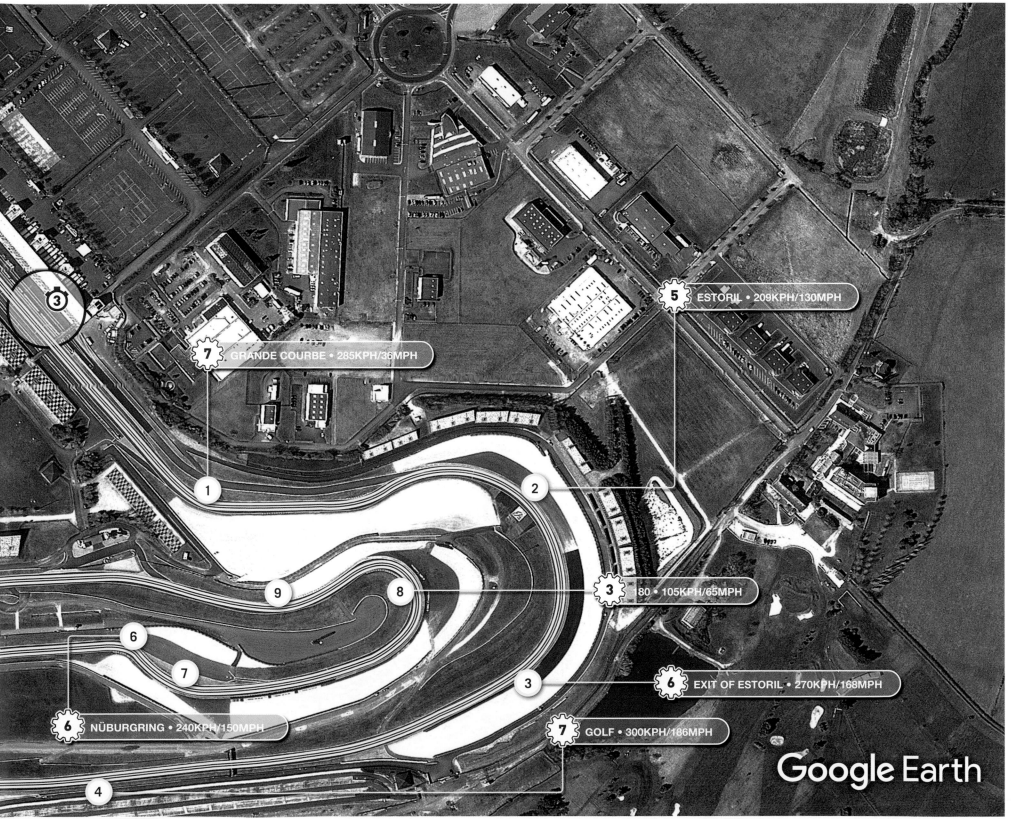

5 ESTORIL • 209KPH/130MPH

7 GRANDE COURBE • 285KPH/36MPH

1

2

9

8

3 180 • 105KPH/65MPH

6

7

3

6 EXIT OF ESTORIL • 270KPH/168MPH

6 NÜBURGRING • 240KPH/150MPH

7 GOLF • 300KPH/186MPH

4

Google Earth

Image © 2014 DigitalGlobe © Google 2014

Circuit Guide

One of the most notable features of this open, sweeping circuit was its smooth surface, helping drivers to place their cars where they wanted them as they negotiated the impressive combination of corners, with only the final corner of the lap a disappointment.

Turn 1 • Grande Courbe
Gear: **7**
Speed: **285kph (177mph)**

The first corner is a tricky one because it's a fast lefthander that offers few sighting points: drivers get to see it only after passing the end of the pitwall. Taken in seventh gear, the track drops away through the corner, with drivers needing to set themselves up almost immediately for the corner that follows, Estoril. Those who are slow away from the grid at the start can get swamped here, especially with the track being wide enough for drivers to attack around the outside.

Turn 2/3 • Estoril
Gear: **5**
Speed: **209kph (130mph)**

A short straight from Grande Courbe brings the cars to the start of Estoril, where the line starts to arc to the right. The middle of this uniform corner is the lowest part of the lap and drivers then have to balance their cars while they accelerate as hard as they dare onto the lap's only long straight. Carrying good momentum is vital for drivers to be able to get close enough to the car in front to catch a tow up to the Adelaide hairpin.

Turn 5 • Adelaide
Gear: **2**
Speed: **72kph (45mph)**

After staying flat-out through the righthand kink called Golf, drivers brake as late as possible into the hairpin at the top of the hill, either to defend their position from attack or to finish off a passing move enabled by the slipstream tow they'd achieved up the hill. Drivers have to decide whether to make their moves wide in/tight out or the other way around. In 1992, a chicane located just beyond the exit was removed, leaving drivers free to accelerate hard down the hill.

Turn 6/7 • Nürburgring
Gear: **6**
Speed: **230kph (143mph)**

The descent from Adelaide to 180 is interrupted by the Nürburgring esse. Approached down a gentle slope in sixth gear, the first part of the sequence, a righthander, requires an incredibly accurate entry line and is followed almost immediately by a slightly more open left turn. It's a fun, flowing part of the lap; there's not enough space for an overtaking move, but a mistake through here can let the chasing car close in for the next corner, 180.

Opposite: Williams to the fore in 1992 as Riccardo Patrese heads Nigel Mansell in the early laps. ***Above left:*** Ferrari's Felipe Massa acknowledges the flag official as he secures second place in 2007. ***Above right:*** Gerhard Berger never won at Magny-Cours. He's shown here rounding the pre-change version of Lycée in his Benetton as he heads to fourth place in 1996.

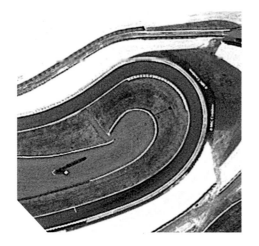

Turn 8 • **180**

Gear: **3**
Speed: **105kph (65mph)**

Located effectively on the infield of Estoril corner, this third gear hairpin turns the cars back in the direction from which they came. The straight down from the exit of the Nürburgring esse is too short to permit much overtaking, but some have tried it when lapping slower cars and got away with it. From the apex onwards, the track then starts to angle upwards again for the start of the climb through some sweepers back up to the top of the slope, Chateau d'Eau.

Turn 10/11 • **Imola**

Gear: **6**
Speed: **230kph (143mph)**

This esse is a matching pair for the Nürburgring esse, with its right/left sequence differing chiefly in that it's taken uphill. Drivers are slightly unsighted as they arrive here because the track dips away after the kerbs of the first part of the esse, and if they clip the kerbing too hard, cars have been known to get airborne here, providing the fans and the TV cameramen with an exciting spectacle but the driver with a problem to sort out as they need to turn immediately left.

Turn 12 • **Château d'Eau**

Gear: **2**
Speed: **80kph (50mph)**

Matching the Adelaide hairpin for altitude, Château d'Eau was the last corner of the lap on the original circuit layout. It's located very close to the exit of the Imola esse, and drivers need to haul their cars over to the lefthand side of the track promptly in order to gain the widest entry line into this longish righthander at the crest of the slope. It's a great spot for spectators on the banking by the circuit museum to see a car cornering under load.

Turn 13 • **Lycée Pin**

Gear: **2**
Speed: **89kph (55mph)**

The approach to the final corner of the lap was changed in 2003, when the right/left esse before it was removed and the notably tight and slow righthander onto the start/finish straight was altered as well. Instead, the revised layout meant that the approach was through a gently arcing stretch of track that fed into a tight right that was followed almost immediately by a right/left chicane at the foot of the podium. This gentler approach at least allowed a chasing driver a chance to pass.

Hockenheim

This long-time home of the German GP is a circuit that has undergone a considerable transformation over the decades. As a result, its races feel so different that they fall into the ages either before or after the change, thus either with the forest loop or without it.

❝ Arriving back into the stadium and seeing all the people there feels good because all the way to the Ostkurve there are no spectators and it feels very lonely. **❞**

Damon Hill

Like rival German circuit the Nürburgring, Hockenheim dates back to the 1920s, opening for racing in 1929. They couldn't have been more contrasting, though, as their only similarity was that they both ran through forests and Hockenheim was flat and simple in lay-out, with effectively two arcing straights joined by a curve at either end. Mercedes-Benz was its most frequent customer, using the circuit for testing purposes.

After the Second World War, Hockenheim had a quiet life, running national race meetings while the Nürburgring hosted the German GP and international sportscar races. The first major change followed in 1966, when it was shortened by the construction of an autobahn between the circuit and the town of Hockenheim, slicing off its western end. Large grandstands were built at this curtailed end and the track made to run in a small loop in front of them at the end of the lap.

Tragically, what made the circuit famous was when the ultimate driver of the day, Jim Clark, already a two-time World Champion, turned up to race for Lotus in a Formula Two race in the spring of 1968 and was killed when his car speared off into the trees.

Aware that speeds down the straights needed to be kept in check, the organizers inserted two chicanes on the loop through the forest in 1970, with one on the outward leg past the point where Clark had crashed and the other on the return run.

After the one-off German GP held here in 1970, Hockenheim had to wait until 1977 to take over the German GP once Niki Lauda had shown once and for all that the Nürburgring was no longer safe enough for F1 (see page 43). Even though it was nine years on from Clark's death, his presence still lingered here, but this gradually dissipated over the following years as Hockenheim hosted some thrilling grands prix.

Yet Hockenheim continued to present dangers of its own and Patrick Depailler crashed his Alfa Romeo at the Ostkurve during a test in 1980, and was killed. As a result of this, a third chicane was inserted, at the Ostkurve, thus making the circuit safer but removing the one long, fast corner. Yet, one of the drivers' perpetual fears about the place remained. This was a fear of running in the rain, since they would be flat-out on the back section, topping 320kph (200mph), with any spray contained by the trees flanking the track and thus incredibly limiting visibility. It was in just such a scenario that Didier Pironi's F1 career was brought to an end in 1982 during practice when he was unsighted by spray and went to overtake Derek Daly's Williams, only to find another car – Alain Prost's Renault – travelling slowly alongside. He slammed his Ferrari into it as they approached the stadium, suffering awful injuries to his feet and ankles.

The racing here was typified by furious dicing for position on the run to the first corner on the opening lap, then more late braking and occasional place-changing on arrival at the first chicane. Thereafter, overtaking tended to happen only at the three chicanes, but the slipstreaming groups certainly looked spectacular as they raced flat-out through the forest. Finally, in 1995, Michael Schumacher gave the crowds the result they so craved, a first home win for a German driver.

Then, partly to pander to environmentalists, the circuit was forced to make radical alterations in 2002. At a stroke, half of its lap was pared away, the forest section axed and a revised lay-out created by ubiquitous circuit architect Hermann Tilke. Instead of accelerating up to maximum speed and remaining there for the blast from the Nordkurve all the way to the first chicane, drivers soon had to start braking hard when not even halfway along this flat-out stretch and turn sharply right. A kilometre-long arcing run to a hairpin follows before bringing the cars back to the entry point to the stadium via a sequence of twisting curves that are dull but undeniably safer. Thus the very nature of the place was transformed, but the plus side was that the cars would come past the grandstands more often, with the grand prix changing from 45 laps to 67. ■

Opposite: Michael Schumacher leads the dash down to Nordkurve in 2002, trailed by brother Ralf and Rubens Barrichello.

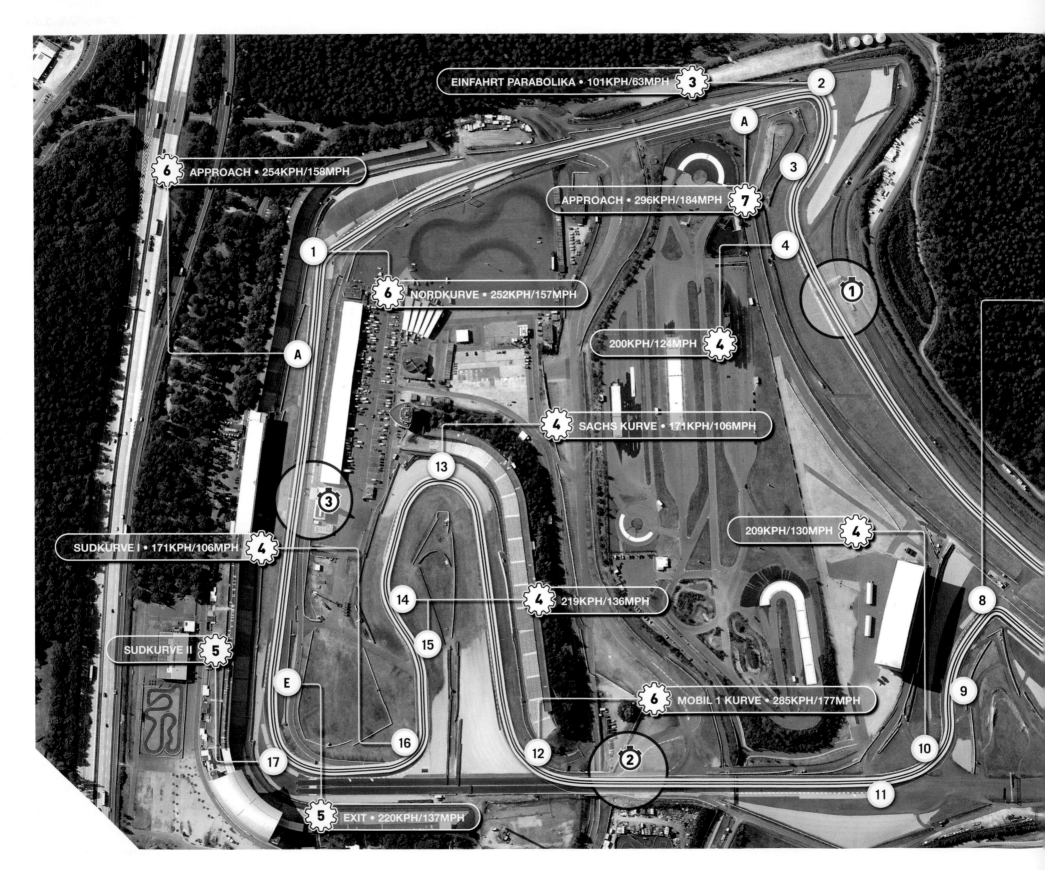

EINFAHRT PARABOLIKA • 101KPH/63MPH **3**

APPROACH • 254KPH/158MPH **6**

APPROACH • 296KPH/184MPH **7**

NORDKURVE • 252KPH/157MPH **6**

200KPH/124MPH **4**

SACHS KURVE • 171KPH/106MPH **4**

209KPH/130MPH **4**

SUDKURVE I • 171KPH/106MPH **4**

219KPH/136MPH **4**

SUDKURVE II **5**

MOBIL 1 KURVE • 285KPH/177MPH **6**

EXIT • 220KPH/137MPH **5**

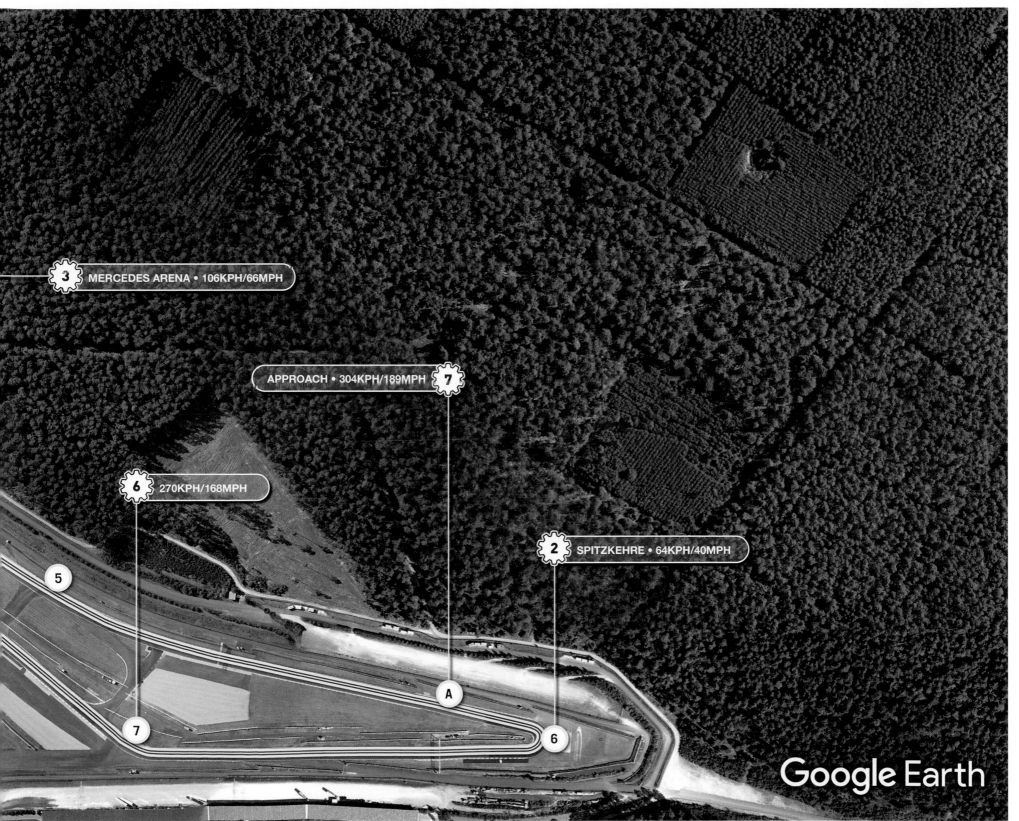

3 MERCEDES ARENA • 106KPH/66MPH

APPROACH • 304KPH/189MPH **7**

6 270KPH/168MPH

2 SPITZKEHRE • 64KPH/40MPH

5

A

7

6

Google Earth

Circuit Guide

Hockenheim's lap can be split into two parts. The division comes after the first corner when the cars leave the stadium section and head out to quieter zones, only to move back in front of grandstands full of noisy fans when they reach Mobil 1 Kurve.

Turn 1 • **Nordkurve**
Gear: **6**
Speed: **254kph (158mph)**

This can be an explosive corner on the opening lap of a grand prix as drivers jostle for position, which has been shown numerous times. Luciano Burti's aerobatic accident in 2001, when he hit Michael Schumacher's faltering Ferrari, offers proof of what can happen when cars come together. On regular racing laps, drivers want to be as far to the left as possible to give them the widest possible line to help them carry the most speed through the corner onto the straight beyond.

Turn 2/3/4 • **Einfahrt Parabolika**
Gear: **3**
Speed: **101kph (63mph)**

The first corner of what many still consider to be the "new" part of the circuit is a corner that is largely alien to the nature of the previous layout. It's a tight one, almost a hairpin, with drivers again needing to turn in from wide out (unless moving to the inside line to block a passing attempt), to get through not only the corner but the tightening angle immediately after that and the lefthander onto the back "straight" that follows.

Turn 5 • **Parabolika**
Gear: **6**
Speed: **280kph (174mph)**

Hockenheim, both old and new, is always thought of as somewhere with plenty of lengthy straights for flat-out motoring, but the truth is that they were usually anything but straight, all arcing one direction or the other. Whereas the ones on the old circuit arced to the right, Parabolika arcs the other way. Trees are set back from the lefthand side of the track and these angle back as the run to the Spitzkehre straightens out, giving drivers warning that they will soon need to brake.

Turn 6 • **Spitzkehre**
Gear: **2**
Speed: **304kph (40mph)**

Overtaking action can almost always be guaranteed if there's a long straight leading into a hairpin, and this is just the formula for Spitzkehre, with drivers needing to brake from 320kph (189mph) in sixth gear to slow all the way down to 64kph (40mph) for this sharp right. The trouble is, the corner onto Parabolika is so tight that cars usually come out line astern, thus making it hard for cars racing rather than lapping to find the performance advantage to catch a tow and pull off a move.

Opposite: Emerson Fittipaldi gets a little sideways at the Sackskurve in 1970 en route to fourth on his second outing for Lotus. ***Above left:*** Alan Jones, shown at the third chicane, remembers the 1979 German GP fondly because it was his first win for Williams. ***Above right:*** Ferrari's René Arnoux leads Andrea de Cesaris' Alfa Romeo, Nelson Piquet's Brabham and the Renaults into Sudkurve in 1983.

Turn 8 • Mercedes Arena
Gear: **3**
Speed: **108kph (68mph)**

Having looked straight ahead to the old circuit as they turn in to Spitzkehre, drivers then scrabble for traction as they get the power down on the hairpin's exit to run through the sixth gear kink at Turn 7 and look to make a move in front of the Mercedes grandstand. The corner changes the flow again as drivers have to drop to third gear, again staying out wide on the right as late as possible because they know they'll have to change direction again almost immediately.

Turn 13 • Sachs Kurve
Gear: **4**
Speed: **71kph (106mph)**

Ever since this corner was inserted in 1966, it has been frustratingly slow and technical. Right at the foot of the grandstands, it looks simple enough, if slow, but this fourth gear lefthander is made more interesting by there being a drop down to the apex and then an equivalent incline on the way out again, with the bend usefully lightly banked to help get the cars around it. Overtaking is hard to do here, but not impossible if the driver ahead makes a mistake.

Turn 12 • Mobil 1 Kurve
Gear: **6**
Speed: **285kph (177mph)**

This fast righthander used to mark the end of the forest section on the old circuit, giving the drivers something of a shock as they burst out in front of the spectators filling the giant grandstands in the stadium section. Now, the contrast isn't as great, but the drivers still notice a sudden increase in noise as they come out of this easy righthander, trying not to run too far over the flat kerbs on the exit because this would spin their cars around.

Turn 17 • Sudkurve
Gear: **4**
Speed: **171kph (106mph)**

The corner preceding any straight is clearly worthy of considerable study because momentum lost will never be regained. In many ways, the Sudkurve can be treated as two different corners, with the first a righthander over a slight brow, then a brief drop before the track cuts right again, this time dropping away slightly between turn in and exit, with a small degree of banking enabling drivers to find more grip that helps them to get the power down for the blast past the pits.

Great Drivers & Great Moments

The long straights and chicanes used to provide extremely dramatic races, but throw in fist fights, a pit fire, a track invasion and the suggestion of team orders, and it's not surprising that racing at Hockenheim has always been considered exciting with the outcome frequently changing late in the race.

Great Drivers

 Michael **Schumacher**
Hockenheim wins – 4

 Nelson **Piquet**
Hockenheim wins – 3

 Ayrton **Senna**
Hockenheim wins – 3

 Nigel **Mansell**
Hockenheim wins – 2

Fittingly, as it's his home grand prix, Michael Schumacher holds the record for the most German GP wins at Hockenheim. He managed this for the first time in 1995 for Benetton, reaching the finish 30 seconds clear of Damon Hill's Williams, and then had the embarrassment of stalling his engine as he waved to his fans and so had to be towed in. He then repeated this success for Ferrari in 2002, 2004 and 2006, with team-mate Felipe Massa running obligingly on his heels in the last of these.

Nelson Piquet managed to win three times at Hockenheim, so there's a certain irony that, to many, the most famous thing that he did here was to punch Eliseo Salazar in 1982 after they clashed when he came up to lap the ATS driver. The Brazilian's three wins came in 1981, 1986 and 1987, with the last being extremely fortunate: it was gifted to him when Alain Prost's McLaren suffered alternator failure with five laps to go, leaving Nelson to win easily for Williams.

Ayrton Senna failed to finish higher than second at Hockenheim for Lotus, but won here three times for McLaren. The first came in his first year with the team, in 1998, when he started from pole and led every lap. He repeated the feat in 1989, albeit with team-mate Alain Prost heading him through the middle of the race, then made it three in a row in 1990, when he again had to regain the lead, this time from Benetton's Alessandro Nannini who got ahead by not pitting.

Hockenheim wasn't a happy hunting ground for this tenacious British driver; it took until his tenth visit, in 1991, for him to be first to the chequered flag. This race for Williams proved easy, and he led away from pole and cruised home ahead of team-mate Riccardo Patrese. Mansell would make it two in a row in 1992 when he was all but untouchable after getting past fast-starting Patrese on the opening lap and his victory took him to the brink of his drivers' title.

Great Moments

1970 Jochen **Rindt** pips Jacky **Ickx** to win by 0.7 secs

1994 Jos **Verstappen** survives a dramatic pit fire

2000 Rubens **Barrichello** helped by a track invasion

2014 Lewis **Hamilton** advances from the tail

In 1970, the German GP was moved to Hockenheim because the owners of the Nürburgring had failed to carry out required safety modifications to the Nordschleife. So the F1 teams turned up to this circuit that was the polar opposite to the Nordschleife. The race was between front row starters Jacky Ickx and Jochen Rindt, with the former leading from pole in his Ferrari, but the lead changed between them 12 times before the Austrian edged ahead in his Lotus to win by 0.7 seconds.

The 1994 season had already claimed the lives of both Ayrton Senna and Roland Ratzenberger at Imola, and left Karl Wendlinger in an induced coma, so it certainly didn't need any more injuries, yet trouble reared its head at the German GP when Benetton rookie Jos Verstappen and his pitcrew were engulfed in flame after a dramatic fire during a pitstop. Fortunately, they all escaped with relatively minor burns, but the team was later found to have tampered with its refuelling rig.

F1 can be shaped by bizarre events, and this was definitely the case in 2000, when a former Mercedes employee staged a protest by running along the grass verges before the first chicane. This brought out the safety car and the race soon turned from one of McLaren domination to one that fell into Rubens Barrichello's hands as Mika Hakkinen pitted for wet weather tyres when it started to rain, losing a 30-second lead. Barrichello stayed out to score his first F1 win for Ferrari.

Nico Rosberg made it nine wins from the first 10 rounds for Mercedes, crossing the finish line almost 20 seconds clear of Valtteri Bottas's Williams. Yet the drive of the race came from his team-mate Lewis Hamilton, for the English ace crashed in qualifying and started from 20th on the grid. That he was able to tiger his way up to third place, less than 2 seconds down on Bottas impressed all who watched it, and showed how much he wanted that second F1 title that he'd go on to claim.

Nürburgring

Built in the 1980s to keep the Nürburgring on the international stage, this was criticized at first for being a homogenized, safety-first sort of circuit – as it obviously is in comparison to the original Nordschleife with which it shared the start/finish area – but it has become accepted as one of the homes of the German GP.

> **" The current circuit may be less epic than the original 14-mile [22.5km] layout, but it can still bite you and the weather can turn in a matter of moments. "**
>
> *Lewis Hamilton*

The rumblings had gone on for years that the Nürburgring Nordschleife was becoming too dangerous for F1 – or, looked at another way, the cars too fast for the circuit. Indeed, the drivers had campaigned for safety improvements in 1969, with Jackie Stewart leading the crusade that led to the track being widened in places, crash barriers added, crests flattened and trees felled. Yet, within a few years, the rumblings were just as strong again. Then Niki Lauda's near-fatal accident in the 1976 German GP showed that the end was nigh. Hockenheim had taken over and there appeared to be no comeback.

However, the circuit owners elected to do what many fans considered to be "the unthinkable": they built a new circuit on the site. This shared the same start/finish line and the same name, but the Nordschleife was merely an anachronism disappearing into the trees in the background. The new circuit was seen by its promoters as the brave new world, a safe place to go racing and one on which fans could see the cars for much of the lap and get to see them 67 times per grand prix – a contrast to the 14 laps allocated to grands prix held on the Nordschleife.

Many fans were stunned when they saw it for the first time in the autumn of 1984, pointing out that this facility looked as though it had been designed for a different sport. Some said that the gravel traps

surrounding almost the entire lap were so large that the fans in the grandstands could scarcely make out the cars. It certainly wasn't love as first sight. Not that Alain Prost cared: he won that first race – run as the European GP – for McLaren after leading every lap.

Brand-new pit buildings gave the new circuit an entirely new feel, all but masking the one part of the track that was shared with the Nordschleife, with a modern hotel nestled into the banks on the far side of the track. The new track then dipped and twisted its way down a gentle slope to the Dunlop Kehre, a hairpin, without a single tree in sight, save for those poking over the tops of the grandstands for the climb back up that slope to what is now Michelin-Kurve. From here, at least, the circuit opened out a little, with a fabulous, dropping sweep from Warsteiner-Kurve allowing the drivers to really let their cars run, and offering the feel of the old circuit again as they were freed from running in front of grandstands and had the backdrop of the Eifel forest across a grassy expanse to their left. After an uphill chicane, the drivers could see the point at which the Nordschleife arced away to the left and off into the forest, but their lap was coming to an end rather than just starting. It was nothing like its full-blood predecessor, but actually not a bad circuit in the modern idiom. It just took years before F1 insiders and racing romantics were prepared to accept this.

Like the Nordschleife, this new circuit also was prone to the arrival of race-shaping downpours, and yet they were never as life-threatening due to the expanses of space either side of the track. There were no hedges running up to the edge of the track here… Indeed, one of the most fondly remembered races was in 1999, when constantly changing conditions not only produced an enthralling race but a surprise winner in Johnny Herbert for Stewart GP.

The circuit changed again in 2002, when the first corner was transformed, being made to double back on itself before feeding into a three-corner loop that brings the cars back to the previous layout where it had exited the first corner esse.

Financial troubles have beset the Nürburgring recently and the heady days in the first decade of the twenty-first century, when Schumachermania encouraged the FIA to allocate Germany two grands prix per year, with the one at the Nürburgring running as the European GP, seem long gone. Indeed, the financial situation of both here and Hockenheim have deteriorated so much that they now alternate the grand prix, with only a local government bail-out enabling the Nürburgring to host the race in 2013.

Opposite: Red Bull Racing's Sebastian Vettel leads the way through the Yokohama-S from Lotus duo Romain Grosjean and Kimi Raikkonen in 2013.

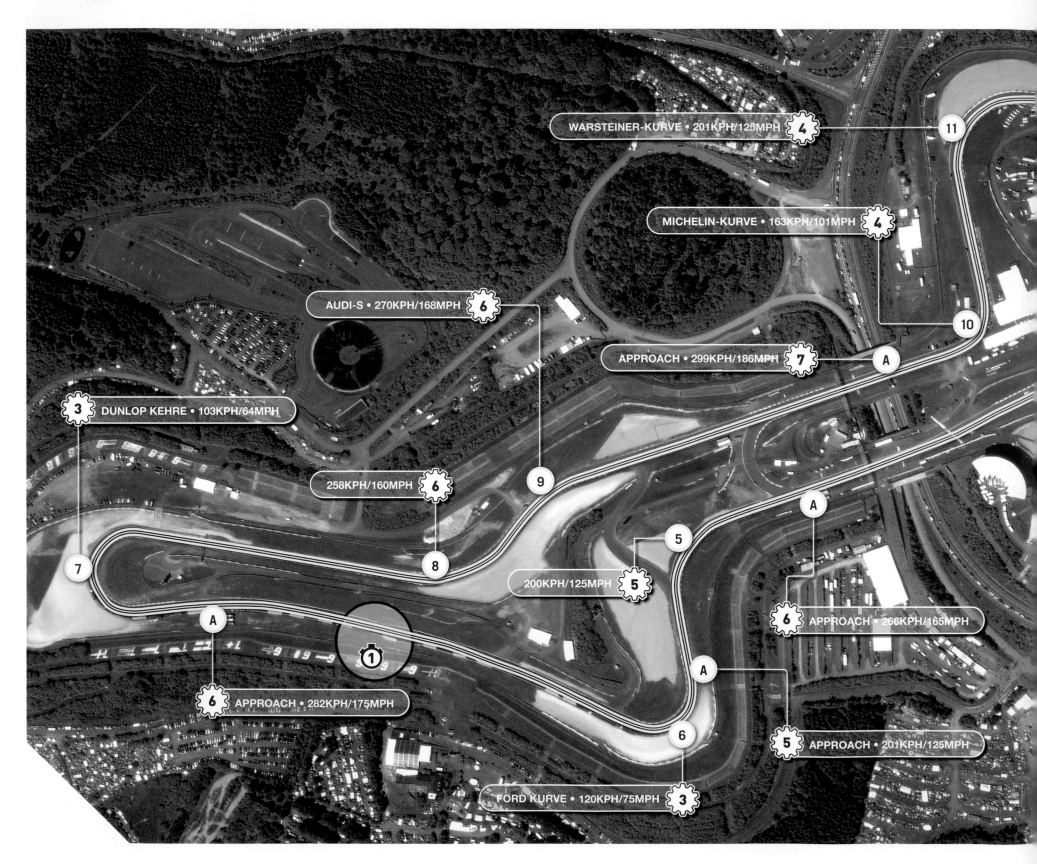

WARSTEINER-KURVE • 201KPH/125MPH **4**

MICHELIN-KURVE • 163KPH/101MPH **4**

AUDI-S • 270KPH/168MPH **6**

APPROACH • 299KPH/186MPH **7**

3 DUNLOP KEHRE • 103KPH/64MPH

258KPH/160MPH **6**

200KPH/125MPH **5**

6 APPROACH • 266KPH/165MPH

6 APPROACH • 282KPH/175MPH

5 APPROACH • 201KPH/125MPH

FORD KURVE • 120KPH/75MPH **3**

2

12 6 ADVAN-BOGEN • 285KPH/177MPH

2 NGK SCHIKANE • 105KPH/65MPH

3 MERCEDES ARENA II • 89KPH/55MPH

2

3 152KPH/94MPH

APPROACH • 240KPH/149MPH 5

4 3 MERCEDES ARENA I • 129KPH/80MPH

2 14

13

1 2 YOKOHAMA-S • 76KPH/47MPH

A

A 3

7 APPROACH • 301KPH/187MPH

15

COCA-COLA KURVE • 129KPH/80MPH 3

Google Earth

Circuit Guide

The Nürburgring is very much a contemporary circuit, with plenty of run-off space and huge gravel traps around its lap, thus lacking the intimacy of its forebears, but it provides the drivers with a worthwhile challenge as it traverses the rolling terrain.

Turn 1 • Yokohama-S
Gear: **2**
Speed: **76kph (47mph)**

The opening corner of the Nürburgring started life as a right/left esse in the 1980s, with many a scrap between drivers ending up with one or other of the cars marooned in the gravel trap. However, it was changed comprehensively for 2002 and now requires drivers to brake hard for a righthand hairpin, with a gently dipping entry, wary that they have to position themselves for the exit, often with a driver trying to pass them, thus forcing them to drive defensively and cover the inside line.

Turn 7 • Dunlop Kehre
Gear: **3**
Speed: **103kph (64mph)**

This is a difficult corner because drivers have to slow from around 280kph (175mph) on the downhill approach to get down to third gear for this broad hairpin. In fact, it's a two-apex corner and drivers need to get balanced as soon as possible so that they can get back on the throttle to accelerate back up the hill. One of the best moves here was by Juan Pablo Montoya in 2003, when he drove his Williams around the outside of Michael Schumacher's Ferrari.

Turn 6 • Ford Kurve
Gear: **3**
Speed: **120kph (75mph)**

This righthander has remained unchanged since the new circuit was built and it's the tightest corner on the descent that runs from the exit of the Mercedes Arena to the Dunlop Kehre at the foot of the hill. The corner before is fast, taken in fifth gear, but then drivers have only a short distance to haul their cars across the track to the left side to get into position to take this much tighter right, wary that the track drops away on its exit.

Turn 10 • Michelin Kurve
Gear: **4**
Speed: **163kph (101mph)**

Known until recently as the RTL-Kurve, this lefthander at the crest of the hill is a seemingly simple corner, but it requires precision; keeping momentum going is vital because drivers approach in seventh gear and need to drop three cogs. Going in to the corner a shade too fast, though – especially on the often greasy track surface that prevails in the mornings when the circuit hosted the grand prix in the autumn – can lead to a trip across the grass on the exit.

Opposite: A view of Dunlop Kehre, from inside the track near the Audi-S in 1996. *Above left:* Sebastian Vettel's continued stunning form for Red Bull Racing meant that he had plenty of fans supporting him in 2013, like this one at Dunlop Kehre. *Above right:* Job done, as Vettel delivers and takes the chequered flag in front in 2013.

Turn 11 • **Warsteiner-Kurve**
Gear: **4**
Speed: **201kph (125mph)**

Warsteiner-Kurve is another fourth-gear corner that is perhaps even more key to a fast lap than the Michelin-Kurve that precedes it, because it's the way onto the fast back section of the circuit. Drivers need to move from the right of the track at the exit of Michelin to get hard left for the turn-in point and resist the desire to take in too much speed, because traction on the exit is vital for accelerating as soon as possible for the straight onto which it leads.

Turn 12 • **Advan-Bogen**
Gear: **6**
Speed: **285kph (177mph)**

This is yet another corner that has been renamed recently as the Nürburgring struggles to keep its head above water financially. Formerly known as the ITT-Bogen, it's an open righthand kink taken in top gear with a good view to the forest beyond. Drivers enjoy the supportive feeling of their cars sitting extra low as they take the compression here and consider how they might pass any rivals into the uphill chicane that follows, whether to try on the left or the right.

Turn 13/14 • **NGK Schikane**
Gear: **2**
Speed: **105kph (65mph)**

This chicane offers a passing opportunity, with its high-speed approach after the flat-out blast down from Warsteiner-Kurve, bottoming at Advan-Bogen, then the climb to the entry point beneath the spectators sitting in the grandstands. Drivers have to haul their cars down from 280kph (175mph) in top gear to 105kph (65mph) in second, then find the shortest line through this left/right sequence, remembering to stay off the kerbs if it has been raining. Accelerating out too soon can lead to a

Turn 15 • **Coca-Cola Kurve**
Gear: **3**
Speed: **129kph (80mph)**

The Coca-Cola Kurve is the final corner of the lap and the highest point of the circuit and because of this is approached up a gentle incline via the short run from the chicane, with the slope levelling off at the entry point. When running without a pursuer, drivers need to place their car as far to the left as they can, then take the shallowest angle to the apex and use the full width of the exit to get the fastest exit onto the start/finish straight.

Great Drivers & Great Moments

Michael Schumacher is way clear on the number of wins achieved at the Nürburgring, but history shows that others have had a look-in too and that changing weather has shaped more than a few of the grands prix held here.

Great Drivers

Michael **Schumacher**
Nürburgring wins – 4

Fernando **Alonso**
Nürburgring wins – 2

Ralf **Schumacher**
Nürburgring wins – 1

Mark **Webber**
Nürburgring wins – 1

Michael Schumacher undoubtedly enjoyed winning the German GP at Hockenheim, but the Nürburgring was far more local to his hometown of Kerpen and so he delighted family and friends by winning four grands prix here. The first came in 1995 as he chased after his second drivers' title. He then joined Ferrari for 1996 but had to wait until 2000 for his next Nürburgring win. But he promptly added another in 2001 and a fourth in 2004, when his and Ferrari's dominance enabled him to cruise home.

Kimi Raikkonen must curse the Nürburgring, for he should have won here in 2003 and then again in 2005, when his car broke on the final lap. The driver who benefited in the latter, Fernando Alonso, would go on to become only the second driver thus far to score multiple wins here. The Renault racer looked confined to second place when he spotted Raikkonen's McLaren spinning at the first corner and motored past. The Spaniard then won again here two years later, this time for McLaren.

Ralf Schumacher's six grand prix wins are way short of his brother Michael's tally of 91, but he had a fine campaign for Williams in 2003 and this included victory in the European GP at the Nürburgring. Key to this was the fact that the Michelin tyres his team used were superior to the Bridgestones fitted to brother Michael's Ferrari. Stung by criticism that he'd shown little attack following Michael home in Canada, he pressed harder and was rewarded when Kimi Raikkonen's leading McLaren expired.

There are drivers through F1 history who stand out for being good enough to win a grand prix but being denied their chance to do so. Red Bull's Mark Webber looked as though this might include him, but it finally all came right at the Nürburgring in 2009. It had seemed as though another win had got away from him when he was made to pit for a drive-through penalty after clashing with Rubens Barrichello at the start, but he served that and was still fast enough to win.

Great Moments

1984 German GP – Alain **Prost** draws first F1 blood

1998 Luxembourg GP – Mika **Hakkinen** edges title rival

1999 European GP – Johnny **Herbert** wins for Stewart

2013 German GP – Sebastian **Vettel's** first home win

The praise for the new circuit was thin on the ground during F1's first visit, but Alain Prost found reason to like the place because he closed the gap on his McLaren team-mate and title rival Niki Lauda by winning the inaugural grand prix here after getting the jump on polesitter Nelson Piquet's Brabham on the run to the first corner, then leading all the way. By contrast, Lauda qualified only 15th and spun passing a backmarker, so he had to make do with fourth place.

Run as the Luxembourg GP in 1998, this looked set to be a poor meeting for title challengers McLaren when Ferrari outqualified both of its cars. However, Mika Hakkinen overcame his car's lack of pace to pick off early leader Eddie Irvine, then catch Michael Schumacher. By running the four laps between Schumacher's pitstop and his own as if they were qualifying laps, he emerged in front and thereafter kept pressing to pull clear and so take a four-point lead to the final round.

This remains the Nürburgring's greatest race yet, because it never stopped surprising from start to finish. Heinz-Harald Frentzen led the first half of the race as others changed to rain tyres with varying degrees of success. Then his Jordan's electrics failed and David Coulthard took over, but it rained again and he slid off, letting Ralf Schumacher hit the front. But he picked up a puncture and Giancarlo Fisichella moved in front, then spun and so Johnny Herbert came through to give Stewart GP its only win.

The 2013 German GP was Sebastian Vettel's sixth on home soil, but it holds a special place in his heart because it was the first time that he managed to win it, after winning 29 grands prix in other countries. Even then, he was kept on tenterhooks all the way to the chequered flag because Kimi Raikkonen gave chase and was just a second behind at the finish after his Lotus showed far less of an appetite for its tyres than Sebastian Vettel's Red Bull did.

Red Bull Ring

This stunning Austrian circuit began life as the Österreichring, one of the world's most flowing stretches of tarmac. Considered too fast to be safe, it was cut back considerably to become the A1-Ring in 1996, then shut shop after 2003 before being given its third lease of life in 2014 thanks to Red Bull investment.

> **"**I always enjoy driving here, not only as it's my home race, but because it has overtaking opportunities due to the three long straights that begin and end with slow corners.**"**
>
> *Alexander Wurz*

Neighbouring Switzerland was involved in the Formula One World Championship from the outset, with its testing Bremgarten circuit outside Bern. Then came the Le Mans disaster of 1955 in which more than 80 spectators were killed. This led to Switzerland banning racing within its borders. So, Austria took up the challenge of keeping F1 in the Alps. It took years of planning and the development of various facilities in the rural region of Styria north-west of Graz.

The first of these was at Zeltweg, on a simple circuit laid out on a military airfield in 1958. Used at first for club racing, it hosted a non-championship F1 race in 1963, won by Jack Brabham. Granted a World Championship round in 1964, its short length (1.998 miles) and extremely bumpy surface made it extremely unpopular.

Fortunately, just up the slope at Spielberg, a purpose-built circuit opened its doors in 1969 as the nation's excitement about Jochen Rindt grew by the week and attracted 100,000 fans through the turnstiles. This was the Österreichring, and it couldn't have been more different. Almost twice the length, at 3.673 miles, it traversed the mountainside in artistic, flowing straights and parabolas. It was fast, very fast, and the lap record before it was dropped by F1 after the 1987 Austrian GP was just over 150mph. It was also made tricky by its mountainous location being prone to summer storms.

Sadly, Rindt was killed at Monza in 1970 and it took until 1984 for Austrian fans to get to cheer a home win, when Niki Lauda triumphed for McLaren. As F1 was insisting on ever more stringent circuit safety, and the Österreichring didn't have the money to make the required modifications, it dropped out of the World Championship after Nigel Mansell's win for Williams in 1987. Furthermore, its narrow start straight was perhaps the cause of the shunts that required several starts that year.

Austrian fans were thus left without a race of their own, but investment from the country's A1 mobile telecommunications group led to racing's return to the circuit, albeit in severely truncated form. The A1-Ring used much of the old layout, but the track was shorn of one mile of its old lap, with the track turning sharply right before the old first corner and rejoining the Österreichring layout a quarter of the way along the old top straight. Other parts to be trimmed included the old Bosch Kurve, a corner considered to be its most fearsome, and the sweeping Jochen Rindt Kurve that concluded the lap, was squared off and made into two, slower turns. The magical flow of old was gone and long-time F1 fans felt shortchanged, but it still produced great moments, though many weren't aggrieved when it was dropped after the 2003 race.

Lauda seemed to be eternally disappointed at his home race, with the Österreichring producing three

first-time winners in the 1970s in Vittorio Brambilla (1975), John Watson (1976) and Alan Jones (1977). Gerhard Berger hoped to buck the trend but, like Lauda, his home race was to thwart him from 1984 through until 1997. Alexander Wurz's family was involved in the shaping of the A1-Ring, but he too was empty-handed when the race lost its slot.

In the summer of 2011, racing returned to a track with new pits, main grandstand and media centre. Now known as the Red Bull Ring, in deference to the source of its revival budget from the Red Bull energy drink company co-founded by Austrian enthusiast Dietrich Mateschitz, it hosted rounds of the DTM touring car series and Formula Renault 3.5 series. When it returned to the World Championship calendar, for 2014, people spoke more favourably of the place, not just because it was a greatly improved place to work, but because it brought back the old school feel that F1 has been shedding in its pursuit of global spread. It's as hard as ever to locate hotel accommodation in the surrounding area, but the vibe is welcome as a counterbalance to the increasing number of flyaway races. Nico Rosberg loves it, though, as he won for Mercedes in both 2014 and 2015. ■

Opposite: Nico Rosberg leads Mercedes team-mate Lewis Hamilton into Remus at the first lap of the 2015 Austrian GP on his way to victory.

REMUS • 75KPH/47MPH **2** 2

RAUCH • 175KPH/109MPH **5** 5

1

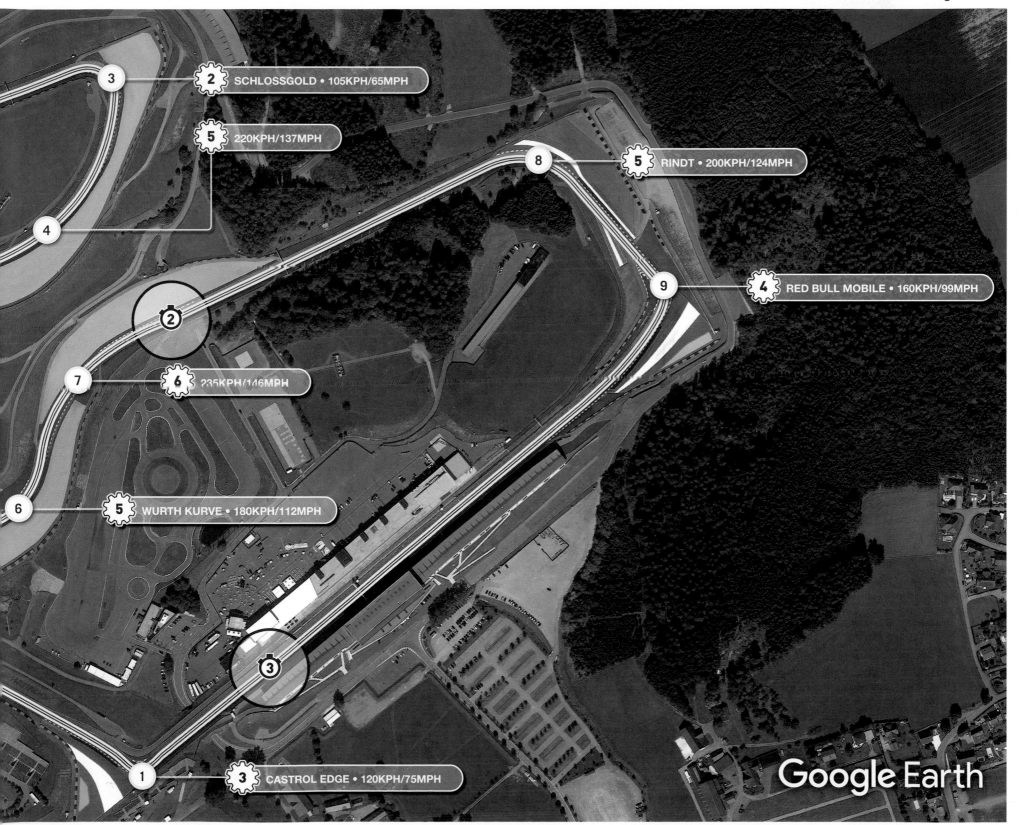

SCHLOSSGOLD • 105KPH/65MPH

220KPH/137MPH

RINDT • 200KPH/124MPH

RED BULL MOBILE • 160KPH/99MPH

235KPH/146MPH

WURTH KURVE • 180KPH/112MPH

CASTROL EDGE • 120KPH/75MPH

Google Earth

Image © 2014 DigitalGlobe © Google 2014

Circuit Guide

The scenery is truly magnificent around the Red Bull Ring, but the drivers have little time to enjoy it as they navigate their way around the mountainside, with an almost constant flow of medium-speed corners and changes of gradient to keep them busy in the cockpit.

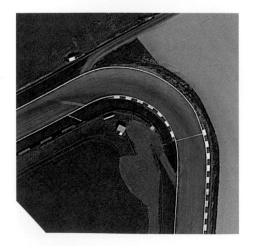

Turn 1 • Castrol Edge
Gear: **3**
Speed: **120kph (75mph)**

Braking has to be heavy into this uphill righthander, as drivers approach it at 190mph. Caution is required, as the exit isn't visible as drivers on approach. Having crested the brow, to see trees straight ahead rather than just the sky, there's plenty of run-off, but drivers need to turn sharply to the right, something that isn't always easy in the busy traffic of the opening lap. Some chose second gear, some third, at what is one of the best spots for passing.

Turn 2 • Remus
Gear: **2**
Speed: **75kph (47mph)**

After the long, kinked run up from the first corner, the drivers have climbed appreciably to reach Remus. This is another tight corner that conceals its exit until drivers have reached the apex. This righthander is the tightest corner of the lap and its restricted nature frequently leads to contact as those who made a better exit out of the first corner then got a tow up the hill look to strike. Getting braking right here is critical, and many don't, adding to the fun.

Turn 3 • Schlossgold
Gear: **2**
Speed: **105kph (65mph)**

After another kinked straight, this time across the hillside, the drivers start a gentle drop into the third corner, Schlossgold. With the track continuing to drop away from the entry of the corner to the exit, drivers find this long second gear turn a challenging one as they struggle to keep their car balanced. The old grandstand that used to have the fearsome Bosche Kurve right at the fans' feet, is a more sensible distance back behind a gravel trap.

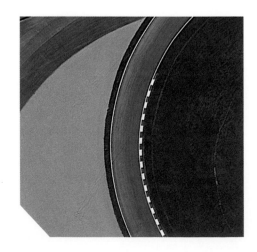

Turn 5 • Rauch
Gear: **5**
Speed: **175kph (109mph)**

After running through a stretch of track flanked Turn 4 is a kink to the right as the descent from Schlossghold turns into a run across the hillside again. Then, as drivers hit 165mph, they have to consider the first part of a pair of right-handers. Rauch can be taken in fourth, but is generally a fifth-gear turn, pitching the drivers down the hill and offering them a clear view of the paddock, grandstands and valley below. When a driver gets Turns 4 to 6 right, there's a wonderful flow.

Opposite: Mika Hakkinen leads into Turn 1 for McLaren in 1998, after deposing Benetton's poleman Giancarlo Fisichella. ***Above left:*** Takuma Sato's Jordan takes a hit from Nick Heidfeld's Sauber at Remus midway through the race in 2002. Sato had to be cut out of his car but, luckily, wasn't badly injured. ***Above right:*** The montains were still snow-capped when F1 visited in 2003, providing a stunning backdrop as Michael Schumacher raced to victory.

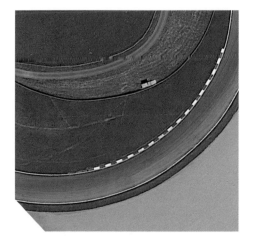

Turn 6 • **Wurth Kurve**
Gear: **5**
Speed: **180kph (112mph)**

This second consecutive left-hand turn echoes the shape of Rauch, but differs in that it cups the cars slightly as it arrests their descent and turns them back across the hillside again. Entry is important, but a good exit is vital, as Wurth Kurve feeds almost immediately into a slight ascent up to the following corner. In many ways, they're close enough to be treated as a pair. A glance to the left gives drivers a clear view of the giant Red Bull sculpture above them.

Turn 7
Gear: **6**
Speed: **235kph (146mph)**

The quick left flick out of Wurth Kurve into a righthander up over a crest at this seventh turn puts the drivers' bodies through heavy G-loading. However, it's considered fairly easy by the drivers as they start to focus on the final two corners that await them. The nature of the track changes here as the track leaves the open meadows of the first part of the lap and enters a short stretch through a patch of woodland.

Turn 8 • **Rindt**
Gear: **5**
Speed: **200kph (124mph)**

Where once there was simply one long, long downhill right-hand corner to complete the lap, there have been two since the Österreichring was transformed to its current format in 1996. Named after Austria's first World Champion, Jochen Rindt Kurve is taken in fifth gear, plunging the drivers down the final slope. There's plenty of space on the exit if drivers should get it wrong, suitably painted in patriotic red-and-white stripes, but a clean line here is required to get the last turn right.

Turn 9 • **Red Bull Mobile**
Gear: **4**
Speed: **160kph (99mph)**

The final corner is tighter than the one before it and it's made extra tricky by a compression that is right next to the apex. It's tempting for drivers to try to negotiate it, but if should they get it wrong, their cars can be spat out towards the outside of the track, with the result than many of them are then spinning back across towards the pit wall. However, a good exit can give drivers a clear opportunity to get a run on the car ahead on the 190mph approach to the first corner.

Great Drivers & Great Moments

Alain Prost won three times at the Österreichring, but no driver has yet managed to equal that tally in the nine grands prix that have been held to date on its shortened successor and Nico Rosberg is the only driver to win twice on this new layout. Outcomes have included Ferrari asking its drivers to swap positions.

Great Drivers

Mika **Hakkinen**
Red Bull Ring wins – 2

The Finn seemed to take forever to score his first F1 win. That came in the last race of 1997. In 1998, his McLaren–Mercedes was the car to have and Mika made the most of it. His win here came from third on the grid after he took the lead from pole-man Giancarlo Fisichella's Benetton on lap 1. Michael Schumacher put him under pressure, but slid off. In 2000, victory came more easily as he led all the way to win easily from McLaren team-mate David Coulthard.

Nico **Rosberg**
Red Bull Ring wins – 2

Two wins in two years reflect a tidy return for Keke Rosberg's son after the reopening of the circuit as the Red Bull Ring. The first came in 2014 after Williams locked out the front row, but had no answer to Mercedes' pace in the race, with Nico's task made easier as team-mate Lewis Hamilton started ninth after a spin in qualifying. The Mercedes duo finished one–two again in 2015 after Hamilton had too much wheel-spin at the start and so wasted his pole position.

Michael **Schumacher**
Red Bull Ring wins – 2

It was Michael's sixth full season before he got to contest an Austrian GP, but it took him a further five years before he'd win there. This was in 2002 when the race should have been won by team-mate Rubens Barrichello, but Ferrari told him to let Michael by, even though this was only round five and it left him with double the points of his closest rival. Michael's second win came in 2003, and this one was more legitimate, with only McLaren's Kimi Raikkonen able to get close.

Gerhard **Berger**
Red Bull Ring wins – 0

Gerhard never won his home grand prix, and was hampered by its nine-year absence from 1988 to 1996, but he was a huge draw for the fans. His greatest chance of victory came at his third attempt, in 1986 when Benetton had BMW turbo power. Team-mate Teo Fabi took pole but Gerhard grabbed the lead on the opening lap, only to drop back at mid-distance after his battery had to be replaced, leaving him to seventh. Records show that his remained his best finish here.

Great Moments

1997 Jacques **Villeneuve** moves past **Trulli** to win

Austria's first grand prix for since 1987 offered a surprise. Jarno Trulli had replaced injured Olivier Panis at Prost and come fourth in Germany. He leapt from third on the grid into the lead, but the shock couldn't last as Jacques Villeneuve moved ahead for Williams. Then, late in the race, the Prost retired from second with engine failure, leaving Villeneuve to win easily from David Coulthard's McLaren and close to within a point of championship leader Michael Schumacher who could finish only sixth after a stop-go penalty.

1999 **McLaren** clash helps Ferrari's Eddie **Irvine**

It should have been a McLaren victory, but Ferrari triumphed thanks to a clash between the silver-grey cars at Remus on the opening lap. Mika Hakkinen led away from David Coulthard, but the Scot dived up the inside and they collided, dropping Hakkinen to the tail of the field. Coulthard was able to claim the lead, but Ferrari timed Eddie Irvine's pitstop better to put him in front, with Coulthard unable to usurp him. Hakkinen produced the drive of the race to get back to third.

2002 Jean **Todt** triggers fury with team orders

Ferrari was so dominant in 2002 that Michael Schumacher really didn't need any help. However, team boss Jean Todt brought shame on F1 when he insisted that Rubens Barrichello, who'd led all the way from pole, pull over to let him win, despite Schumacher having already won four of the first five rounds. It's better to remember the day for Takuma Sato the good fortune of escaping with light injuries from a car-shattering shunt when his Jordan was T-boned at Remus by Nick Heidfeld's Sauber.

2014 Nico **Rosberg** enjoys F1's return to Austria

Formula One's second return to Austria was only likely to produce victory for one team, such was its competitive advantage. That team was Mercedes and it had won six of the first seven rounds. At the Red Bull Ring, though, Williams filled the front row and first Felipe Massa then Valtteri Bottas led. After the first round of pit stops, Nico Rosberg moved ahead of them, then took the lead when Sergio Perez finally pitted his Force India. From there on, Rosberg had it under control.

🇬🇧 Brands Hatch

For decades, this charismatic circuit alternated with Silverstone in hosting the British GP, and its twisting undulations provided a remarkable contrast to its airfield-derived rival. Perhaps as a consequence, the races here were seldom less than dramatic.

> **❝** Brands Hatch is one of the best circuits anywhere for a driver who really enjoys driving, with corners that go uphill and downhill and so it's not flat and featureless like some modern circuits. **❞**
> *Emerson Fittipaldi*

Brands Hatch is one of the great circuits that have been left behind as Formula One has sought ever greater levels of safety for its drivers. In its heyday in the 1970s, it was where the World Championship was at its most vibrant, with its grandstands and spectator banking packed to capacity to watch racing that was seldom less than enthralling thanks to the complexity of the circuit, with numerous challenging corners. This was a track on which drivers really had to earn their keep.

All of this was a far cry from its early days. Its setting had been used first of all by cyclists in 1926 after they spotted that the natural bowl that was being used as a field to grow mushrooms would be ideal for racing. By 1928, pedal power gave way to motorbikes and a kidney-shaped track layout was marked out at the foot of the bowl.

Car racing finally arrived in 1950 after the track was given a bitumen surface. It was an instant hit, and Brands Hatch's proximity to London meant that it drew large crowds of spectators. Wanting to host national races rather than just club ones, the track was widened and lengthened for 1954, with the climb to Druids hairpin added. The track direction was reversed at this point too, becoming clockwise.

The biggest change came in 1960, when the grand prix loop was opened, more than doubling the lap length to 4.3km (2.7 miles). This gave the lap a two-part feel by taking the cars left when they reached the end of what was then known as Bottom Straight and leading them onto a rising and falling run through six more corners through the woods. The route then returned the drivers to the original amphitheatre midway through the final sweep of corners, and back onto the start/finish straight.

With dynamic entrepreneur John Webb running the show, he pushed Brands Hatch forward and was behind many of the investments that propelled it onto the world stage, with the creation too of a non-championship F1 event, the Race of Champions (1965–83), in the years that it wasn't hosting the British GP.

Good enough by the early 1960s to host F1, it replaced Aintree as the alternative host of the British GP in 1964 (sharing with Silverstone) and Jim Clark led all the way for Lotus to win from BRM's Graham Hill. Of the grands prix that followed, the one in 1970 stands out for Jack Brabham losing the lead when his Brabham ran out of fuel at Stirling's on the final lap, letting Jochen Rindt through to win; there was drama of a disappointing kind in 1974, when Niki Lauda needed a punctured tyre replacing but then couldn't leave the pits because an official's car was blocking the exit; there was then unrest in 1976, when James Hunt's McLaren was damaged in a first corner mêlée triggered by the Ferrari drivers and only the crowd's fury enabled him to take the restart; then there was the start of Mansellmania in 1985, when Nigel Mansell finally scored his first F1 win in the European GP, followed up a year later by another win at the Kent venue for Williams.

In all, there would be 14 grands prix held at Brands Hatch through until 1986, after which Silverstone had a deal to host the British GP exclusively. Many drivers were sad about this, but Gerhard Berger summed up the situation when he reckoned that it was then "the best circuit in the world, but a bit dangerous now for F1".

Since losing the grand prix, Brands Hatch has been reduced to holding largely national race meetings, with a few international events augmenting its diet. A chicane was inserted at Dingle Dell Corner, and Graham Hill Bend was later reprofiled, but any dreams of Brands Hatch ever hosting a grand prix again are long gone. The topography that makes it so interesting means that too much work would be required to enlarge the run-off to modern standards as well as the expensive requirement to relocate the pits; the current paddock is far too small and space is limited. With houses nearby, there are also considerable noise restrictions. ∎

Opposite: Jochen Rindt keeps his Lotus ahead of Ronnie Peterson's March after lapping it as they head out of Brands Hatch's amphitheatre at Surtees in 1970.

PADDOCK HILL BEND • 209KPH/130MPH **5** 1

3

2

DRUIDS • 119KPH/74MPH **2** 2

3 GRAHAM HILL BEND • 179KPH/111MPH

5

SURTEES * 193KPH (120MPH) **4**

4

5 CLEARWAYS • 210KPH/130MPH

CLARK CURVE • 225KPH/140MPH **5** 12

11

HAWTHORN BEND • 225KPH/140MPH

WESTFIELD BEND • 233KPH/145MPH

DINGLE DELL CORNER • 177KPH/110MPH

STIRLING'S BEND • 164KPH/102MPH

Google Earth

Circuit Guide

Brands Hatch is a twisting and turning track that rises and falls as it works its way through a natural bowl lined with grandstands to a blast through a wooded section. Drivers considered it one of their toughest challenges before it was dropped from the F1 rota.

Turn 1 • **Paddock Hill Bend**
Gear: **5**
Speed: **209kph (130mph)**

This is a corner that is far from easy because it's hard to identify any markers on approach over a rise in the start/finish straight. Bumpy at the point where drivers want to brake, with the barriers right alongside the track on the left, drivers have to turn in before they can see around the corner, with the track dropping to the right. It's vital not to take too wide a line, because understeer induced by the track falling away will take a car straight on.

Turn 2 • **Druids**
Gear: **2**
Speed: **119kph (74mph)**

After the drama of Paddock Hill Bend, drivers get their cars back under control, then accelerate through the dip and power up the hill to this righthand hairpin. The ideal line is to brake deep into the corner, keeping the car to the left, then brush the apex and slide wide on the exit. However, a look in the mirrors might reveal someone trying to dive up the inside on the way into the corner, requiring a modification of line towards the right.

Turn 4 • **Surtees**
Gear: **4**
Speed: **193kph (120mph)**

Approached via the curving Cooper Straight that runs behind the paddock, this lefthander takes the cars out of Brands Hatch's amphitheatre onto the country loop. The turn-in looks simple enough, but the corner then not only rises sharply towards its exit but tightens its radius, leaving cars understeering, then, as they crest the rise at the exit and dip under a bridge, oversteering just when they want to be going straight ahead for what follows – the fastest part of the circuit.

Turn 6 • **Hawthorn Bend**
Gear: **5**
Speed: **225kph (140mph)**

After racing flat-out through the compression at the foot of Pilgrim's Drop and then climbing Hawthorn Hill, drivers reach Hawthorn Bend. It's a fast, open righthander, but it's made tricky by the fact that attacking drivers might try a passing move. With drivers seeing trees ahead of them as they approach, it's natural to want to brake harder than required, but they need to keep as much speed as possible for the short straight that follows along to Westfield. Jo Siffert died here in the 1971 Rothmans Victory Race.

Opposite: The South Bank has always been a popular viewing position, as shown here in 1984. *Above left:* Diving into the compression by the apex at Stirling's Bend, Jacky Ickx keeps his Ferrari in front of Jackie Stewart's Tyrrell and Jean-Pierre Beltoise's BRM in 1972. *Above right:* Jackie Oliver leads Jo Siffert and Chris Amon into Druids in 1968.

Turn 7 • **Westfield Bend**
Gear: **4**
Speed: **233kph (145mph)**

With trees lining either side of the track behind broad grass verges, the approach to this corner is benign enough, but its characteristic is entirely different to Hawthorn Bend, after dipping slightly before the turn-in point, it then drops away sharply after the apex and, if it wasn't for this, the corner would otherwise be all but flat-out. Again, a tight line is required to avoid running wide on the exit, because any lifting off the throttle will cost momentum.

Turn 9 • **Dingle Dell Corner**
Gear: **4**
Speed: **177kph (110mph)**

After the slight right kink at Dingle Dell, the track rises to Dingle Dell Corner. This too is a righthander, but requires a lot more attention because it's impossible to see the apex on the way in. Instead, drivers aim for the marshals' post beyond, then brake hard and attempt to put their cars into a slide, immediately trying to regain full control to help to swing the car back across from the left of the track to the right for the following corner.

Turn 10 • **Stirling's Bend**
Gear: **3**
Speed: **164kph (102mph)**

Approached down the short straight after Dingle Dell Corner, this is the last corner of the wooded country loop and the slowest, demanding caution. For the optimal line, drivers need to have their cars on the extreme right of the track, brake hard, then drop to third gear and turn in sharply. Cars would often oversteer here, some drivers even employing opposite lock to straighten them up so that they could start accelerating as soon as possible for the run back towards the circuit's amphitheatre.

Turn 12 • **Clark Curve**
Gear: **5**
Speed: **225kph (140mph)**

After arcing to the right through Clearways, staying away from the outside of the track where it drops away slightly, drivers reach this, the final corner of the lap and want to maximize their entry speed to the Brabham Straight past the pits. Typical of Brands Hatch, this fast righthander is full of camber changes to catch out the unwary, with drivers also experiencing the contrast of being back out in full daylight and the trackside being filled with spectators.

🇬🇧 Silverstone

Dubbed the home of British motor racing, Silverstone is far more than that – it's very much one of the great tracks of the world. Indeed, it's the venue that hosted the opening round of the inaugural World Championship back in 1950.

> ❝The new loop offers some challenging corners as well as overtaking opportunities. What's important is that we have a circuit to test the world.❞
>
> *Damon Hill*

Silverstone is undoubtedly one of the world's great racing circuits. Not only does it offer drivers a real challenge to get their teeth into, but it's steeped in history and has hosted more top international race meetings than almost any other, with world-class sportscar and touring car events alongside its 47 grands prix hosted to date.

After the Second World War, Britain was dotted with airfields with little purpose. The village of Silverstone had one of these and it wasn't long before it was identified by the Royal Automobile Club as a place where a racing circuit might be created around its perimeter roads and up and down its runways. The Air Ministry agreed to a lease and things moved so fast that it hosted the first British GP in its opening year, 1948, with Luigi Villoresi winning for Maserati.

With the dynamic Jimmy Brown as circuit manager, modifications were made for 1949, the stretches along the runways being removed and replaced by the classic Silverstone silhouette that has largely remained to this day, with plenty of sky, plenty of space and plenty of pace. It was then and always has been a place for fast motor racing, offering open corners and room to race as opposed to the strictures offered by many of its rivals.

For 1950, it was given the honour of hosting the first round of the first ever World Championship, with Alfa Romeo showing British fans the levels

that could be attained. In 1952, the temporary pits were moved from after Abbey to between Woodcote and Copse, but then little changed until 1975, when a chicane was inserted at Woodcote – no doubt to prevent a repeat of the massed accident triggered by Jody Scheckter when he'd run wide there in 1973. That 1975 British GP proved equally disastrous, though, as torrential rain hit half of the circuit, with car after car sliding off at Club.

Unlike quite a few of the circuits hosting grands prix, Silverstone is a circuit that is in use most weekends from spring to autumn, running events on its full and its national layouts for everything from international level meetings to club events.

As speeds continued to rise and the FIA asked for improved safety, changes were made, with the straight from Abbey to Woodcote given a chicane called Luffield in 1987 before a far more comprehensive alteration – to the same straight – in 1991, this time making the track go into a dip halfway along its length and turn to the right in a corner called Bridge. This fearsome corner was then followed by a loop made by lefthanders at Priory and Brooklands before returning to Luffield. Stowe was also tightened, with the track dropping into a dip called the Vale, this also making Club a much slower corner. The best change of all, though, was when straight after the high-speed left kink at Maggotts, the track was

made to run through a new sequence of esses at Becketts, a world-class run of corners.

What marks the British GP out is not just the size of the crowd – always a sell-out, with the spectator banking also packed on the Friday and Saturday as well – but its knowledge and passion. Occasionally, this has overflowed, such as in the height of Mansellmania when the crowds flowed onto the track in support of a new national hero as F1 brought in fans new to racing.

Silverstone has been ever-changing since, with a chicane added at Abbey in 1994 and then its most comprehensive alterations in the past five years. These came at the behest of F1 ringmaster Bernie Ecclestone, who was perpetually sniping that Silverstone was lagging behind the facilities that new, government-funded circuits in the Far East were offering. So, in order to secure its long-term future as a grand prix circuit, Silverstone built a giant pit building between Club and Abbey in 2010, with an extra loop added that curled around the infield and then used the old club straight down to Brooklands. The layout has changed and the startline moved, but the nature has not, as Silverstone still has plenty of sky, plenty of space and plenty of pace. ∎

Opposite: The opening of The Wing pit buildings brought Silverstone into the twenty-first century, along with an extended track layout.

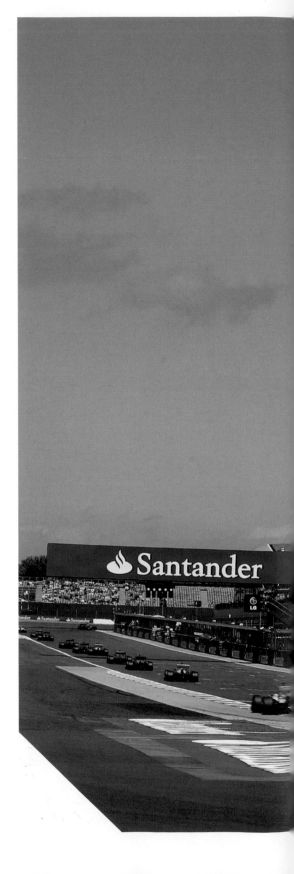

CLUB CORNER • 215KPH/134MPH **5**

APPROACH • 295KPH/183MPH **6**

18

215KPH/134MPH **5** **E**

3

125KPH/77MPH **3** **17**

A

16

ABBEY • 295KPH/183MPH **7**

1

STOWE • 240KPH/149MPH **5**

3 VALE • 102KPH/63MPH

2

FARM • 292KPH/181MPH **7**

15

CHAPEL • 250KPH/155MPH **6**

A

2

7 APPROACH • 302KPH/187MPH

14

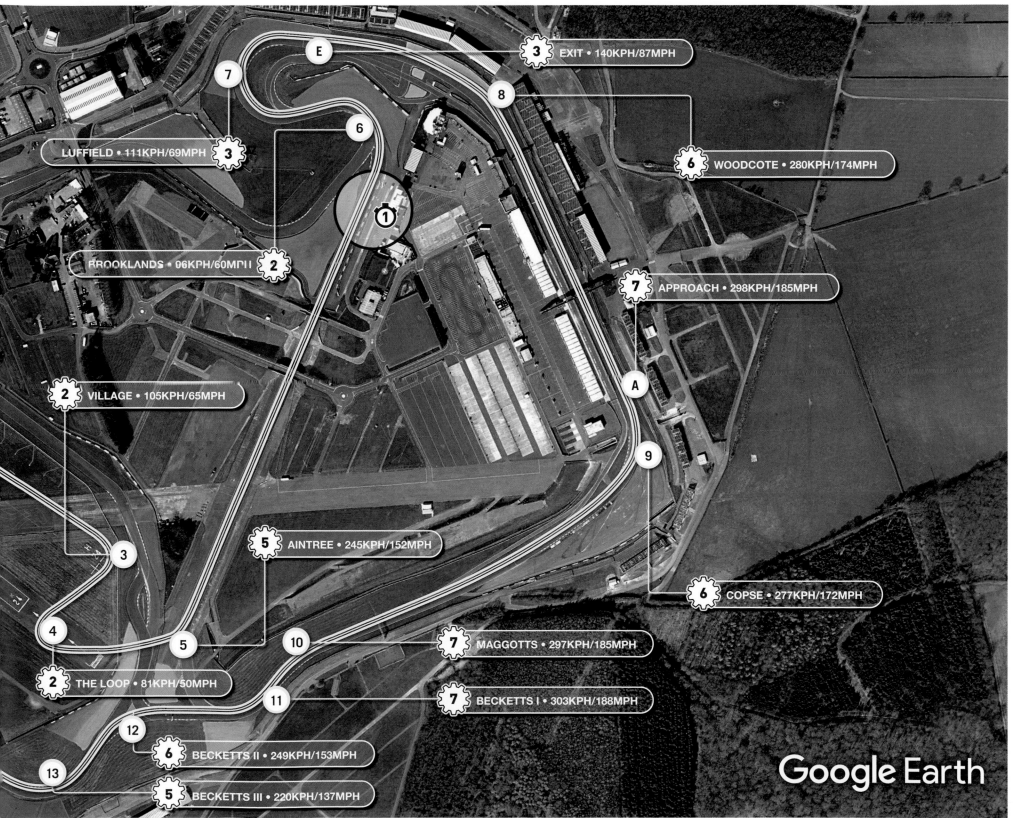

3 EXIT • 140KPH/87MPH

LUFFIELD • 111KPH/69MPH 3

6 WOODCOTE • 280KPH/174MPH

7 APPROACH • 298KPH/185MPH

BROOKLANDS • 96KPH/60MPH 2

2 VILLAGE • 105KPH/65MPH

5 AINTREE • 245KPH/152MPH

6 COPSE • 277KPH/172MPH

7 MAGGOTTS • 297KPH/185MPH

2 THE LOOP • 81KPH/50MPH

7 BECKETTS I • 303KPH/188MPH

6 BECKETTS II • 249KPH/153MPH

5 BECKETTS III • 220KPH/137MPH

Google Earth

Circuit Guide

Its flat, wide open spaces have always been used to make a track full of high-speed corners and, even though its layout has changed on numerous occasions, the spirit of the track that hosted the first British GP back in 1948 still prevails.

Turn 1 • Abbey
Gear: **7**
Speed: **295kph (183mph)**

Until 2010, this was a rapid corner two-thirds of the way around the lap, but since 2011 it has become the first corner, the point at which the track turns into the infield loop. In its initial incarnation, it was a very fast lefthander, where Tony Brooks rolled his BRM in 1956 when its throttle stuck open. In the mid-1990s, it was slowed by the insertion of a chicane, but at last Abbey is a quick corner again, with a bump before entry making drivers exercise caution.

Turn 7 • Luffield
Gear: **3**
Speed: **111kph (69mph)**

This is a tricky corner because drivers are often out of position after exiting Brooklands, and need to get over to the left side of the track before arriving at Luffield so that they can take the widest entry for the optimum line through the righthander. To compound their problems, Luffield is really a two-part corner and those who miss the first apex will be way off the ideal line at the exit, thus delaying them getting the power down for the blast towards Copse.

Turn 6 • Brooklands
Gear: **2**
Speed: **96kph (60mph)**

This long left is a tricky corner in its own right, because it's approached in top gear and requires drivers to lose two-thirds of their speed. Ideally, drivers will be hugging the righthand kerb, ready to take the least severe line around the corner. However, this is a popular overtaking point, so many drivers find themselves having to take a less ideal line as they defend their position, with the consequences of a poor exit line being magnified at the next corner, Luffield.

Turn 9 • Copse
Gear: **6**
Speed: **277kph (172mph)**

The changing layouts used at Silverstone mean that this corner – the first corner of the lap from 1950 until 2010, before that changed to Abbey – is now found halfway around the lap. This doesn't stop it from being a daunting bend all the same, but no longer are drivers arriving for this sixth-gear corner with a turn-in made blind by the end of the pitwall in a pack of jostling cars. It's a corner that requires precision to keep the flow going.

Opposite: The sign says it all as Felipe Massa guides his Ferrari into Becketts in 2007. *Above left:* This aerial view shows Copse in 2001, when it was still the first corner of the lap. *Above right:* Abbey is now the opening corner, and Red Bull Racing's Sebastian Vettel and Mark Webber are shown leading away at the start in 2011.

Turn 11/13 • **Becketts II**
Gear: **6**
Speed: **210kph (163mph)**

There is scarcely a driver who doesn't rank the Becketts esses as one of their greatest challenges of the season. They are approached at speed, with the added difficulty that drivers have just veered left through Maggotts before they have to turn right, then left, then right again, bringing their speed down from 290kph (180mph) or so in seventh at the first part to not much over 220kph (137mph) by the last, taken in fifth, turning as they do so. A great run through here offers immense satisfaction.

Turn 15 • **Stowe**
Gear: **5**
Speed: **240kph (149mph)**

For decades, this fast righthander at the end of the Hangar Straight was the circuit's signature corner, a place where the bold would be rewarded if they carried more speed in. However, since 1991, it has been less of a challenge because it was made to turn back on itself to feed the cars into the Vale. As a consequence, there is less chance of overtaking here, which has sadly reduced the desire for drivers to work themselves into a slipstreaming position down the straight.

Turn 16 • **Vale**
Gear: **3**
Speed: **102kph (62mph)**

Drivers have to really hit the anchors for this righthander, approached down the dipping and increasingly enclosed straight from Stowe. A wide line through the corner is achieved by entering the sharp lefthander from the righthand side of the track, but this can be scuppered if a rival then dives down the inside to take the corner. Their exit speed will then invariably be affected, but to some it's a risk worth taking. Acceleration up the short slope towards Club corner is vital to finish off the lap.

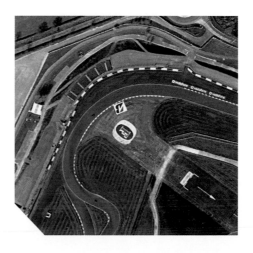

Turn 18 • **Club Corner**
Gear: **5**
Speed: **215kph (134mph)**

The last corner of the lap was another corner that was slowed in the 1991 redevelopment and, like Stowe, was changed from a high-speed corner through which drivers kept their flow going to a corner that is arrived at slowly. Drivers have to hit the brakes and turn sharply left out of the Vale, then start turning right and turning significantly more as they climb a small rise, then wait for the moment to plant the throttle to accelerate onto the start/finish straight.

Great Drivers & Great Moments

The high-speed nature of the circuit and its wide open corners have led to some remarkable races since Silverstone hosted the first ever World Championship race in 1950, and the selection of names and events chosen here is just the tip of the iceberg of the great names who have triumphed here.

Great Drivers

Alain **Prost**
Silverstone wins – 5

Not only did Alain win the British GP at Silverstone five times, twice more than any other driver, but he did so with four teams and achieved this feat over a span of 11 years. His first success here was in 1983, when he was racing for Renault. He then won again in 1985 on F1's next visit, this time for McLaren, and took a third in 1989 after team-mate Ayrton Senna spun out. He completed his tally by winning for Ferrari in 1991 and Williams in 1993.

Nigel **Mansell**
Silverstone wins – 3

Nigel Mansell had won the European GP at Brands Hatch in 1985 and then the British GP there in 1986, but Mansellmania was in its infancy then. By 1987, though, it was in full swing and the way with which Nigel hunted down his Williams team-mate Nelson Piquet at Silverstone in 1987 had the fans on their toes. When he dived down the inside into Stowe with three laps to go, they went wild. He'd win again at Silverstone in 1992.

Michael **Schumacher**
Silverstone wins – 3

This seven-time World Champion ended his career with multiple wins at most grands prix, and he collected three here. After being denied in 1995 when his Benetton was taken out by Damon Hill, he triumphed for Ferrari in 1998 in a finish that was notable because he took the unusual step of serving his stop-go penalty at the end of his final lap. He also won at Silverstone in 2002 and 2004. Michael probably recalls the 1999 race with the least affection, as he crashed at Stowe and broke a leg.

Lewis **Hamilton**
Silverstone wins – 3

When Lewis Hamilton won the British GP for McLaren in 2008, everyone thought that it would be his first of many at Silverstone. Yet, that famous win in fast-changing wet/dry conditions wasn't equalled until he finally won his home race for a second time in 2014. Now racing for Mercedes, he was caught out by a rapidly-drying track and qualified sixth, but closed in on Nico Rosberg before his team-mate's gearbox failed. In 2015, it was all rather easier after Williams gots its tactics wrong.

Great Moments

1950 Alfa Romeo domination in first WC round

When the World Championship arrived for its first ever round in May 1950, it was clear that the Alfa Romeo team would supply the winner, especially when its 158s filled the first four places on the grid. Not even Prince Bira in a Maserati could challenge them and so Giuseppe Farina swapped the lead with team-mates Luigi Fagioli and Jean Manuel Fangio before storming home at the head of an Alfa 1-2-3, with the next finisher – Yves Giraud-Cabantous in a Lago-Talbot – two laps adrift.

1969 Jackie Stewart wins by a whole lap

Only 17 grands prix have ended up with the winner finishing a lap clear, but this happened in 1969, when Jackie Stewart won an enthralling duel with Jochen Rindt. The Austrian had led away in his Lotus, the pair immediately dropping the rest, but the Scot went past on lap 6 in his Matra, only to be repassed 10 laps later. They stayed glued together for the next 46 laps until Rindt pitted with a loose wing endplate, and this left Stewart to win as he pleased.

1973 Jody Scheckter triggers chaos on lap 1

It's safe to say that Jody Scheckter made a massive impact when he broke into F1 as a 22-year-old. The British GP was his third outing of 1973 in McLaren's third car and the South African was pressing hard at the end of the opening lap when he ran wide coming out of Woodcote onto the start/finish straight. In an instant, his M23 spun off the grass and came back across the track, scattering those behind and triggering an eight-car pile-up that stopped the race.

2008 Lewis Hamilton dominates in the wet

Lewis Hamilton had come so close to taking the drivers' title at his first attempt in 2007, so was determined to make amends in 2008 and drove a beautiful race to prove the master of ever-changing conditions for McLaren. Kimi Raikkonen was the only driver to offer even a slight challenge, but Ferrari guessed wrong on tyre choice and Hamilton was left to control proceedings. At the end, he was a minute clear of Sauber's Nick Heidfeld, with Honda's Rubens Barrichello the only other unlapped runner.

Hungaroring

This was a landmark circuit when it was built to host a round of the World Championship in 1986. It took Formula One to a new region, into still-communist Eastern Europe, showing how the sport was opening up and embracing new areas in its desire for a truly global reach.

" The Hungaroring is a circuit where drivers are busy all around the lap, so it's really demanding and there are barely any opportunities to catch your breath."

Michael Schumacher

The World Championship had an established pattern through the 1970s. The vast majority of the grands prix continued to be held in Europe, but after 1980 Watkins Glen was deemed no longer to be safe for the increasing speed of the cars and the search began for a permanent home for the United States GP. Then, in 1985, Australia finally landed a round. With that country's strong racing pedigree, this came as no surprise. What followed in 1986, though, most certainly did.

The shock was the addition of a Hungarian GP: not only had the country's limited racing pedigree faded decades earlier, with its only grand prix being held in Budapest's Nepliget Park in 1936, but the country was behind the Iron Curtain, its government communist and thus opposed to such capitalist pursuits as motor racing. However, when attempts to place a World Championship event in the Soviet Union faltered, the government sanctioned the building of a circuit for the express purpose of hosting a grand prix.

The Hungaroring has a spectacular location in rolling hills to the north-east of Budapest, with its layout (designed by Istvan Papp) taking the drivers along one side of the valley and down the dip across it before traversing the far side, then making the return leg back across the valley again. Because of this, the circuit is one of only a handful of grand prix circuits built over a river. This is found, naturally, at its lowest point, being crossed when the drivers head down into the dip after Turn 3 and then again when they head back towards the pits before Turn 12. This led to a change of track format in 1989, when a chicane immediately after Turn 3 was bypassed, enabling the drivers to carry more speed down into the dip.

This is a circuit where drivers need to set their cars up on soft suspension settings and can run a medium degree of wing because there are many more corners than straights. It's also a track on which drivers need to be alert to the way its surface changes markedly from their opening laps in first practice on the Friday morning of a grand prix meeting through the course of the weekend. Dust is a problem, but it gets grippier as rubber is laid down, although that degree of extra traction can come at a cost to the tyres as temperatures are often sky high here in summer.

The most remarkable thing about the inaugural Hungarian GP was the size of the crowd, with around 200,000 people turning out to witness this novelty, thus dwarfing the turn-out at many of the other European events. It was thus adjudged a hit as Nelson Piquet romped to victory for Williams, but there was one problem then that has affected every grand prix there since: a lack of places to overtake.

With its bowl-like location, viewing from the grandstands on either side of the valley is great but, sadly, the racing is not. While the circuit provides an interesting challenge for drivers attempting to set the fastest lap in qualifying, with the corners coming thick and fast, there's precious little space for overtaking, leading to processional races where the main chance for passing the car ahead comes from a tactically timed pitstop. Nigel Mansell bucked this trend in 1989, when he muscled his way from 12th on the grid to win for Ferrari, but more often than not the race order is static. This was proved comprehensively the following year, when Thierry Boutsen won for Williams, holding back Ayrton Senna's clearly faster McLaren.

Despite the fact that Hungarian driver Ferenc Szisz won the first ever grand prix, the French GP of 1906, Hungarian fans are still waiting for one of their own to run at the front. In the history of the World Championship, there has thus far been just one Hungarian driver. This was Zsolt Baumgartner, who had two races for Jordan in 2003, then a full season for Minardi in 2004, peaking with eighth, three laps down, in a crash-hit US GP. ■

Opposite: Fernando Alonso accelerates his Ferrari F2012 out of the third gear Turn 6/7 chicane in 2012.

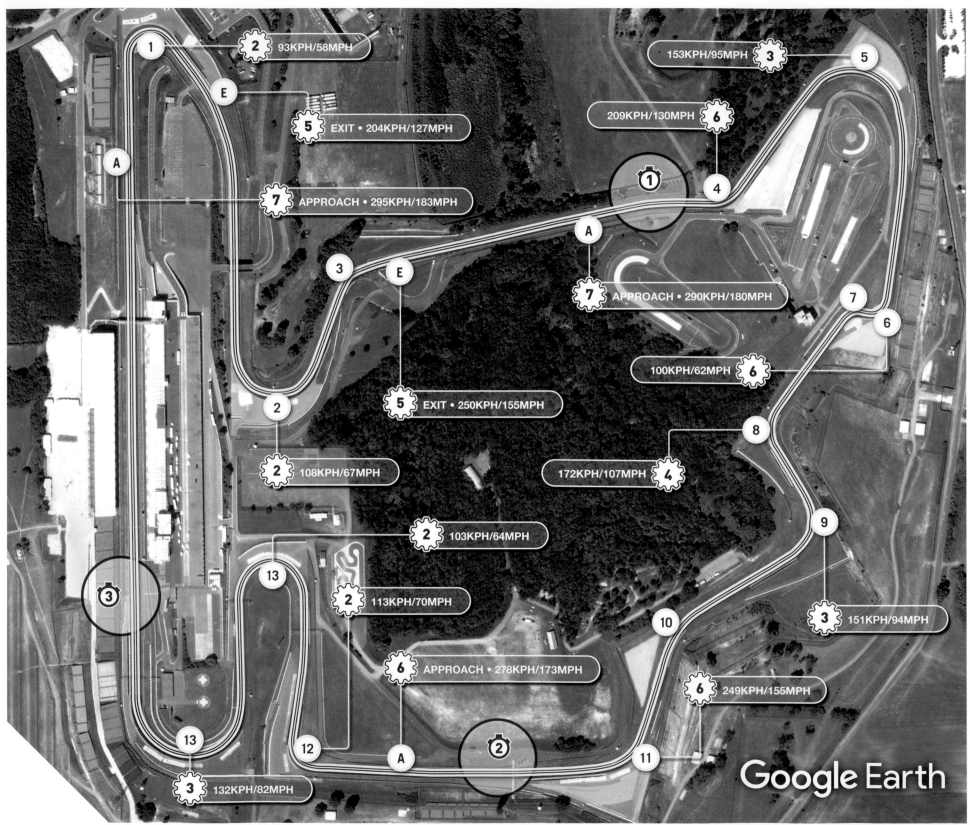

93KPH/58MPH

153KPH/95MPH

EXIT • 204KPH/127MPH

209KPH/130MPH

APPROACH • 295KPH/183MPH

APPROACH • 290KPH/180MPH

EXIT • 250KPH/155MPH

100KPH/62MPH

108KPH/67MPH

172KPH/107MPH

103KPH/64MPH

113KPH/70MPH

151KPH/94MPH

APPROACH • 278KPH/173MPH

249KPH/155MPH

132KPH/82MPH

Image © 2014 DigitalGlobe © Google 2014

Google Earth

Red Bull Racing's Daniel Ricciardo took the lead with just three laps to go to take his second F1 win at the 2014 Hungarian GP.

Circuit Guide

This is a circuit where drivers seem to be turning almost constantly, with only two straights and a host of twisting corners in between. Overtaking is nigh on impossible and the challenge comes from finding the perfect line in qualifying.

Turn 1 •

Gear: **2**
Speed: **93kph (58mph)**

The approach to this corner is down a gentle incline and it represents the only point on the circuit where a driver might realistically think about how best to overtake a car in front. Drivers have to brake as late as they dare, aware that they might have to hamper their exit speed simply to resist an attack from behind. Turn 1 is a two-part corner. It dips from entry to exit as it doubles back and drivers start to position themselves for Turn 2.

Turn 2 •

Gear: **2**
Speed: **108kph (67mph)**

Having arrived down a gentle slope, this lefthander is made all the more interesting because it drops away sharply from the apex. Drivers try to arrive on the far right of the circuit to get the most open and thus fastest run through the corner, but cars tend to dive in from all angles on the opening lap according to the line they occupied when they came out of Turn 1. Contact is not unknown here, but a good move can pay real dividends.

Turn 4 •

Gear: **6**
Speed: **209kph (130mph)**

This is a real rarity at the Hungaroring, a truly fast corner. Drivers arrive after the track has bottomed out at the foot of the valley and hit 290kph (180mph) up the start of the ascent of the opposite slope before dropping down a gear to take this lefthand kink. It's hard for drivers to get a clear view around this corner, especially because the angle of the slope flattens out midway around it, and this makes it extra difficult for balancing the car too.

Turn 6/7 •

Gear: **2**
Speed: **100kph (62mph)**

Having turned through uphill Turn 5 onto the first flat stretch of the circuit since leaving the starting grid, drivers immediately have to get busy through this sequence of fiddly corners set at the foot of natural spectator banking. This right/left chicane is the start of a twisting section of the circuit and forces drivers to run in single file, with numerous clashes over the years when some have tried not to do so, especially if being delayed by a backmarker.

Opposite: Mark Webber brakes hard as he chases Felipe Massa into Turn 1 in 2013. *Above left:* A panoramic view of the Turn 2, with the far side of the track from Turn 5 in the background. *Above right:* There is always jostling for position on the approach to Turn 2 on lap 1, as shown in 2013.

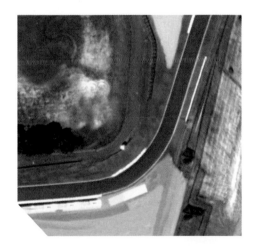

Turn 11 •

Gear: **6**
Speed: **249kph (155mph)**

Having swerved their way along the far side of the valley to the pits, drivers start building up speed after coming out of Turn 9 before carrying it through the sweep of Turn 10. They ought to be hitting 249kph (155mph) when they reach Turn 11, a righthander. With the circuit dropping away at its exit and a short straight following, it's essential that drivers manage to turn in from the lefthand side of the track, clip the apex and then run up to the kerb on the exit.

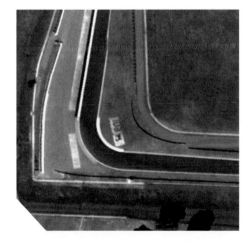

Turn 12 •

Gear: **2**
Speed: **113kph (70mph)**

This is one of the few corners that have been modified since the circuit opened. Originally a fairly open righthand kink, it was changed in 2003 to a tighter corner by the downhill straight from Turn 11 being extended and then this extra stretch of track taking drivers to a 90-degree righthander. At a stroke, it changed it from a third-gear bend to a second gear one and reduced the chances of a chasing driver being able to line up a move into Turn 13.

Turn 13 •

Gear: **2**
Speed: **103kph (64mph)**

The penultimate corner of the lap offers drivers a view of the rear of the paddock high above them as they arrive down the short straight from Turn 12. Drivers must resist the urge to carry too much speed into this upward-turning corner because it's imperative to get the power on as soon as possible once they have passed the apex and can see the exit to get right onto the tail of a rival if they want to be close enough to line up a pass into Turn 1.

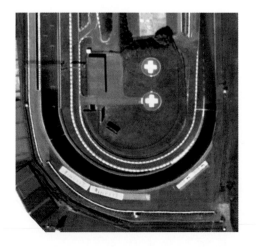

Turn 14 •

Gear: **3**
Speed: **132kph (82mph)**

Still climbing as they leave Turn 13, drivers need to move from the righthand side of the track to the left so that they can take the widest line through this uphill corner. Any extra fraction of momentum that can be built up through this long righthander is vital, because the track flattens out on exit and, providing a chasing driver doesn't lose control over the exit kerbs, they then ought to be able to get into the slipstream of the car ahead.

Great Drivers & Great Moments

Such is the narrow and twisting nature of the Hungaroring that drivers really need to qualify on pole position, then survive attacks through the first two corners to stand a chance of winning, but there have also been some remarkable drivers coming through the field among those on the victory roll.

Great Drivers

 Michael **Schumacher**
Hungaroring wins – 4

Michael spread his wins here across 11 years, from his victory for Benetton in 1994 to his win for Ferrari in 2004. That first win cheered Benetton after its German GP pitfire, then his second for Ferrari in 1998 was produced by an attacking three-stop tactic to get him ahead of the McLarens. He'd win twice more here for Ferrari – in 2001, when a one-two ahead of team-mate Rubens Barrichello clinched his fourth F1 title; and again in 2004, when the season's 13th race brought his 12th win.

 Lewis **Hamilton**
Hungaroring wins – 3

When Lewis Hamilton won here in 2007, it was confirmation that his maiden season was no flash in the pan. His breakthrough win had come in the sixth round in Canada, but he was a two-time winner by the time the teams reached Hungary for round 11. He got in front and stayed there, resisting Kimi Raikkonen's Ferrari. Hamilton won here again in 2012 for McLaren and then followed that up by taking a third Hungarian success in 2013 after moving to Mercedes.

 Ayrton **Senna**
Hungaroring wins – 3

After a pair of second place finishes on his first two visits to the Hungaroring, Ayrton struck gold when he moved from Lotus to McLaren for 1988, leading every lap after starting from pole. Second in both 1989 and 1990, Ayrton won again in 1991 and then completed his Hungaroring hat trick in 1992, when he resisted the otherwise dominant Nigel Mansell's pace-setting Williams to win and so prevent the Englishman from claiming his long-awaited drivers' title with a victory.

 Mika **Hakkinen**
Hungaroring wins – 2

This fast Finn first raced at the Hungaroring in 1991, for Lotus, but didn't take his first win there until eight years later. His success in 1999 came on the second occasion he qualified on pole on this hard-to-pass circuit, and his McLaren team-mate David Coulthard was able to get close only after getting past fast-starting Giancarlo Fisichella and Heinz-Harald Frentzen. Hakkinen made it two in a row in 2000, when a repeat finish was scuppered by Coulthard being delayed by both Minardi drivers.

Great Moments

1986 Nelson **Piquet** wins in front of a huge crowd

Ayrton Senna took pole for the inaugural Hungarian GP, then led away as Nigel Mansell powered past Williams team-mate Nelson Piquet and Alain Prost's McLaren to grab second. Two laps later, Piquet demoted Mansell. While he chased Senna, Prost passed Mansell too. Then, on lap 12 of 76, Piquet hit the front. Electrical problems forced Prost to pit and then Senna did enough to emerge from his tyre-change ahead of Piquet, but the Williams driver then overtook him to win as he pleased.

1997 Damon **Hill** just loses out for Arrows

Jacques Villeneuve winning for Williams in 1997 came as no surprise but, had the race been just one lap shorter, Damon Hill winning for Arrows certainly would have been. Hill qualified third, his best grid position by six places, then moved straight into second behind Michael Schumacher's Ferrari, and then hit the front on lap 11 as Michael struggled on the harder tyres. He built a 35-second cushion, only for a hydraulic glitch to hit on lap 75 of 77. Villeneuve swept past on the final lap.

2006 Jenson **Button** gives Honda its only win

Honda Racing scored its first win here in 2006, and Jenson Button did too, yet this twin triumph was made all the more epic by the fact that they achieved it in a race made unpredictable by wet weather. Kimi Raikkonen led from pole for McLaren, but Fernando Alonso rose from 15th after a qualifying penalty to take over. Then Raikkonen crashed and Alonso's lead was negated by a safety car period. But Alonso later lost a wheel and so Button and Honda got to celebrate.

2014 Daniel **Ricciardo** leaves it late for Red Bull

With Mercedes dominating, F1 needed variety and the fans were treated to plenty of that. Nico Rosberg took pole for Mercedes, but Hamilton's car caught fire and he lined up last. While Hamilton echoed his feat of the previous race by making it up to third, victory went to a car of a different hue as Daniel Ricciardo benefitted as the first four runners passed the pit entrance before a safety car period was announced. The Australian overtook Alonso's Ferrari with three laps to go.

█▌Imola

This is a circuit that Formula One folk used to love, because it not only heralded the first European grand prix of the year but did so in a glorious setting often bathed in spring weather. However, it also had its dark side and will forever be remembered as the circuit where Ayrton Senna died.

❝ Imola is a tricky circuit where it is so easy to make a mistake and completely spoil your lap time, your tyres and your mood. ❞

Nelson Piquet

Anyone fortunate enough to visit the Autodromo Enzo e Dino Ferrari on a sunny spring day will appreciate why this circuit was held in such affection, for it exists as part of the countryside rather than simply being a tailor-made facility in the middle of nowhere. Built on the edge of the town of Imola, with its lower edge only 50 metres (165 ft) or so from the riverbank and its upper side twisting its way through farmland and orchards, it felt connected to its landscape, something that was all the more appreciated when the teams had returned from the season-opening flyaway races. This was where they could bring their trucks for the first time and thus have all the equipment they needed. They could bring their motorhomes too, and so life felt less compromised.

Imola has always operated in the shadow of Monza, the pre-eminent Italian temple to motor racing. Built 30 years after its illustrious rival, Imola opened in 1952 and operated very much as a national level circuit, bar a non-championship F1 race won by Lotus ace Jim Clark in 1963, until it finally gained international standing when its facilities were upgraded in 1979 and it hosted another non-championship F1 race won by Niki Lauda for Brabham. With Monza still in some confusion after Ronnie Peterson's death at the start of the 1978 Italian GP, Imola then took over the Italian GP in 1980, and Brabham won again, this

time with Nelson Piquet taking the chequered flag. Then, with the sport's governing body showing a degree of favouritism to all things Ferrari, Imola remained in F1 after the Italian GP returned to Monza, because it was granted a grand prix of its own from 1981 – called the San Marino GP, named after the small landlocked principality located 80 kilometres (49 miles) to the south-east. This arrangement would continue until 2006, after which the FIA couldn't justify Italy having two grands prix and looked to drop European events to make way for new grands prix in Asia.

By this time, the facilities at Imola had dropped below the level expected, with the paddock seen as its most major drawback. It was incredibly cramped and had little scope to be expanded because it already filled all the space between the back of the pits grandstand and the river behind. So, it was inevitable that its F1 days were numbered, even though its hillsides and grandstands continued to be packed by raucous *tifosi* – and thus F1 lost one of its most characterful venues.

Two of Imola's notable features were that it used to be extremely high on fuel consumption, because so much of the lap was driven at full throttle. It was also immensely hard on the brakes due to heavy retardation being required into Tosa as well as into the Variante Alta and Variante Bassa chicanes. After the insertion of further

chicanes at Tamburello and Villeneuve following the double deaths of Roland Ratzenberger and Ayrton Senna in 1994, the amount of full throttle running was reduced, to 61 per cent of the lap, and the intensity of braking into Tosa cut back. However, it remained a place that made the cars work as hard as the drivers, with the plunge from Piratella down to Acque Minerali, then up again to Variante Alta being incredibly challenging.

While the deaths that rocked F1 in 1994 remain the most poignant, the circuit had had major accidents from which drivers had been fortunate to escape, including Gilles Villeneuve slamming into the barriers at the kink before Tosa in 1980 and Gerhard Berger surviving a fiery crash at Tamburello in 1989. For Ferrari fans, though, a dark moment came in 1991, when disaster struck even before the start as Alain Prost spun out at Rivazza on the parade lap while rain fell and Jean Alesi slid out of the race at Tosa a few laps later. Older *tifosi* might prefer to forget the bad feeling in their camp after Didier Pironi allegedly reneged on a pre-race agreement with team-mate Villeneuve to beat him in the race from which the Formula One Constructors Association (FOCA) teams stayed away. ■

Opposite: F1 at Imola heralded the start of the European season and the arrival of spring. Jarno Trulli's Toyota is shown flashing past the pits at speed in 2006.

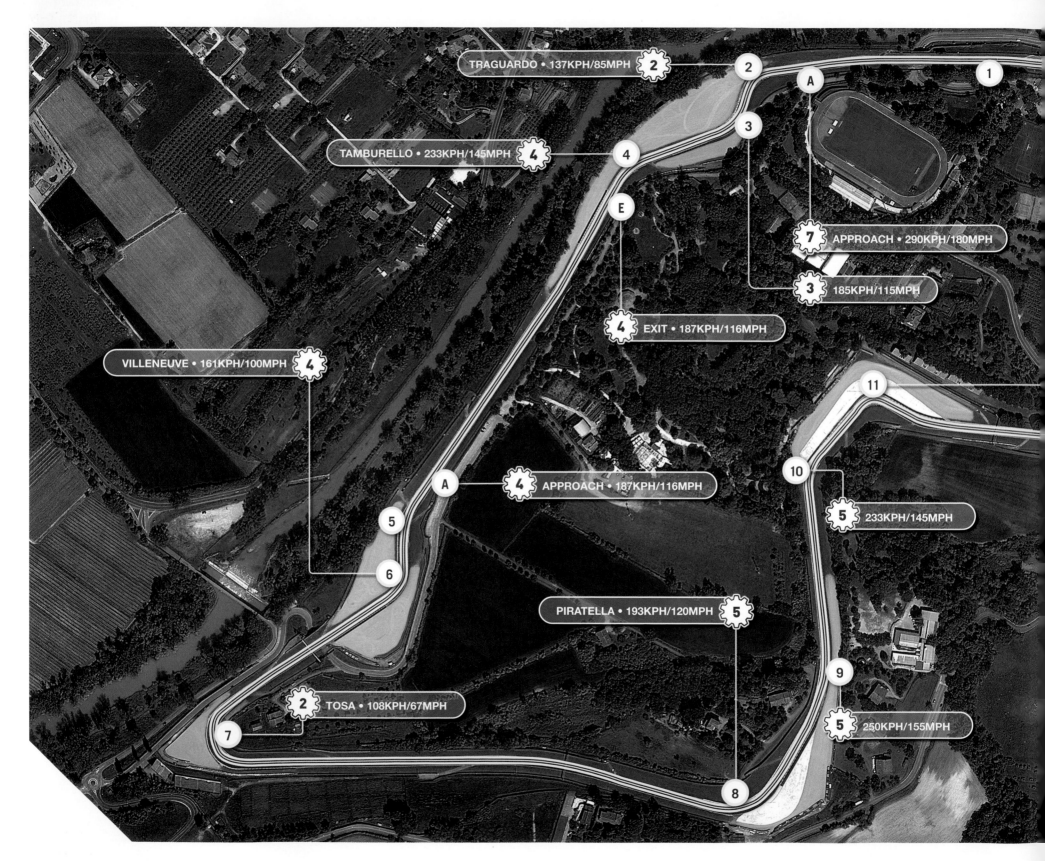

TRAGUARDO • 137KPH/85MPH **2** 2

A 1

3

TAMBURELLO • 233KPH/145MPH **4** 4

A

7 APPROACH • 290KPH/180MPH

E

3 185KPH/115MPH

4 EXIT • 187KPH/116MPH

VILLENEUVE • 161KPH/100MPH **4**

11

10

A **4** APPROACH • 187KPH/116MPH

5 233KPH/145MPH

5

6

PIRATELLA • 193KPH/120MPH **5**

9

TOSA • 108KPH/67MPH **2**

5 250KPH/155MPH

7

8

RIVAZZA II • 140KPH/87MPH **3**

15

17

113KPH/70MPH **2**

18

16

6 282KPH/175MPH

2 VARIANTE BASSA • 113KPH/70MPH

14

3 ACQUE MINERALI • 135KPH/84MPH

RIVAZZA I • 121KPH/75MPH **2**

12

13

3 VARIANTE ALTA • 153KPH/95MPH

3 153KPH/95MPH

Google Earth

Image © 2014 DigitalGlobe © Google 2014

Circuit Guide

Imola is a circuit that offers the joys of incline and immense variety of corners, from the flat-out Tamburello to uphill Tosa and downhill Acque Minerali, with the already buzzing atmosphere made all the more vibrant whenever Ferrari was involved.

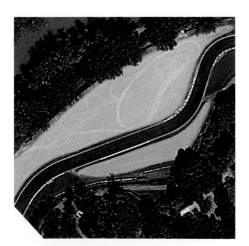

Turn 3/4 • **Tamburello**
Gear: **4**
Speed: **233kph (145mph)**

Built as a flat-out kink, taken in top gear, this lefthander was changed forever after Ayrton Senna was killed when his Williams speared off the track into the barriers in 1994. By the time Formula One returned in 1995, a chicane had been inserted in its place, forcing drivers to drop to second gear to turn left and up to third to go right, then a more open left on the way out. Being the first corner of the circuit, this is often a place of contact on the opening lap.

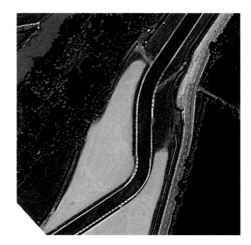

Turn 5/6 • **Villeneuve**
Gear: **4**
Speed: **161kph (100mph)**

The flat-out sprint along the bottom of the valley from the startline to Tosa used to be nearly at its end when the cars reached this kink, with drivers flicking their cars to the right at close to 322kph (200mph) before standing on their brakes for tight Tosa that follows. Then, after Simtek's F1 rookie Roland Ratzenberger crashed fatally here in qualifying in 1994, it was replaced by a second chicane, a left/right combination, thus completing the transformation of the nature of the lap.

Turn 7 • **Tosa**
Gear: **2**
Speed: **108kph (67mph)**

This used to be the first slow corner, a lefthand hairpin with an uphill exit. Fans used to book their grandstand seats there to see who'd dare to brake latest at the end of the blast from the startline. It's still a good place to watch, despite the more broken-up approach, because the drivers have to pick their line carefully to be able to get onto the power as early as possible for the climb towards Piratella, though this was reduced as a spectacle by traction control.

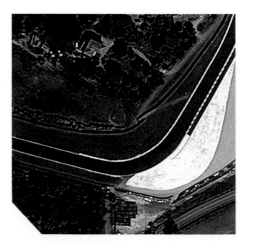

Turn 8 • **Piratella**
Gear: **5**
Speed: **193kph (120mph)**

The highest point of the lap is approached up a long ascent, with woods closing in on the drivers' left as they approach the summit and an earth bank towering over their right side. Feeling hemmed in, they then have to locate the turn-in point around this blind corner. The track drops away downhill to the left and they have to balance the desire to carry momentum with the need to haul their cars back to the left of the track before the next corner.

Opposite: One for the *tifosi* as Ferraris are first and third at the start in 2003, with his brother Ralf's Williams getting between Michael Schumacher and Rubens Barrichello. *Above left:* The spectator banks are always packed. This is at Rivazza. *Above right:* The cars accelerate hard out of Tosa and up the hill towards Piratella.

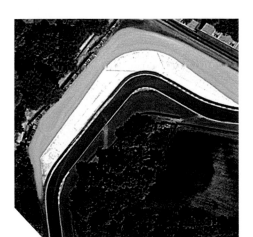

Turn 11 • **Acque Minerali**
Gear: **3**
Speed: **135kph (84mph)**

This has always been one of the trademark corners, and its approach comes up at the drivers quickly as they plunge towards it down the descent from Piratella. Actually, it's really a two-part corner because there's a righthand kink as the track continues its descent, then a tighter right as it reaches the bottom of the dip. Drivers have to drop to third gear in order to negotiate this and manage the compression as they immediately look to accelerate up the next incline.

Turn 12/13 • **Variante Alta**
Gear: 3
Speed: **153kph (95mph)**

The nature of the lap changes again as the drivers power up the hill out of Acque Minerali and leave the meadow on their right behind them and return to having trees on both of their flanks. As the slope reaches its crest, they are suddenly confronted by a chicane. Inserted into the lap in 1974, this flicks right, then left and is all but blind on entry, with drivers having to thump the kerbs to make the line through it as short as possible.

Turn 14/15 • **Rivazza**
Gear: **2**
Speed: **121kph (75mph)**

The flow from the Variante Alta is downhill to the next corner. Not as steep as the plunge from Piratella, it's a slope of note all the same and drivers could hit 306kph (190mph) before they had to brake for the first of this two-part combination of lefthanders. Drivers look to turn in from the far right and the track becomes steeper again after the apex, with a huge gravel trap there to catch any who went in too fast. The second left exits onto level ground.

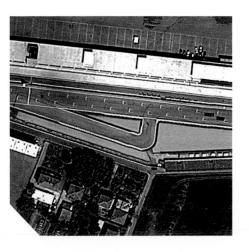

Turn 17/18 • **Variante Bassa**
Gear: **2**
Speed: **113kph (70mph)**

This chicane has been breaking the flow of the final blast towards the end of the lap since it was inserted in 1973, albeit with a format that has changed several times in the intervening years. Initially a right/left, then left/right combination, it was changed to a gentler righthand kink feeding into a short straight and then a tighter left/right chicane onto the start/finish straight in 1995 in response to Rubens Barrichello's lucky escape in 1994. The straight was realigned in 2008.

Great Drivers & Great Moments

There was a time at the start of the twenty-first century when Imola seemed to be Michael Schumacher's personal fiefdom, but the circuit has provided wins for others and some very exciting ones too, as the teams prepared their cars for the European season.

Opposite top: Michael Schumacher had to race really hard in 2006, with Renault's Fernando Alonso pushing his Ferrari all the way to the chequered flag.

Opposite bottom left: Ayrton Senna was in control in 1991, winning for McLaren, but the circuit would claim his life three years later.

Opposite bottom right: The Ferraris dominated a depleted field in 1982. Gilles Villeneuve is shown leading Didier Pironi, but the order was reversed by the finish.

Great Drivers

 Michael **Schumacher**
Imola wins – 7

 Alain **Prost**
Imola wins – 3

 Ayrton **Senna**
Imola wins – 3

 Nigel **Mansell**
Imola wins – 2

The German's run of success began in 1994, when he and Benetton won the awful race that claimed Ayrton Senna's life. He wouldn't win there again until his fourth season with Ferrari, in 1999, when Mika Hakkinen crashed out and Michael got the better of the Finn's McLaren team-mate David Coulthard. After that, he had a remarkable run of wins that was broken only in 2001, when brother Ralf won, and 2005, when he was a close second. He won the final race there in 2006.

This four-time World Champion finished second at Imola in 1983, for Renault, but came good the following year after moving to McLaren to beat René Arnoux's Ferrari. The Frenchman was first in 1985 but was disqualified for his car being underweight, gifting victory to Lotus's Elio de Angelis. He made amends the following year, though, beating Nelson Piquet's Williams by 8 seconds. Prost's third Imola victory came in 1993, when he overcame his Williams team-mate Damon Hill.

Imola was the only circuit at which Ayrton ever failed to qualify, after his Toleman suffered engine failure, but he always went well here after that, finishing in second place for Lotus in 1987 and then winning on three of his next four visits. In both 1988 and 1989, he led all the way from pole position. He missed out in 1990, then won again in 1991. Tragically, this would be the circuit that claimed his life when he crashed his Williams out of the lead in 1994.

Nelson Piquet, Nigel Mansell and Damon Hill all collected two wins at Imola, but Mansell deserves special mention for his dominant victory in 1987, when he finished 27 seconds clear of Ayrton Senna's Lotus. He would retire on each of his next four visits before mounting the top step of Imola's podium again in 1992, after a race for which he qualified on pole and then led every lap to beat his Williams team-mate Riccardo Patrese by 10 seconds for his fifth win in that year's first five rounds.

Great Moments

1980 Nelson **Piquet** wins Imola's inaugural grand prix

1982 Gilles **Villeneuve** falls out with Dider **Pironi**

1994 The weekend from hell claims two lives

2005 Fernando **Alonso** holds off Michael **Schumacher**

This was the only Italian GP to be held here, with all others known as the San Marino GP. Renault filled the front row and René Arnoux led the first two laps, before team-mate Jean-Pierre Jabouille took over, but then Nelson Piquet hit the front and would stay there for the remainder of the race to win easily for Brabham, crossing the line 29 seconds ahead of Alan Jones's Williams. Gilles Villeneuve was lucky to escape a huge shunt at the kink before Tosa, scattering debris.

This race had been boycotted by the FOCA teams and so Ferrari's Didier Pironi and Gilles Villeneuve had only the Renaults as real opposition. Once René Arnoux dropped out, Villeneuve was in the lead and obeyed orders to "slow" as the Ferraris were marginal on fuel. Pironi caught him, then went past. Twice, Villeneuve retook the lead, then slowed to preserve fuel. However, Pironi elected to ignore orders and took the lead on the final lap. Villeneuve was livid and never spoke to him again.

The 1994 San Marino GP was jinxed. First Rubens Barrichello was fortunate to survive a huge crash in his Jordan on the Friday. Then Simtek rookie Roland Ratzenberger was killed in qualifying before Ayrton Senna made it two deaths in two days when he crashed his Williams out of the lead early in the race. Add to that spectators being injured when debris flew into the crowd at the start and mechanics being knocked over by Michael Alboreto's errant wheel in the pitlane, and it was truly a weekend from hell.

History relates that the 2005 grand prix was to be the penultimate one held at Imola, but no one knew that at the time. What it will be remembered for, though, is a fantastic battle between Fernando Alonso's Renault and Michael Schumacher's Ferrari. Kimi Raikkonen had set the pace, but his McLaren broke a driveshaft and then Alonso led as Schumacher passed Jenson Button before closing right in. Yet, despite having the faster car, the German could not quite find a way past the wily Spaniard.

⬛▯⬛Monza

This fine Italian circuit is the oldest European circuit still in use, making it drip with history, and it continues to offer a distinctive driving challenge. Monza also has the added advantage that the racing here is often riveting, offering scope for drivers to challenge one another down the straights into the chicanes.

❝Monza is a circuit I like very much. Having good brakes and traction are important factors here and crucial for a good race.❞
Rubens Barrichello

Most dedicated race fans will tell you that some circuits offer great racing while others offer a special aura. Monza, or the Autodromo Nazionale di Monza to give it its full name, offers both. It really is an exceptionally special place. Certainly, its facilities are increasingly rough around the edges, despite constant updates, but it offers so much more than almost all of the recently built, tailor-made circuits that have been commissioned around the world. You don't even have to spot the fabled banked circuit of old lurking in the infield to appreciate that this is a serious temple to motorsport.

As long ago as 1922, urged by the nascent Italian automotive industry's desire to show off its sporting aspirations, the Automobile Club of Milan selected a site in a walled park adjoining the Villa Reale estate outside the town of Monza as the ideal place to build a racing circuit. The project was completed in only 110 days thanks to 3,500 people labouring on the project and so Italy had a circuit of which to be proud. It gave rise to a nation that really worshipped motor racing, becoming in time the home of the *tifosi*, the Ferrari-worshipping fans who have eyes for no other cars. Even in recent years when Ferrari hasn't offered its drivers a competitive car, the huge grandstand opposite the pits has been packed with fans clad in Ferrari's red colours. Over the years, *tifosi* without seats in that main grandstand have

even climbed trees or scaled advertising hoardings in order to get a better view of the action, famously booing any driver from a rival team should their car retire from the race.

One notable feature of the original circuit was that it had two main components: the circuit outline that is little changed today and a second element, a banked oval that could either be run as just that or be included as the second half of each lap. If both parts were used, Monza's full lap distance was 10km (6.214 miles).

In 1955, the last corner of the lap, Curva Vedano, was transformed from two asymmetric corners, with the first sharper than the second, into one, long righthander that was, fittingly, named Curva Parabolica, and this is perhaps the least changed corner of the lap, a real slingshot of a corner if a driver gets it right. As the circuit has such a fast layout, though, cars are generally sent out with a low downforce set-up. This means that they have minimal wing angle – they're fast down the straights but struggle through the corners – making it a real balancing act to keep turning right through the Parabolica without running wide into the gravel trap.

The banked circuit was used until 1961 and remains as a reminder of wilder days, decaying gradually as it arcs to the right at around the point of the first chicane.

The other main change to the circuit came in 1972, when the drivers were confronted for the first time with three chicanes that had been inserted around the lap to slow the cars. More than that, they were aimed to break up the packs of slipstreaming cars and thus eliminate the high-speed collisions that had given the circuit such a black name. Indeed, the list of drivers who have perished racing at Monza is way too long. Among the fallen are Giuseppe Campari, who went over the banking at the old South Curve in 1933; Wolfgang von Trips, who cartwheeled into the crowd on the approach to Parabolica in 1961, killing 13; Jochen Rindt, who crashed to his death at the same corner in 1970 and became the sport's only posthumous world champion; and Ronnie Peterson, who was involved in a massed collision on the blast to the first chicane in 1978 and died from his injuries.

Yet, despite the occasional tinkering with the outline of the circuit, Monza's nature remains much as it has always been: a high-speed lap on a ribbon of tarmac cutting through wooded parkland. It has a magic made by a heady mix of its immense history, the challenge of its greatest corners, the passion of its fans and its beautiful setting. ■

Opposite: Jean Alesi exits the Parabolica onto the pit straight in his Benetton in 1996.

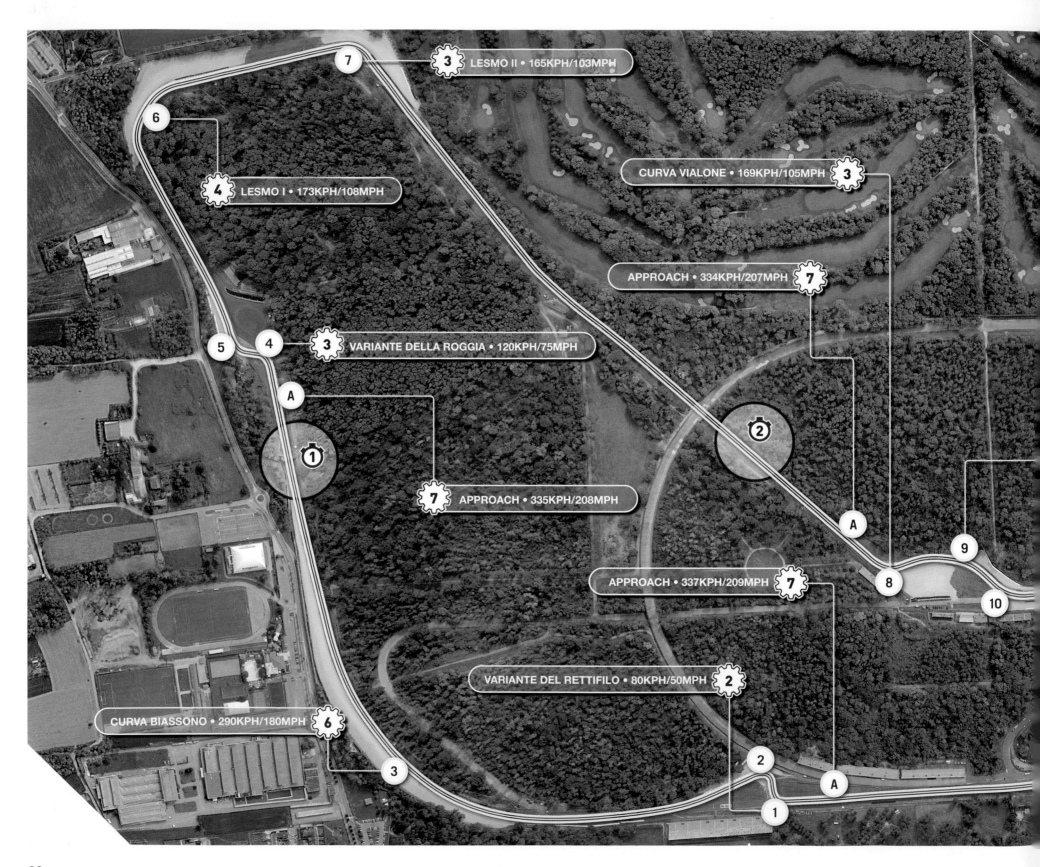

LESMO II • 165KPH/103MPH

CURVA VIALONE • 169KPH/105MPH

LESMO I • 173KPH/108MPH

APPROACH • 334KPH/207MPH

VARIANTE DELLA ROGGIA • 120KPH/75MPH

APPROACH • 335KPH/208MPH

APPROACH • 337KPH/209MPH

VARIANTE DEL RETTIFILO • 80KPH/50MPH

CURVA BIASSONO • 290KPH/180MPH

APPROACH • 336KPH/208MPH **7**

4 VARIANTE ASCARI • 200KPH/124MPH

A

CURVA PARABOLICA • 187KPH/116MPH **4** **11**

3

Google Earth

Image © 2014 DigitalGlobe © Google 2014

Circuit Guide

This is a circuit with a flow to it, one that allows drivers to build up speed and offers the space in which to try to overtake. There are slow parts too, but the overall nature is high-speed with the Parabolica a masterpiece.

Turn 1 • Variante del Rettifilo
Gear: **2**
Speed: **80kph (50mph)**

This was merely part of the start/finish straight until 1972, when a chicane was inserted to break up the slipstreaming packs of cars and cut speeds through Curva Grande. First a double right/left combination, it was altered in 2000 to a single right/left chicane, with a far tighter first turn. This invariably catches out several cars on the opening lap; there is fortunately an escape road should they need to take evasive action, with drivers then having to weave through giant blocks before rejoining.

Turn 4/5 • Variante della Roggia
Gear: **3**
Speed: **120kph (75mph)**

Like the Variante del Rettifilo, this was inserted in 1972 to cut speeds and break up the packs of cars. This second chicane is the opposite of the first: it's a left/right combination, with an approach that offers even less of a view of what follows. With trees still not far from the track on the righthand side, this chicane is often shaded, adding a level of difficulty on bright days. Like the first chicane, it can provide drama, especially on the opening lap.

Turn 3 • Curva Biassono
Gear: **6**
Speed: **290kph (180mph)**

Despite the trees having been moved back from the outside edge of this corner to improve safety, this righthand sweep formerly known as Curva Grande remains a fine bend. Taken in sixth gear, it's not as challenging as it was long ago, because this once majestic but fairly scary bend now has a far shorter approach following the insertion of the Variante del Rettifilo in 1972. Yet it remains a corner that is essential to master to build speed for the run to the second chicane.

Turn 6 • Lesmo I
Gear: **4**
Speed: **173kph (108mph)**

The Lesmos are often combined in descriptions of the circuit, but they are two, distinct corners. Reached at the furthest point away from the pits, they are both righthanders, but both offer a different challenge. This first one is the faster of the pair and offers drivers little view other than of trees as they approach, but a broader one as they hit the apex because the run to the second Lesmo offers plenty of open space to the drivers' left.

Opposite: Monza's banked section was last used in a grand prix in 1961 and now lies decaying in the infield. *Above left:* Jacky Ickx's Ferrari leads the field away from the grid in 1970 on the long, pre-chicane, blast to what was then known as Curva Grande. *Above right:* Valtteri Bottas' Williams FW35 Renault leads Charles Pic's Caterham CT03 Renault into Curva Parabolica in 2013.

Turn 7 • Lesmo II

Gear: **3**
Speed: **165kph (103mph)**

The second Lesmo was tightened in 1995, meaning that drivers could carry less speed through the corner but offering greater safety as it left more run-off space for any driver who had gone into the corner too fast. Like most corners at this still classically flowing circuit, speed out of the corner is the aim of every driver, especially because here it feeds the cars onto the kinked straight that takes the cars under the bridge carrying the banked section of the old circuit towards Curva Vialone.

Turn 8 • Curva Vialone

Gear: **3**
Speed: **169kph (105mph)**

Drivers arrive at this third gear lefthander after a dipping and shaded straight that drives under the banked oval, with a rapid exit from Lesmo II offering a chance to try to line up a passing move here. This is the first point at which the drivers can see the sky clearly again because it's where the track emerges from its loop through the woods that started before the second chicane. Dropping four gears, they have to be on the right line or risk arriving at the next corner out of shape.

Turn 9/10 • Variante Ascari

Gear: **4**
Speed: **200kph (124mph)**

Straight out of Curva Vialone, the drivers have to tackle the lap's third chicane, turning right and then almost immediately left again. One of the best recent improvements, from the drivers' point-of-view, is the lowering of the kerbs, allowing them to thump their way across them to take a more direct line through the corner without as much risk of unsettling their cars or, even worse, damaging them. Race engineers have the cars set up on a soft suspension to cope with them.

Turn 11 • Curva Parabolica

Gear: **4**
Speed: **187kph (116mph)**

Accelerating hard out of the third chicane, the drivers accelerate from fourth gear to seventh and can hit 336kph (208mph) before they have to think about slowing for the final corner of the lap. This is one of the few untouched corners, having remained in the same format since 1955. Braking later than a rival here can be an advantage, but momentum out of this corner onto the long and wide start/finish straight is the absolute key for a passing manoeuvre into the first chicane.

Great Drivers & Great Moments

With a history of close and enthralling races filled with overtaking and counter-overtaking, Monza has hosted some epic grands prix over the decades. Unfortunately, though, its high-speed layout has also resulted in numerous accidents and, tragically, many fatalities.

Great Drivers

 Michael **Schumacher**
Monza wins – 5

 Rubens **Barrichello**
Monza wins – 3

 Juan Manuel **Fangio**
Monza – 3

 Stirling **Moss**
Monza wins – 3

Not only did Michael Schumacher race to a record five wins at Monza, but he made them doubly valuable to the fans there by claiming all of these while leading Ferrari's F1 attack. His first Monza success came in 1996, in his first year with the Prancing Horse, when he headed home former Ferrari favourite Jean Alesi. He'd win again in 1998 after both McLarens faltered, then dominated proceedings in 2000, 2003 and 2006, with the team announcing his retirement after the last of these.

Rubens was always an emotional individual, sobbing after claiming his maiden F1 win at Hockenheim in 2000. So, imagine how emotional he must have felt to add wins at Monza in front of Ferrari's home fans in 2002, when team-mate Schumacher had already been crowned champion, and again in 2004, and so feel the unbridled love of the *tifosi*. Then, in a later stage of his career, he claimed a third Monza win when Brawn GP enjoyed spectacular technical superiority in its lone season in 2009.

Fangio scored a hat-trick at Monza. His first win here was in 1953, when he won a race-long scrap with Ferrari's Alberto Ascari and Giuseppe Farina plus Maserati team-mate Onofre Marimon, going through when Ascari and Farina clashed at the final corner after a race that had had 19 changes of the lead. He followed this up by winning by a lap in his Mercedes in 1954 after wrapping up his second F1 title in the previous round. He made it three in a row in 1955.

Having played understudy to Fangio when they were together at Mercedes-Benz, this English ace claimed the first of his three Monza wins when he triumphed in 1956 after running out of fuel. Fortunately, he was pushed to the pits by team-mate Luigi Piotti and benefited when Luigi Musso retired his Lancia with steering failure. Stirling would also win in 1957 for Vanwall, well clear of Fangio's Maserati, and again in 1959, when he managed the tyres of his Rob Walker-entered Cooper better than Ferrari did theirs.

Great Moments

1961 Phil **Hill** scores sad win for Ferrari

1967 Jim **Clark** fights back from a lap down

1971 Peter **Gethin** heads a five-way finish

2008 Sebastian **Vettel** wins for Toro Rosso

Held as the penultimate race of the 1961 season, it was effectively a shoot-out to decide which Ferrari driver would become World Champion. Wolfgang von Trips qualified on pole while rival Phil Hill was only fourth fastest. Hill worked his way into the lead after they reached the banking on the opening lap, but von Trips and Jim Clark's Lotus collided as they approached Parabolica on lap 2, spearing off and killing the German and 13 spectators. Victory for Hill was enough to make him World Champion.

Jim Clark had dark memories of Monza, as he'd been involved in Wolfgang von Trips's fatal accident in 1961. However, he won in 1963 and ought to have added victory four years later. Having qualified on pole, he was leading when his Lotus picked up a puncture on lap 13. The pitstop left him a lap down, but he powered his way back into the lead, only to be slowed by a fuel pump problem, leaving him to be passed by John Surtees and Jack Brabham.

The open nature of Monza that lent itself to slipstreaming was never shown more clearly. As the race entered its final five laps, a pack consisting of five drivers who'd never won a grand prix broke clear. They were Ronnie Peterson (March), Francois Cevert (Tyrrell), Howden Ganley and Peter Gethin (both BRM) and Mike Hailwood (Surtees). Into the final corner, Cevert and Peterson were ahead, but Gethin carried more momentum out of Parabolica and edged in front on the line to win by just 0.01 seconds.

Only the use of hindsight makes this win anything other than extraordinary. Of course, Vettel would move to Red Bull Racing and score four drivers' titles in a row. However, in 2008 he was racing for Scuderia Toro Rosso, a team that had been a tailender when racing as Minardi. Still, the youthful German not only stuck his car on pole but then controlled the race from the start behind the safety car as the rain was so heavy, all the way to the finish. No one got close.

Monaco

Walk the streets of Monte Carlo and there's no obvious space for a grand prix, but the street circuit that climbs high through the town before dicing down to the harbourside is Formula One's most iconic venue, the scene of an annual dose of glamour and drama since 1929.

> ❝ Monaco presents you with everything that you find along a public road: lamp posts, trees, kerbs, gutters, night clubs… It's a road race in the true meaning of the term. ❞
>
> *Graham Hill*

Most modern F1 circuits are tailor-made, their every turn and undulation crafted by architects, turning a blank piece of land into a state-of-the-art facility. Monaco could not be more different, its limitations obvious from the moment that the royal family gave cigarette manufacturer Antony Noghes permission to run a grand prix around the streets of its principality. That was back in 1929 and even people not interested in motor racing can conjure images of F1's annual visits. In short, there's no track like Monaco's and no grand prix that fans would rather attend, even though almost all overtaking is completed by the first corner of the opening lap because the track is too narrow and twisting to allow for passing moves.

That the World Championship has been happy to visit this restrictive venue ever since its inaugural season in 1950, when Juan Manuel Fangio won for Alfa Romeo, is proof that the appeal of all that happens beyond the racing outweighs its narrow track, tiny pitlane and cramped paddock. The patrons and later the teams' sponsors have always loved Monaco for being able to entertain their friends and business associates on a yacht in the harbour, on a balcony in the Hôtel de Paris or in the casino that it overlooks. It is a venue like no other.

The circuit itself makes for fabulous TV footage, a forward-facing on-board camera showing how even the smallest slip by a driver will cause their car to clang into the crash barriers, as rookie Johnny Servoz-Gavin discovered in 1968, when his race-leading Matra brushed a barrier as he sprinted clear and he went from hero to zero. There is ever-present excitement on this circuit: the spectacle of cars climbing the steep ascent from Ste Dévote to Massenet, diving into the black hole of the tunnel under the Grand Hotel and bursting back out into the sunlight for the slope down to the harbourside chicane – Monaco is unique.

Add to this the rich and lengthy history of the event and the fact that it's in the heart of a vibrant and exciting city, and its appeal is all the more obvious. That many of the drivers live in Monaco because of its generous tax laws makes it a home race for them, adding to their delight if they should win there. Jenson Button summed it up well in 2009, when he finished first for Brawn GP. "Before the weekend, I said that this grand prix isn't different to any other," commented the Englishman, "but that was a bit of a lie, as I was just trying to take the pressure off myself. Winning here is very special."

While the friends and families of all involved join the fans in enjoying this extraordinary venue, the teams and drivers have to work extra hard. Racing at Monaco used to be physically tiring when drivers had to change gear with a lever, the palm of their right hand often raw by the end of the race. Since the advent of semi-automatic gearboxes in the late 1980s, though, it has become less of a test.

Furthermore, the drivers don't suffer the strain of heavy g-force loading that they do at circuits with faster corners. The major strain these days is to get the race tactics right, to chose which compound of tyres to start on and guess when it would be best to pit; getting the timing wrong could lead to a pace-setting driver emerging back onto the track behind a backmarker and being stuck there for laps, losing time as he tries to find a place to overtake. Indeed, the gambling is as great on the track as in the casino, and that's before taking into account how the sudden arrival of a safety car period could alter the order and so scupper all best-laid plans. ∎

Opposite: This view, from high above the start/finish straight, shows Ste Dévote on the left plus the run from Tabac to Piscine and the harbour beyond.

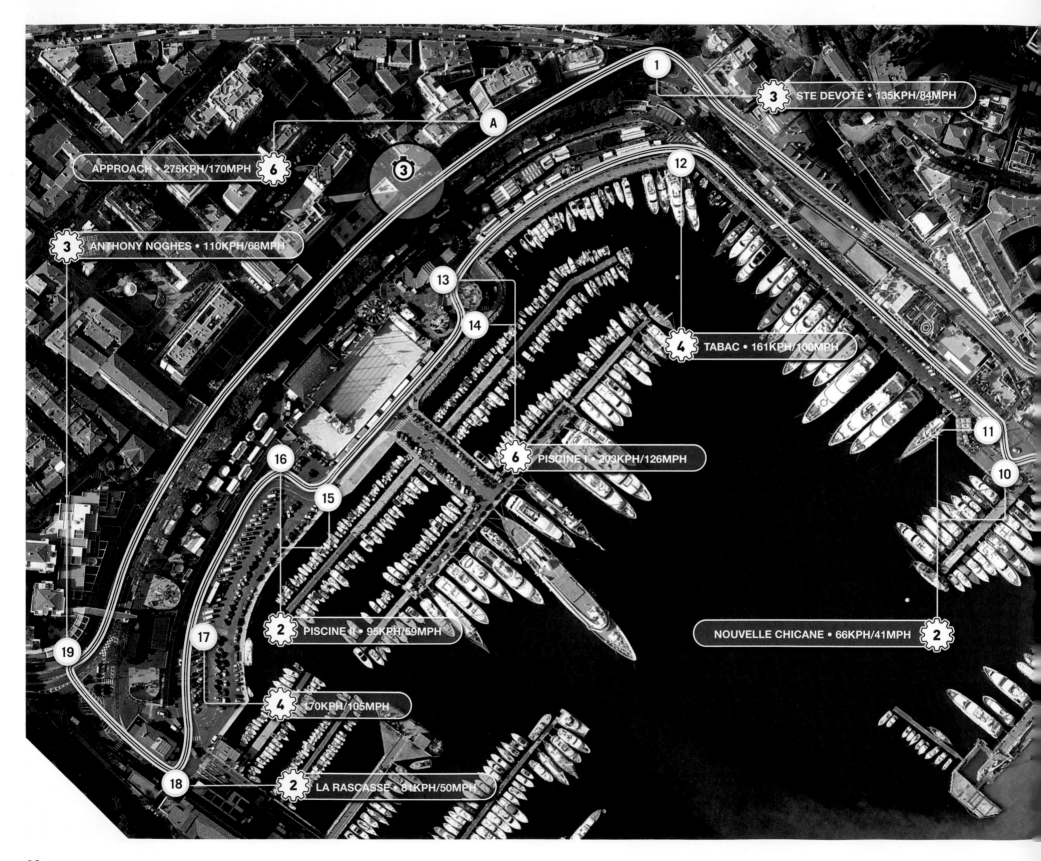

STE DEVOTE • 135KPH/84MPH

APPROACH • 275KPH/170MPH

ANTHONY NOGHES • 110KPH/68MPH

TABAC • 161KPH/100MPH

PISCINE I • 203KPH/126MPH

PISCINE II • 95KPH/59MPH

NOUVELLE CHICANE • 66KPH/41MPH

170KPH/105MPH

LA RASCASSE • 81KPH/50MPH

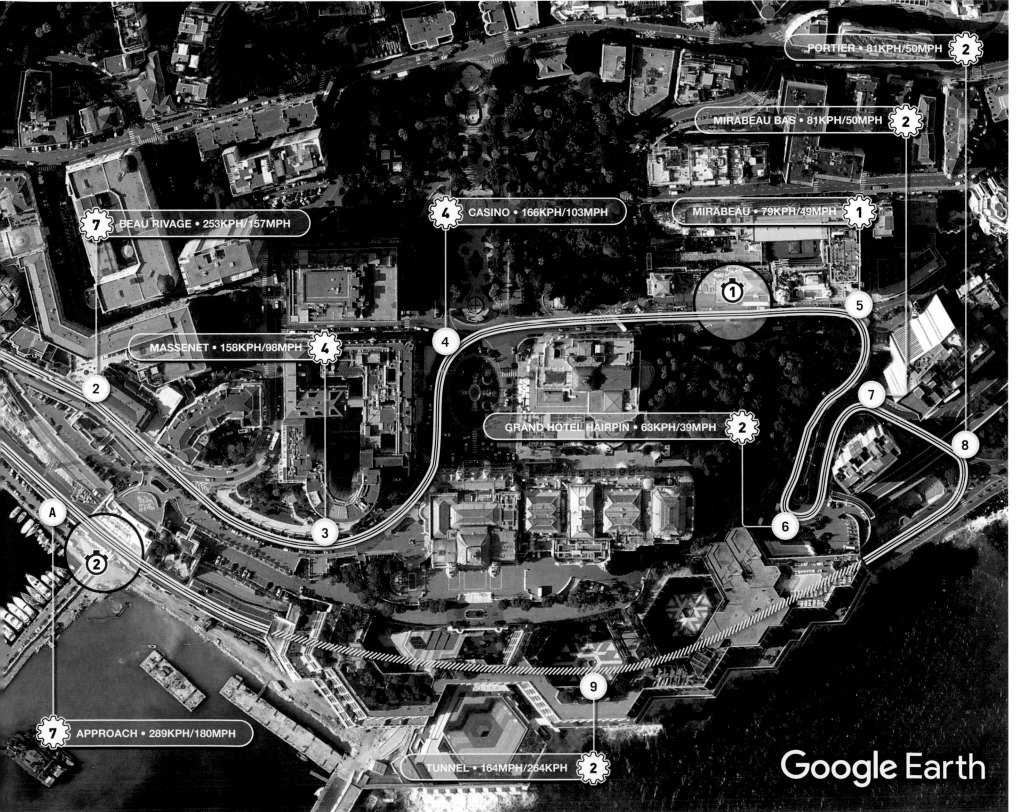

PORTIER • 81KPH/50MPH **2**

MIRABEAU BAS • 81KPH/50MPH **2**

CASINO • 166KPH/103MPH **4**

MIRABEAU • 79KPH/49MPH **1**

BEAU RIVAGE • 253KPH/157MPH **7**

1

5

MASSENET • 158KPH/98MPH **4**

2

4

7

GRAND HOTEL HAIRPIN • 63KPH/39MPH **2**

8

3

6

A

2

9

7 APPROACH • 289KPH/180MPH

TUNNEL • 164MPH/264KPH **2**

Google Earth

Circuit Guide

Monaco is a circuit unlike even other street circuits and the corners that make up its undulating lap are a mixture of low- and medium-speed, with only short straights and a curving tunnel in between.

Turn 1 • Ste Dévote
Gear: **3**
Speed: **135kph (84mph)**

A 135kph (84mph) corner would be considered slow on almost any F1 circuit, but this righthander is one of the quicker ones at Monaco. Its approach down the curving start/finish straight is made more daunting by the buildings that rise sheer from behind the barriers on the left and by the burning desire for drivers to make a move into here on the opening lap. Fortunately there's an escape road for when those desperate moves go wrong and drivers have to pull out of their manoeuvre.

Turn 3 • Massenet
Gear: **4**
Speed: **158kph (98mph)**

The blast up the hill from Ste Dévote is thought of as a straight but, being Monaco, even this contains a swerve in it. Arriving at the crest of the hill at 273kph (170mph) and with the shape of Monte Carlo's Casino looming ahead of them, the drivers have to drop down to fourth gear and commit to turning into this lefthander. The track is narrow and the turn-in blind, and drivers have to get into position immediately for the following corner.

Turn 4 • Casino
Gear: **4**
Speed: **166kph (103mph)**

This is one of the most famous parts of the circuit, but the drivers have no time to admire the casino and gardens to their right. They have to master the change in the gradient as the track turns left and starts to drop gently downhill in order to stop their cars from drifting towards the barriers while they attempt to keep them on a tight line. On exit they run out towards the left as they start their descent from the highest point on the circuit.

Turn 6 • Grand Hotel Hairpin
Gear: **2**
Speed: **63kph (39mph)**

After negotiating the righthand hairpin at Mirabeau, the drivers reach the second downhill hairpin in succession, this one an even tighter left. Drivers sometimes try to overtake here, especially if the driver they are chasing makes a poor exit from Mirabeau, but there's precious little space. Those gazing from the roof terraces of the Grand Hotel witness many collisions here, with drivers becoming delayed further by their cars being stuck together, their wheels interlocked.

Opposite: There's a stark change from daylight to darkness when the cars power away from Portier into the tunnel, but lighting helps to reduce the transition. *Above left:* Felipe Massa tackles the downhill hairpin in front of the Grand Hotel. *Above right:* The view down from the balconies of the apartments overlooking the start/finish straight, the sweep to Piscine and the harbour beyond is unrivalled.

Turn 8 • **Portier**
Gear: **2**
Speed: **81kph (50mph)**

After the track dives under a flyover, it turns sharply right here as it hits the seafront for the first time in its lap, with drivers having to be exceedingly cautious not to glance the outside barrier, which Ayrton Senna did in 1988. Early acceleration out of here is vital to carry extra speed into the tunnel that follows. Ayrton Senna famously clipped the barrier when in a dominant lead here in 1988, the damage forcing him into a retirement.

Turn 10/11 • **Nouvelle Chicane**
Gear: **2**
Speed: **66kph (41mph)**

Still accelerating as they exit the tunnel back into the sunlight, the cars hit 281kph (175mph) before drivers have to brake hard as the gentle downward slope levels out and steer left, then immediately right. Fortunately, there is an escape road directly ahead for those who fail to slow enough to turn into the chichane. The kerbs are low and drivers try to avoid hitting them too hard, which might delay their acceleration onto the short straight to Tabac.

Turn 12 • **Tabac**
Gear: **4**
Speed: **161kph (100mph)**

Flanked by yachts on its left and a grandstand crammed into the narrow space inside Ste Dévote on its right, this fourth-gear lefthander is named after a tobacconist's kiosk that used to stand there. The corner is made extra tricky because drivers can't see around it. Until 1972, this was the final corner of the lap because the start/finish line was then on the harbourfront. Martin Brundle famously got it wrong while qualifying in 1984, when he arrived here with his Tyrrell on its side.

Turn 13/14 • **Piscine**
Gear: **6**
Speed: **203kph (126mph)**

The construction of a public swimming pool on the harbourfront in 1972 meant the insertion of a pair of esses around it, with a left/right flick, followed by a short straight and then a right/left one at its far end. To make matters trickier still for the drivers, the turn-in is all but blind for each esse, making the 257kph (160mph) approach seem all the more excessive due to the complete lack of run-off there. The cars look extra dynamic here.

Great Drivers & Great Moments

A circuit as out of the ordinary as Monaco's has produced some staggering drives and some equally unexpected results across the decades. Here are a selection of the drivers and the grands prix that have stood out on a circuit where even a slight brush with the surrounding crash barriers can lead to embarrassed retirement.

Opposite top: The climax of the 1992 Monaco GP was this battle between Williams racer Nigel Mansell and McLaren's Ayrton Senna after the Englishman returned to the track from an unscheduled pitstop.

Opposite bottom left: Alberto Ascari's Lancia Ferrari is winched from the harbour after his spectacular departure from the track in 1955. He was fortunate to have swum clear.

Opposite bottom right: Nico Rosberg completed a Monaco hat-trick in 2015 when he profited from Lewis Hamilton losing out in a safety car deployment.

Great Drivers

 Ayrton **Senna**
Monaco wins – 6

This exceptional Brazilian holds the record of six Monaco wins, but it could easily have been eight – he was denied victory when the 1984 race was red-flagged early because of wet conditions just as he moved his Toleman past Alain Prost's McLaren for the lead. Four years later, having won in 1987, he clipped the barrier at Portier and was forced out. Having learnt his lesson, he then won this most prestigious grand prix every year from 1989 to 1993.

 Graham **Hill**
Monaco wins – 5

This moustachioed Englishman made the streets of Monaco pretty much his own in the 1960s, starting in 1963, when he won for BRM after Jim Clark hit gearbox trouble. He then added wins in 1964 and 1965, also for BRM, before winning for Lotus in 1968 and 1969 to earn the nickname of Mr Monaco. Sadly, his 1975 outing was hit by engine troubles and resulted in non-qualification of his Hill GH1 and so he elected to retire from racing there and then.

 Stirling **Moss**
Monaco wins – 3

Victory at Monaco in 1956 marked Stirling's first grand prix win and he added to this victory for Maserati with another in 1960, when entrant Rob Walker decided he ought to change from a Cooper to a Lotus. Moss fought his way to the front after a poor start, only for rain to interject. Brabham then took the lead in his works Cooper then spun, but it took a chase back after a plug lead change for Moss to make it two victories. He won again for Rob Walker in 1961.

 Nico **Rosberg**
Monaco wins – 3

With a German mother and a Finnish father, it's hard to apportion Nico a home race. However, he was brought up in Monaco, so he sees this as his home event. Second in 2012 was his best result in eight attempts, but that was bettered in 2013 when this second generation F1 racer won after taking pole. In 2014, team-mate Hamilton felt he'd been denied pole, but Rosberg used it to good effect. Nico completed his hat-trick in 2015 when Hamilton was denied by a tactical blunder.

Great Moments

 1955 Alberto **Ascari** survives a dip in the harbour

One of the most dramatic images of Monaco in the 1950s was provided by the 1952 and 1953 World Champion when he was distracted by smoke from Stirling Moss's Mercedes as it expired and so lost concentration at the chicane – his Lancia Ferrari flying into the harbour. He survived the dunking with nothing more than a loss of pride and minor facial injuries, but his luck was to run out just four days later when he was killed testing a Ferrari sportscar at Monza.

1970 Jack **Brabham** throws it away on the last lap

Jackie Stewart led away from pole in his March from Chris Amon's similar car, but a misfire delayed him and Brabham took the lead. Jochen Rindt moved his Lotus to 9 seconds behind with four laps to go, amazingly catching Brabham as they started the final lap; the pressure told, and Brabham braked too late for the Gasworks Hairpin and slid into the bales, letting Rindt dive by for victory before he could reverse out to finish second, 23 seconds behind.

1992 Nigel **Mansell** just fails to pass Ayrton **Senna**

Nigel Mansell had won the first five grands prix of the season, so when he claimed pole it was expected that he'd make it six in a row in his Williams. However, with seven laps to go and a healthy lead over Ayrton Senna's McLaren, the rear of his car felt strange and so he pitted. A corner weight had come loose. By the time he rejoined, Senna was in the lead. Mansell then did everything except drive over the McLaren to get back in front, but still failed.

1996 Olivier **Panis** comes through to win

Olivier Panis rides his luck to come out on top Michael Schumacher and Damon Hill started on the front row, but the German crashed out halfway around lap 1 and Hill's Williams lost a clear lead when its engine failed. So Jean Alesi led for Benetton, but Olivier Panis was first to change from wet tyres to slicks and advanced past McLaren's David Coulthard to second. Then Alesi's suspension collapsed with 16 laps to go and Olivier seized the moment.

Zandvoort

Here is a circuit that still operates today, albeit in an abbreviated fashion. What remains, though, is a clear reminder of this once wonderful circuit that snakes its way through the sand dunes on the North Sea coast and which used to be one of the best attended of all the European grand prix circuits.

"Out at the back of the circuit, you had a sequence of quick corners which in our cars were taken at 160mph [257kph] and there was little in terms of safety."

John Watson

Some parts of some grand prix circuits look alike, but not one of Zandvoort's corners could be mistaken for being anywhere else, which isn't surprising: none of the other top circuits to host Formula One twisted their way through sand dunes. Bridgehampton in the USA was also laid out among dunes, but that hosted Can-Am sportscars rather than F1. So, if ever you see a shot of a Ferrari, Vanwall or Lotus being guided through some twisters flanked by tufted dunes, you can be sure that it was taken at the Netherlands' premier circuit.

Zandvoort was a fabulous and distinctive place to go racing and, even now, in its current truncated form, it has a special character that is made all the more redolent of bygone glory as it has been off the World Championship rota for almost three decades.

Opened for business in 1948, it was created from link roads that had been built between gun emplacements just in from the sea west of Amsterdam by the German army during the Second World War. The clear character of its circuit design was the way that it was made up largely of high-speed sweepers which undulated through the dunes. The final corner, Bos Uit, was a wonderfully long corner feeding the cars onto the lengthy start/finish straight at appreciable speed for

slipstreaming all the way down to the double-right called Tarzan at its far end. Late-braking overtaking moves have always been a feature of racing here, with every move being made potentially fraught by sand blowing off the dunes. It was very much a drivers' circuit and the thousands of fans who turned out even in foul weather to watch the action added a special atmosphere too.

After holding a couple of non-championship Formula One races in 1950 and 1951, both won by Louis Rosier in a Lago-Talbot, Zandvoort joined the World Championship in 1952, when Alberto Ascari scored the first of two consecutive wins for Ferrari. The circuit was popular straight away, but it was also a place with a sad side, as shown when Piers Courage met a fiery death in 1970 and then Roger Williamson likewise in 1973, when an atrocious standard of marshalling left his greatest chance of surviving in the hands of David Purley. (Purley stopped his own car to run back and try to turn the inverted March back over to rescue him while marshals clad in shirtsleeves stood and stared, and a nearby fire tender elected not to go against the flow of the circuit to attempt to save him.) On a happier note, Zandvoort made history when Lotus gave F1's most successful engine its debut when Jim Clark gave the Ford Cosworth DFV a winning start in 1967.

The racing was invariably competitive and great scraps included James Hunt's McLaren against John Watson's Penske in 1976. Yet, as money ran short, the final Dutch GP came in 1985, when Niki Lauda claimed the final win of his F1 career.

The circuit then fell on hard financial times and had to be taken over by the town council. This was pivotal; it was already under pressure from noise abatement. Fortunately, it lived to fight another day, albeit in truncated form. To address noise concerns, a dune was created between the circuit and the town, with the lap losing more than 1.6km (1 mile) from its length; the track was made to turn right at Hunserug before running through a new loop that brought it back to the original circuit just after the exit of the final corner. That was in 1989, but a decade later it was given its dignity back and the current layout was adopted, with the original run from Hunserug to Scheivlak and then Marlborobocht being reinstated before the track turned right onto another new loop that twisted its way back around to the 1989 loop. There was no chance of returning to the original layout, because houses were built on its furthest reaches after the 1989 transformation. ■

Opposite: Niki Lauda keeps his McLaren ahead of Ayrton Senna's Lotus in 1985 as he races towards his 25th and final grand prix win.

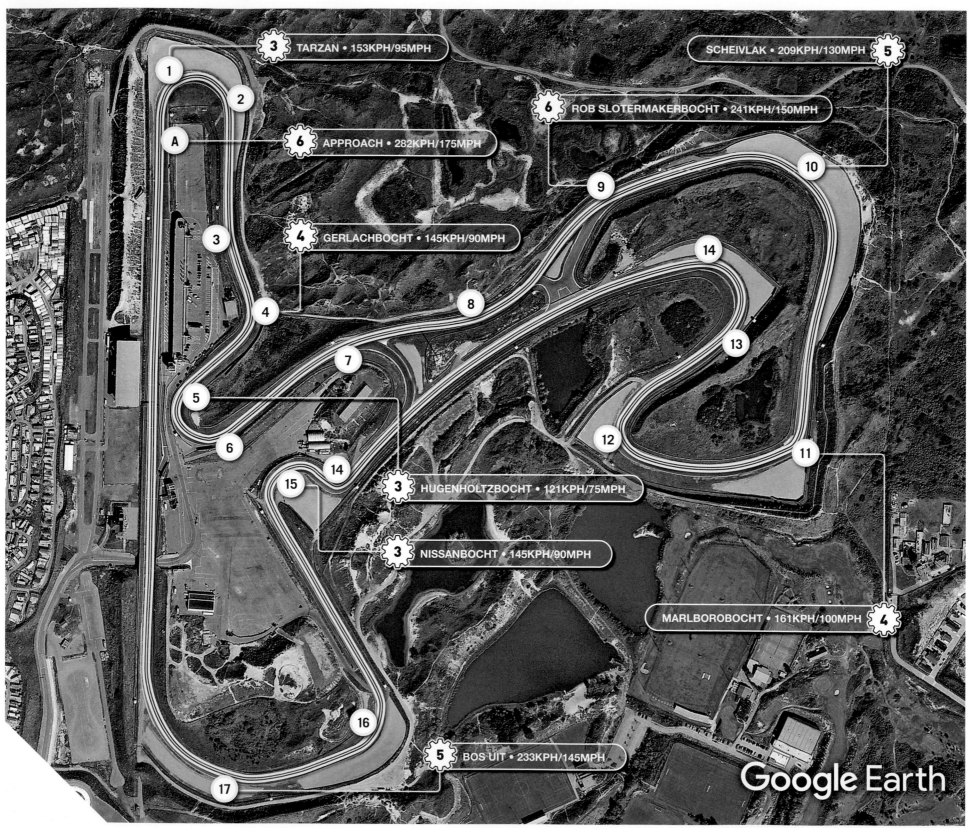

TARZAN • 153KPH/95MPH

SCHEIVLAK • 209KPH/130MPH

ROB SLOTERMAKERBOCHT • 241KPH/150MPH

APPROACH • 282KPH/175MPH

GERLACHBOCHT • 145KPH/90MPH

HUGENHOLTZBOCHT • 121KPH/75MPH

NISSANBOCHT • 145KPH/90MPH

MARLBOROBOCHT • 161KPH/100MPH

BOS UIT • 233KPH/145MPH

Image © Data SIO, NOAA, U.S. Navy, NGA, GEBCO © Google 2014

98

Renault's Alain Prost and René Arnoux lead
Alan Jones's Williams and Nelson Piquet's
Brabham into Gerlachbocht in 1981.

Circuit Guide

From the flat-out blast to Tarzan through the sweepers behind the pits and the undulating loop through the dunes, Zandvoort was always a circuit that the drivers loved. Add passionate fans and a fun town, and F1 lost a great place when it was dropped from the World Championship rota.

Turn 1 • Tarzan
Gear: **3**
Speed: **153kph (95mph)**

The most fabled of Zandvoort's corners, this is approached down the main straight. Sitting beneath the dunes, it's wide open on entry, but its double-apex format makes the inside line the preferred one for overtaking, although bold drivers like Gilles Villeneuve in 1979 occasionally opted to brave it out around the outside. The corner rises from the first apex and this extra camber helps to hold the cars in, although anyone riding too high will be slow onto the return straight.

Turn 5/6 • Hugenholtzbocht
Gear: **3**
Speed: **121kph (75mph)**

Dropping into a dip at the foot of the circuit's control tower, this double-apex lefthander offers absolutely no run-off area on its righthand side, making passing moves on the way in potentially damaging. The corner is something of a bowl, with the track rising immediately after its midway point, cupping the cars as the drivers look to start accelerating out of the corner for the flat-out blast all the way to Scheivlak. Any driver running wide on the exit will be massively compromised.

Turn 4 • Gerlachbocht
Gear: **4**
Speed: **145kph (90mph)**

Rising over a slight crest after a lefthand kink behind the paddock, this is a tricky corner. The track drops away slightly on the exit as the corner tightens, leaving drivers to balance their cars and move them across towards the righthand side of the track to get onto the optimum line for the following corner. It can get extremely busy here on the opening lap of the race, with very little space to correct any departures from the intended line.

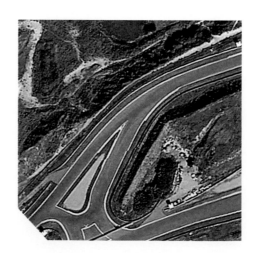

Turn 9 • Rob Slotermakerbocht
Gear: **6**
Speed: **241kph (150mph)**

After the rise out of Hugenholtzbocht, the crest at Hunserug and the left flick through Zijn Veld, the track rises again on the approach to this sixth-gear righthand sweeper. With the pits, paddock and grandstands now far behind as the drivers head into the dunes, the fast flow is made to feel all the faster by the barriers nestling so low on either flank. The corner is named after the racer who ran Zandvoort's skid school but died in a touring car race in 1979.

Opposite: Jo Siffert powers his privately entered Lotus out of Hugenholtzbocht en route to second place behind Jackie Stewart's Matra in 1969. *Above left:* This shot of John Surtees's Ferrari in 1963 shows the twists approaching Gerlachbocht. *Above right:* This is the compression between the dunes between Hunserug and Rob Slotermakerbocht in 1970.

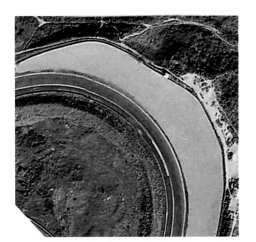

Turn 10 • Scheivlak
Gear: **5**
Speed: **209kph (130mph)**

Many reckon that this righthand corner was the most difficult twist of the lap. Approached in top gear, with a huge sand dune filling the drivers' eyeline as they arrive at speed, the corner dips to the right and drops away on exit into a cutting between the dunes. For a quick lap, as much speed as possible needed to be carried through here, but the perennial Zandvoort problem of sand blowing onto the track made this a notably scary option here.

Turn 11 • Marlborobocht
Gear: **4**
Speed: **161kph (100mph)**

At the foot of the compression after Scheivlak, this is more straightforward, being a fast flick to the left in the circuit's original format. Since 1999, though, this has been a tighter turn to the right taken about 100 metres (328ft) earlier on a level piece of ground in the shadow of the dunes. This marks the point at which the latest iteration of the track starts its return journey towards the pits and is where the greatest difference comes, as fast and open becomes tight and twisty.

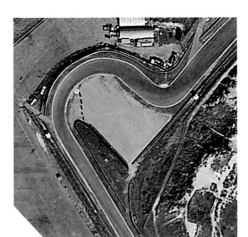

Turn 15 • Nissanbocht
Gear: **3**
Speed: **145kph (90mph)**

The 1999 loop offered a decent straight down to a notably tightening righthander. This then feeds almost immediately into this double-apex lefthander and drivers can afford to cut the kerbs at the first part of this. For the tighter, second part of the corner, it's hard for drivers to pull their cars across to the ideal racing line without slowing, but it's worth doing so to ensure they can get the power down as early as possible to accelerate onto the straight towards Mitsubishibocht.

Turn 17 • Bos Uit
Gear: **5**
Speed: **233kph (145mph)**

This is not the fearsome corner that it was in the circuit's original format. Built several hundred metres closer to the pits than the old corner, due to the construction of a complex of holiday bungalows, it echoes the same arc, but the key in its emasculation lies in the fact that it is now approached only via a short blast rather than the much longer straight of old from the long lost corner called Pulleveld. A balanced car on the exit will earn dividends down the straight.

Great Drivers & Great Moments

Although Zandvoort hosted grands prix from 1952 until 1985, its heyday was in the 1960s and 1970s, when the likes of Jim Clark and Jackie Stewart were frequently to be found in the lead in front of thousands of fans lining the dunes.

Opposite top: The 1967 Dutch GP was a landmark event, Jim Clark giving the Ford Cosworth DFV a winning debut by bringing his Lotus home 23 seconds clear of Jack Brabham.

Opposite bottom left: James Hunt got ahead of Niki Lauda's Ferrari in the 1975 Dutch GP and remained there to score his first and Hesketh's only grand prix win.

Opposite bottom right: BRM had long sought victory in F1 and it all came right here in 1959 when Jo Bonnier qualified his P25 on pole then won as others faltered.

Great Drivers

 Jim **Clark**
Zandvoort wins – 4

 Jackie **Stewart**
Zandvoort wins – 3

 Alberto **Ascari**
Zandvoort wins – 2

 Jack **Brabham**
Zandvoort wins – 2

This great Scot was the master of every venue he tackled, but he had remarkable success here, winning four times. The first of these was in 1963, when he lapped the entire field in his Lotus 25 on the way to his first drivers' title. He followed this up in 1964 by putting everyone bar Ferrari's John Surtees a lap behind him, then made it a hat-trick in 1965 although BRM's Jackie Stewart at least kept him in sight. He then added a fourth in 1967 (see below).

Scots clearly have an affinity with this Dutch circuit, as Jackie Stewart was the second most successful driver here. He scored his first Zandvoort win in 1968, when he worked his way past Graham Hill's Lotus to win ahead of Matra team-mate Jean-Pierre Beltoise. Stewart and Matra won again in 1969 after Hill again made the early running and Jochen Rindt led until his Lotus broke. Stewart's third came in his final year, 1973, when he headed a Tyrrell one-two.

Ferrari's team leader was on a roll by the time the teams arrived at Zandvoort in 1952, as he had won the first four rounds. So it came as little surprise after he qualified on pole that he led each of the 90 laps, with only team-mates Giuseppe Farina and Luigi Villoresi finishing on the lead lap. In 1953, the Italian did it again when he continued his winning streak into a second season, again starting from pole position and leading all the way to the finish.

Second behind Jo Bonnier in 1959, the reigning World Champion propelled his works Cooper past Stirling Moss's Rob Walker-entered Lotus at the start in 1960, and they pulled clear of the rest until a concrete marker tile flicked up by Brabham gave Moss a puncture and so the Australian won easily. Six years later, Brabham won again as his Repco-powered Brabham proved to be the pick of the machines in this first year in which 3-litre engines were allowed.

Great Moments

1959 Jo **Bonnier** lands BRM its maiden victory

1967 Jim **Clark** gives Ford Cosworth DFV a debut win

1975 James **Hunt** holds off Niki **Lauda's** charge

1985 Niki **Lauda** heads a McLaren one-two

BRM had spent a fortune attempting to win a grand prix and it all came together when Jo Bonnier qualified on pole and then, after a race of swapping the lead, was first to the chequered flag. He was passed early on by Masten Gregory but retook the lead when Gregory's Cooper suffered gear-change problems. Gregory's team-mate Jack Brabham then passed before suffering the same problem. Then Rob Walker Racing's Stirling Moss took the lead but his gearbox broke and so BRM made its breakthrough.

Lotus was going nowhere fast when it started 1967 with BRM power, but it turned up at the third round with the all-new Ford Cosworth DFV in its Type 49s and turned F1 on its head. Graham Hill grabbed pole and led 10 laps, but his engine cut out with camshaft trouble and so Jack Brabham took over. Lotus team-mate Jim Clark had missed most of qualifying and started eighth, but he passed the Brabham for the lead on the 16th lap and won by 23 seconds.

Hesketh was the team the establishment said would never win, reckoning it was simply a way for Lord Hesketh to go partying. Yet James Hunt had won the International Trophy in 1974 and opened the 1975 season by finishing second in Argentina. Having qualified third here behind Ferrari's Niki Lauda and Clay Regazzoni, he watched Lauda lead in the wet and then pitted early to change to slicks as the track dried and took the lead. Lauda was on his tail for the last 15 laps, but Hunt held on.

The final grand prix held at Zandvoort produced a surprise result when Niki Lauda followed up the announcement at the previous grand prix of his retirement from racing by producing a masterful performance to race to the front from 10th on the grid – and then resist the challenge of his usually faster McLaren team-mate, Alain Prost. Keke Rosberg led until his Williams blew its engine, then Prost took over, but Lauda went in front when Prost had a slow pitstop and stayed there for his 25th win.

Estoril

Rough and ready, this circuit strafed by winds blowing in off the Atlantic was a popular stop for the Formula One circus from 1984 until 1996. With a lack of Portuguese drivers to cheer, it became the place for Brazilian fans to make their annual European sortie to cheer on Ayrton Senna in particular.

"Estoril is quite challenging, especially through the long corners at the start and the end of the lap, with the bumps that are everywhere making it even more tiring."

Damon Hill

Portugal had hosted a grand prix before Estoril came into being, on a street circuit in Oporto in 1958 and 1960 and once in a park at Monsanto near Lisbon in the intervening year. Then the country dropped away from the scene, with only national racing and no star drivers of its own.

In 1972, though, the country's first purpose-built circuit was created. This was Estoril, built on a rocky plateau just inland from the coastal resort of Cascais and the casino town of Estoril on the Atlantic coast to the west of Lisbon. The layout consists of a long start/finish straight that dips towards the opening corner and then doubles back from a low point at its third corner to hit an interior straight, before rounding out its lap with a twisting return leg from the other low point at Orelha. Apart from the first two corners, the lap is made up of medium- and low-speed bends, but the gradient changes added interest and it became a popular place to go racing, helped in no small part by Cascais and Estoril being such fun places for the teams to stay.

Estoril hosted a round of the European Formula Two Championship in 1973 and then from 1975 to 1977, each of which was won by French drivers who would race in Formula One – Jean-Pierre Jarier, Jacques Laffite, René Arnoux and Didier Pironi. Then, with its finances in a parlous state, the circuit fell into a state of disrepair. Unusually, what brought it back onto the international scene

was hosting a special stage of the Portuguese Rally. Then, with teams seeking a place to conduct close-season testing in its usually clement winter climate following political pressure not to use Kyalami in South Africa, the circuit attracted the investment needed to bring it up to contemporary standards. It was rewarded with its inclusion on the F1 World Championship calendar in 1984. That this was a momentous race in which Niki Lauda did just enough to pip his McLaren team-mate Alain Prost to the drivers' title only added to the start of its second life.

However, what really put Estoril back on the map was Ayrton Senna's remarkable maiden win there for Lotus in streaming wet conditions early in the 1985 season. This alone encouraged Brazilian fans to make the journey to what some still considered their mother country and they filled the grandstands with colour and noise as they supported mainly Senna but Nelson Piquet too, and later Rubens Barrichello. The local fans didn't have so much to cheer, though: after Pedro Chaves failed to qualify for every race of the 1991 season with an uncompetitive Coloni, the only Portuguese driver to race in the grand prix during the circuit's reign was Pedro Lamy. He was a driver of great promise who won races in Formula 3000 and reached F1 with Lotus in 1993. However, he had a major career setback when he crashed when testing at Silverstone

in 1994, breaking his knees and a wrist; the recovery period cost him all momentum and he was never able to challenge when he returned with Minardi.

Momentous races at Estoril include the one in 1989, when race leader Nigel Mansell overshot his pitstop and was disqualified for being pushed backwards in the pitlane, leaving Ferrari team-mate Gerhard Berger to win. Although he'd win here the following year, it went wrong for Mansell again in 1991, when his Williams had a wheel come loose as he left the pits and he was disqualified again. The final Portuguese GP, in 1996, was marked by a fantastic drive from Jacques Villeneuve, which was capped when he drove his Williams around the outside of Michael Schumacher at the daunting final corner to go on to win.

Then Estoril's time at the sport's top table was over, and it has fallen from grace spectacularly. No international series go there now, preferring the Algarve International Circuit near Portimao because it's a more challenging track with modern facilities, leaving Estoril mainly as a venue for national racing series. Sadly, it has fallen even further than Brands Hatch did after losing the British GP. ■

Opposite: Michael Schumacher's Ferrari is chased up the hill to Saca-Rolhas by Jacques Villeneuve's Williams and Gerhard Berger's Benetton early in the 1996 Portuguese GP.

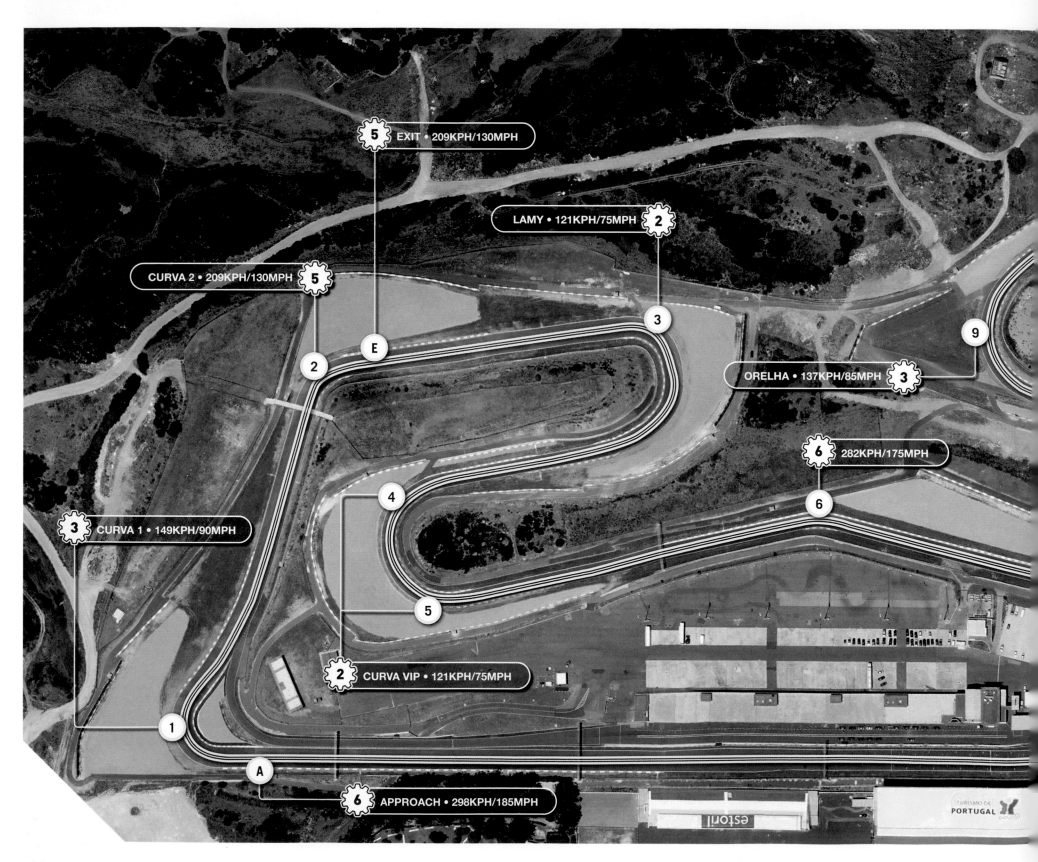

5 EXIT • 209KPH/130MPH

LAMY • 121KPH/75MPH 2

CURVA 2 • 209KPH/130MPH 5

2

E

3

ORELHA • 137KPH/85MPH 3

9

6 282KPH/175MPH

6

4

3 CURVA 1 • 149KPH/90MPH

5

2 CURVA VIP • 121KPH/75MPH

1

A

6 APPROACH • 298KPH/185MPH

estoril

TURISMO DE
PORTUGAL

3 CURVA DO TANQUE • 153KPH/95MPH

13

10

12

11

1 SACA-ROLHAS • 80KPH/50MPH

5 PARABOLICA AYRTON SENNA • 209KPH/130MPH

3 ESSES • 169KPH/105MPH

14

8

15

2 PARABOLICA INTERIOR • 121KPH/75MPH

7

Circuito Estoril

Google Earth

Circuit Guide

From the flat-out blast to Turn 1 and the fearsome passage down through Turn 2 to the inner straight and then the twisting climb back up the rocky hillside to the seemingly never-ending corner onto the start/finish straight, Estoril is full of challenges.

Turn 1 • **Curva 1**
Gear: **3**
Speed: **149kph (90mph)**

For drivers arriving down the dipping start/finish straight at 306kph (190mph), with trees on their lefthand side and a rocky outcrop to their right, this was a fearsome corner when the circuit hosted the Portuguese GP. They knew that they had to carry as much speed through it as possible and hope not to slide out into the gravel trap. In 2000, though, the approach was lengthened before the track was made to double back through a much tighter corner, taken in third gear rather than fifth.

Turn 2 • **Curva 2**
Gear: **5**
Speed: **209kph (130mph)**

Because Turn 1 is so much tighter than it was when the World Championship raced here, the second turn is no longer the one that drivers fear the most: the arrival speed down the sloping approach is so much less. Also, there is some run-off now on the exit, a luxury that the F1 drivers didn't get to enjoy – they held their breath and simply hoped for the best as they tried to carry as much speed through the corner and onto the straight beyond.

Turn 3 • **Lamy**
Gear: **2**
Speed: **121kph (75mph)**

At the foot of the short straight down the slope from Turn 2, this two-part corner is the start of the climb back up the slope again. If entered from the extreme left, the corner is wide, though. So, providing not too much speed is carried into the first part in an attempted overtaking manoeuvre, drivers can accelerate hard through the more open second part before they start moving to the righthand side of the track for the next corner.

Turn 4/5 • **Curva VIP**
Gear: **2**
Speed: **121kph (75mph)**

After the climb from Lamy, the circuit flattens out just before this long lefthander, and drivers need to enter this parabolic corner from the far right. Taken in second gear, this corner has an open feel after the climb through the cutting. It isn't a difficult corner other than the fact that it comes so soon after Lamy, but getting a clean exit from it is absolutely essential for a good lap time because it feeds the cars onto the kinked interior straight, the lap's second longest flat-out blast.

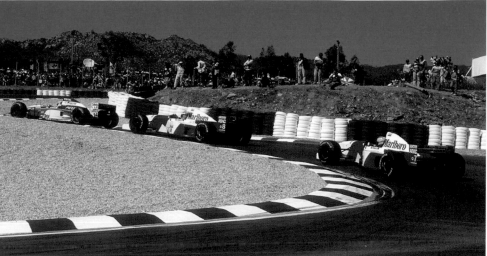

Opposite: Keke Rosberg turns his alternative-liveried McLaren through Turn 1 ahead of Stefan Johansson's Ferrari in 1986. ***Above left:*** Rubens Barrichello steers his Jordan through the Esses in 1993. ***Above right:*** Barrichello again, this time in 1995, leading the McLarens of Mika Hakkinen and Mark Blundell out of Saca-Rolhas.

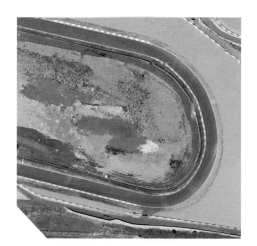

Turn 7/8 • **Parabolica Interior**
Gear: **2**
Speed: **121kph (75mph)**

The interior straight is interrupted by a flat-out righthand kink, then descends gently towards this corner. It's a downhill double left that is a definite overtaking opportunity if a driver has managed to catch a tow down the straight. Each apex is distinctive, even though the corner is a parabola; drivers must stay tight through the first but can then afford to run a little wide out of the second part of the corner as they accelerate onto the dropping straight that follows.

Turn 9 • **Orelha**
Gear: **3**
Speed: **137kph (85mph)**

Orelha is the sixth corner of the lap with a downhill entry, making it harder than it would be on the level for drivers to find any grip as they decelerate. This is the lowest point of the lap and it's a third-gear righthander that really requires a smooth line through it. Drivers are careful not to hit the unusually high kerbs either at the entry or at the exit before they put the power down again to climb the steep slope that follows.

Turn 14 • **Esses**
Gear: **3**
Speed: **169kph (105mph)**

Since the unpopular detour to Curva 9 (Saca-Rolhas) was inserted in 1994 to replace a fast uphill sweeper that had absolutely no run-off, this right and then left sequence has proved to be less of a challenge because the cars don't arrive at such great speed after their tighter and steeper approach. No sooner has this corner been exited than drivers have to cross the track from the righthand side to the far left in order to get ready for the final corner.

Turn 15 • **Parabolica Ayrton Senna**
Gear: **5**
Speed: **209kph (130mph)**

This final corner is one that drivers feel goes on and on. It's a long righthand arc through which drivers have to get their cars balanced and then hold them there until they dare to accelerate out of the corner, which they try to do as early as possible in order to start building momentum for the long start/finish straight that follows. Jacques Villeneuve showed no fear in taking rival Michael Schumacher around the outside here in 1996.

Barcelona

Spain had hosted its grand prix at four other circuits before the Circuit de Catalunya was built at Montmelo outside Barcelona, but this has been the race's home ever since its debut in 1991 and the rise of Fernando Alonso has done something that had happened at no Spanish GP before – filled the grandstands.

> **"** It's a very enjoyable circuit, with Turns 3 and 9 a real test, but it's also hard to set the car up for, as there are high-speed, medium-speed and low-speed corners.**"**
>
> *Pastor Malonado*

Formula One hasn't always enjoyed its current popularity in Spain, with Fernando Alonso a national hero, but only those with longer memories will recall the times when grands prix would be held there with no Spanish involvement and thus only part-filled grandstands.

Had Alfonso de Portago not been killed during the 1957 Mille Miglia sportscar road race, it's quite possible that he would have gone on to win grands prix for Ferrari and so Spain would have had more reason to love and support F1. Unfortunately, he did meet his end and Spanish drivers were absent from the pinnacle of the sport through the 1960s and 1970s. The nation's motorsporting success was instead driven by its motorbike racers, with tens of thousands turning out to watch the likes of 13-time World Champion Angel Nieto, Ricardo Tormo and Sito Pons but largely ignoring their four-wheeled racers.

Despite this lack of popularity, the Spanish GPs held at Pedralbes in Barcelona's western suburbs in 1951 and 1954 were finally followed by the country's World Championship return in 1968, using the Jarama circuit that had been built outside Madrid. This then alternated with the Montjuich Park circuit in Barcelona until 1975, when spectators were killed at the latter. However, meagre crowds, due to the fans having no national hero to cheer, led

to a lack of investment and Jarama lost its race after 1981. Fortunately for Spanish fans, the mayor of Jerez de la Frontera in the south-west of the country wanted to promote his sherry-producing region and so financed the building of a circuit that would host the Spanish GP from 1986 to 1990.

But then Barcelona struck back with a tailor-made circuit of its own: the Circuit de Catalunya. Financed by local and governmental grants, it offered superior facilities and an interesting layout. Better still, it was located far closer to the bulk of Spain's population and offered excellent viewing. It was then treated to a vibrant debut grand prix in 1991, when Nigel Mansell and Ayrton Senna fought wheel-to-wheel.

Like Estoril before it in neighbouring Portugal, this circuit has long been a popular venue for winter testing. Indeed, its weather is more predictable than Estoril's was, although the wind here often swaps direction (blowing as a headwind down the start/finish straight in the morning, and a tailwind in the afternoon), thus hampering the teams' findings. However, the variety of corners and changes of gradient around the lap mean that the engineers can work on all sorts of chassis and aerodynamic set-ups that they will need through the course of the season.

Mansell won the first two Spanish GPs held here, Michael Schumacher added a pair in 1995

and 1996 and Mika Hakkinen won three in a row for McLaren from 1998. Yet Spanish fans still had no one of their own at the sharp end of the field, even though Barcelona-born Pedro de la Rosa was trying his best for assorted midfield teams, including Arrows and then Jaguar Racing.

What it took to interest the Spanish fans was the arrival of former World Kart Champion Fernando Alonso, who burst onto the car racing scene with such aplomb that he was an F1 driver by the start of his third year. His form then took off in 2003, when he started winning races for Renault. The crowd numbers exploded and he sent them home deliriously happy when he won the Spanish GP in 2006, a feat that he repeated with Ferrari in 2013.

Although this was a huge success, the Spanish economy was entering a dip and the circuit then faced a challenge to its supremacy because a street circuit was created in Valencia. This gave Spanish fans a second race, as it was run as the European GP from 2008, but that lasted only until 2012 and it has now been dropped, returning the Circuit de Catalunya to its previous position of supremacy. ∎

Opposite: Sergio Perez steers his McLaren out of the Turn 14/15 chicane ahead of Adrian Sutil, Romain Grosjean, Paul di Resta and Mark Webber in 2013.

APPROACH • 294KPH/184MPH **6**

6 EXIT • 280KPH/175MPH

4 REPSOL • 161KPH/100MPH

A

1

4

E

5 RENAULT • 235KPH/146MPH

3

5

3 SEAT • 121KPH/75MPH

150KPH/93MPH **3**

5 254KPH/158MPH

8

2

6

7

4 200KPH/125MPH

ELF • 141KPH/88MPH **3**

WURTH • 145KPH/90MPH **3**

1

5 CAMPSA • 246KPH/153MPH

3 BANC SABADELL • 139KPH/87MPH

6 EXIT • 260KPH/161MPH

CHICANE RACC • 92KPH/57MPH **2**

9

12

E

EUROPCAR • 213KPH/133MPH **5** 13

11

RACC

Circuit de Catalunya

14 15

2

10

LA CAIXA • 133KPH/83MPH **3**

16

3

NEW HOLLAND • 241KPH/150MPH **6**

Google Earth

Circuit Guide

The Circuit de Catalunya is a technical circuit that has every type of corner from low-speed to fast sweeper, and the lap is made all the more interesting by near constant changes of gradient, making it great for driving if not for overtaking.

Turn 1 • Elf
Gear: **3**
Speed: **141kph (88mph)**

This is always an exciting corner, with its 306kph (190mph) approach along the downward-sloping start/finish straight and then heavy braking before drivers dare to start turning into this near 90-degree righthander. With this being the main place for overtaking, it can get very busy here, not just on the opening lap but throughout the race and there have been numerous clashes here over the years. A tight line in helps drivers to get onto a more open line through Turn 2.

Turn 3 • Renault
Gear: **5**
Speed: **235kph (146mph)**

This is a corner that really works the tyres on the outer (lefthand) side of the car as it arcs uphill and around to the right. Drivers pushing too hard risk graining those tyres. Taken in sixth gear, it also tests the strength of drivers' neck muscles. A slow exit from Turn 2 compromises speed through here, but a clean entry not only makes a driver fast through this long, constant radius bend, but boosts speed along the short straight to the following corner.

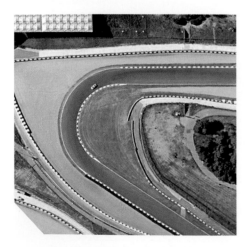

Turn 5 • Seat
Gear: **3**
Speed: **121kph (75mph)**

After rounding the double right fourth corner, the track rises again towards the fifth, Seat. This, like the third corner, can be a place where the cars are buffeted by wind, so drivers have to be prepared for that. A late turn into this tight lefthander is essential for a driver to be able to take the widest possible line out. The track drops away on the exit and feeds the drivers onto a brief, kinked straight on which they can hit 254kph (158mph) in fifth.

Turn 7 • Wurth
Gear: **3**
Speed: **145kph (90mph)**

As soon as the drivers have run through the kink, their view ahead used to be filled not with sky and clear space but with a tall earth bank, focusing their minds on getting their braking just right for this 90-degree left turn. More recently, the earth bank has been moved back and gravel traps inserted to make it less threatening. Dropping to third gear, drivers need to get the car balanced so that they can accelerate hard as soon as possible to power them up the climb that follows.

Opposite: Ferrari's Felipe Massa leads Kimi Raikkonen's McLaren and the Hondas of Rubens Barrichello and Jenson Button out of Turn 2 in 2006. *Above left:* Mika Hakkinen leads McLaren team-mate David Coulthard, Giancarlo Fisichella's Benetton and Michael Schumacher's Ferrari down to the first corner, Elf, in 1998. *Above right:* This was the moment that Fernando Alonso clinched the win that counted most to him in 2013.

Turn 9 • Campsa

Gear: **5**
Speed: **216kph (153mph)**

Taken over the crest of the slope, this may not look particularly tricky on a circuit map, but it's the most difficult corner of the entire lap because the apex can't be seen until the cars are almost upon it and the exit only when the apex is reached. So, placing the car is best done with experience, but there is at least plenty of run-off should drivers get it wrong, although Heikki Kovalainen's McLaren bounced clean across that after experiencing wheel failure in 2008.

Turn 10 • La Caixa

Gear: **4**
Speed: **133kph (83mph)**

At the end of the interior straight, this corner is approached downhill at 298kph (185mph). Drivers need to place their cars to the far righthand side of the track in order to help them take the least sharp angle around this lefthand turn, dropping from top gear to third as they do so. They must also pay attention to wind direction, which can really affect their optimum braking point, most especially if there's a tailwind. Overtaking is occasionally possible here.

Turn 12 • Banc Sabadell

Gear: **3**
Speed: **139kph (87mph)**

This is tighter in angle than the third corner, Renault, but similar in nature in that it's a long righthander taken uphill. The climb returns the circuit to not far short of the altitude of Campsa, but at least its second apex is visible on approach. Drivers used to really wind their cars up through here because it fed into the fast and open final two corners, but since 2007 it has fed onto a shorter straight and then a sharper righthand turn.

Turn 14/15 • Chicane RACC

Gear: **2**
Speed: **92kph (57mph)**

The realignment of the end of the lap in 2007 has been by far the most major change in the circuit's history. Instead of sloping downhill through a fast right, the track was made to cut right before the penultimate corner and then twist through this left/right chicane halfway down the slope to the final righthander. This was thought to be a good idea to help a chasing driver to get close enough to catch a tow down the start/finish straight, but it has done the opposite.

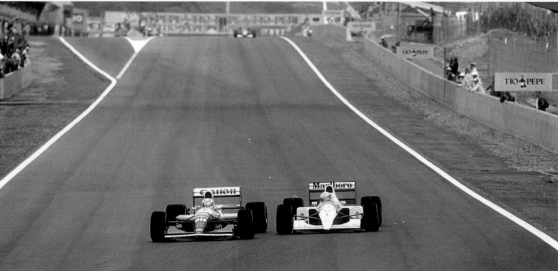

Great Drivers & Great Moments

The Circuit de Catalunya has always been a circuit on which overtaking is extremely difficult, so victories have often been decided by qualifying rather than by inspiration during the grand prix, but there have been some stand-out moments and star performances across its 24-year history.

Great Drivers

 Michael **Schumacher**
Barcelona wins – 6

 Mika **Hakkinen**
Barcelona wins – 3

 Fernando **Alonso**
Barcelona – 2

 Kimi **Raikkonen**
Barcelona wins – 2

Six of Michael's record tally of 91 grand prix wins came in the Spanish GP, making the Circuit de Catalunya his equal second most successful hunting ground (with Suzuka). The victory that stands out is the one he scored in 1996, when he didn't put a wheel wrong in the wet (see below). Michael had already won here for Benetton in 1995 and would go on to win four in a row for Ferrari between 2001 and 2004, with his victory in 1995 his most comprehensive.

This double World Champion had a great record at the Circuit de Catalunya, following up a dominant first win here in 1998 with two more in 1999 and 2000, all ahead of his McLaren team-mate David Coulthard. Indeed, the Finn was all set to make it four wins in a row here in 2001, when he suffered a last lap clutch failure and arch-rival Michael Schumacher motored past to win for Ferrari by a large margin from Juan Pablo Montoya's Williams.

When Fernando triumphed here in 2006, it was the win that the Spanish fans had been waiting for all of their lives. Driving for Renault, he qualified on pole and had an answer for everything that Michael Schumacher could throw at him, and so sent 130,000 people wild with delight as they waved their national and Asturican flags. Fernando had finished as runner-up in both 2003 and 2005 and later added a second win here in 2013 for Ferrari, also winning at Valencia in 2012.

Kimi's first victory in Spain came in 2005, when he was simply in a class of his own in his McLaren. No one else could get close and second-placed finisher Alonso's Renault was fully 27.6 seconds adrift by the chequered flag. The Finn would win here again in 2008, when the challenge from Spain's racing hero Fernando Alonso's Renault was thwarted by an engine problem; Raikkonen won from pole position as he pleased, beating his Ferrari team-mate Felipe Massa in his typically unflappable manner.

Great Moments

1991 Nigel **Mansell** and Ayrton **Senna** do battle

1993 Alain **Prost** wins as Damon **Hill's** engine fails

1996 Michael **Schumacher's** wet weather masterclass

2012 Pastor **Maldonado** holds on to win for Williams

If the fans weren't all convinced that F1 could be spectacular when the circuit opened in 1991, they were certainly so by the end of that year's Spanish GP because they had been treated to some of the decade's closest and most visceral racing. The battling was between Williams racer Nigel Mansell and McLaren's Ayrton Senna, with the pair running almost the length of the start/finish straight, their cars inches apart before a poor tyre choice led to Senna spinning in changing conditions, letting Mansell win.

In 1993, Damon Hill was desperate to prove his talents against his far more experienced Williams team-mate Alain Prost and pushed him harder than ever before. Prost qualified on pole, but Hill blasted past at the start, showing ever-improving form and suggesting that this might be the day he'd take his first win. However, it wasn't to last and Hill's Renault engine failed. Prost was able to relax in the lead because he had easily enough performance in hand to beat Ayrton Senna's McLaren.

Every now and again, when conditions for racing are terrible, a driver rises above it all to produce a drive of sheer genius. In 1996, Michael's first year with Ferrari, he did just that. The F310 wasn't particularly competitive, but the German came on strong as rain fell and conditions worsened, passing Jacques Villeneuve's Williams for the lead at one-fifth distance and then extending his advantage all the way to the finish as others spun, winning by fully 45.3 seconds from Jean Alesi's Benetton.

No one doubted that Venezuelan racer Pastor Maldonado possessed a good turn of speed. However, he had become known for being infuriatingly erratic and making mistakes. Yet, in 2012, not only did Pastor enjoy hitting the front on the rare day that Williams was able to offer him a competitive car with which he had qualified on pole, but he soaked up intense pressure from local hero Fernando Alonso, keeping ahead all the way to give Williams its first win since 2004.

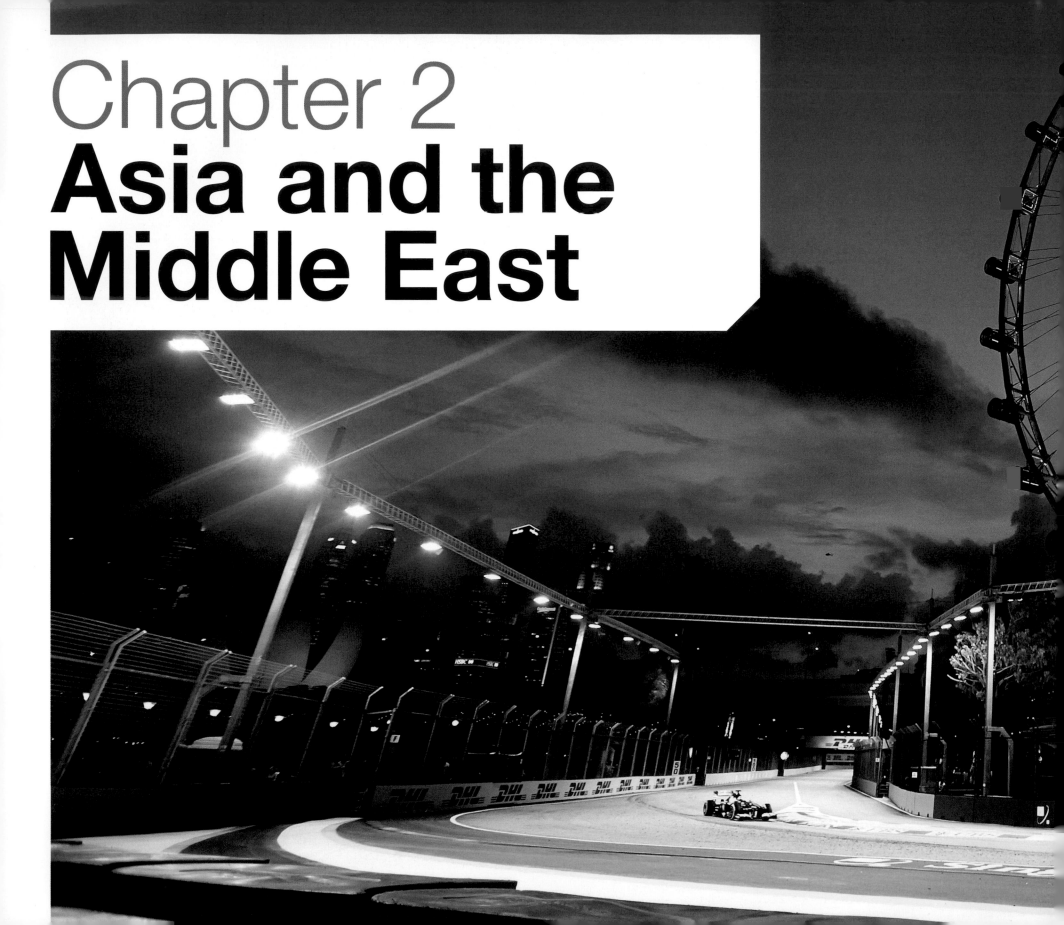

Chapter 2
Asia and the Middle East

Felipe Massa guides his Ferrari through Turn 22 of Marina Bay, Singapore, passing the giant Ferris Wheel.

Yas Marina

With money no object, this oil-rich country decided to host a round of the World Championship to boost its identity and so built a circuit of staggering grandiosity. It immediately impressed the teams when they first visited in 2009, but it is yet to produce a great race.

"This track has a bit of everything, with high-speed and low-speed corners, positive and negative camber, and the walls are pretty close most of the way around.**"**
Jenson Button

As the senior member of the United Arab Emirates, and the one with the greatest oil reserves, Abu Dhabi hasn't had to trumpet its wealth in the past. However, the rampant promotion of flashier junior emirate Dubai seems to have changed Abu Dhabi's approach, and the creation of the Abu Dhabi GP in 2009 was proof of this.

Like all other countries on the Arabian Peninsula, Abu Dhabi has no motorsport history, nothing to build on and no fan base to lure to the racing. Yet, this was seen as no impediment, because it was reckoned from the outset that the bulk of the spectators would be drawn from the tens of thousands of expatriate workers in the Gulf region. Indeed, one of the reasons for hosting a grand prix was to attract tourists to Abu Dhabi. To this end, it created the Yas Marina development that would offer far more than just a state-of-the-art racing facility. As well as the circuit, it would have a marina, a golf course, top-end hotels and even a Ferrari theme park, making Yas Island a place that people might chose for a holiday rather than just a weekend away.

So it was that Formula One's circuit designer of choice, Hermann Tilke, was given the design brief to create something dramatic. And this he did with a 21-corner stretch of tarmac that combines all the ingredients which an entertaining and challenging circuit should have, from a tightish first corner to

a run of esses, a chicane and a hairpin even before the cars have reached the first straight. The run from Turn 7 to Turn 8 is long enough for cars to hit just under 322kph (200mph) before the drivers have to brake very hard for the hairpin/chicane combination in front of a huge grandstand. With this being followed by a long, arcing straight into another tight corner, overtaking was expected to be rife. The final part of the lap is something of a departure, made up of a run of tighter corners, offering a very different challenge. The Yas Marina circuit even broke new ground, with its pitlane exit dipping into a tunnel under the track before delivering the cars to a safer merging point just after Turn 2.

It would take someone of powerful imagination to liken the Yas Marina circuit with Monaco's, yet it does possess two of the principality's key components: it too runs alongside a yacht-filled marina and also runs under a hotel, with a spectacular arch spanning the track between Turn 18 and Turn 19. However, you simply can't manufacture a setting like Monaco, where circuit melds with town and the glamour is for real.

Compared to the Sakhir circuit in fellow Gulf state Bahrain, though, the Yas Marina really benefits from being part of a sports and leisure complex, those yachts being packed with people in Abu Dhabi to have fun.

One other factor that marked out the Yas Marina as being a little different from other Tilke-designed circuits is that the grand prix has always been held as day turns to night, with the backdrop becoming all the more spectacular as darkness falls and the lights come on all around the circuit, with the hotel under which the circuit passes being a shroud of colour.

When the teams got their first sight of the circuit, they were more than a little impressed by its quality and could easily believe the alleged build cost of $1 billion. Abu Dhabi's inaugural grand prix in 2009 was won by Red Bull Racing's Sebastian Vettel after pole starter Lewis Hamilton's McLaren was slowed by a brake problem.

Sadly, the circuit has yet to provide the truly great racing that was expected of it because, although the racing has been close, overtaking has proved far harder than planned. This was shown most clearly in the final round of the 2010 World Championship when Fernando Alonso's title hopes evaporated; his Ferrari became bottled up behind Vitaly Petrov's Renault after a pitstop and he simply couldn't get past, allowing that evening's winner Vettel to pip him to the title by four points. ∎

Opposite: There's no time to admire the architecture as Toro Rosso's Jean-Eric Vergne brakes hard for Turn 1 in 2013.

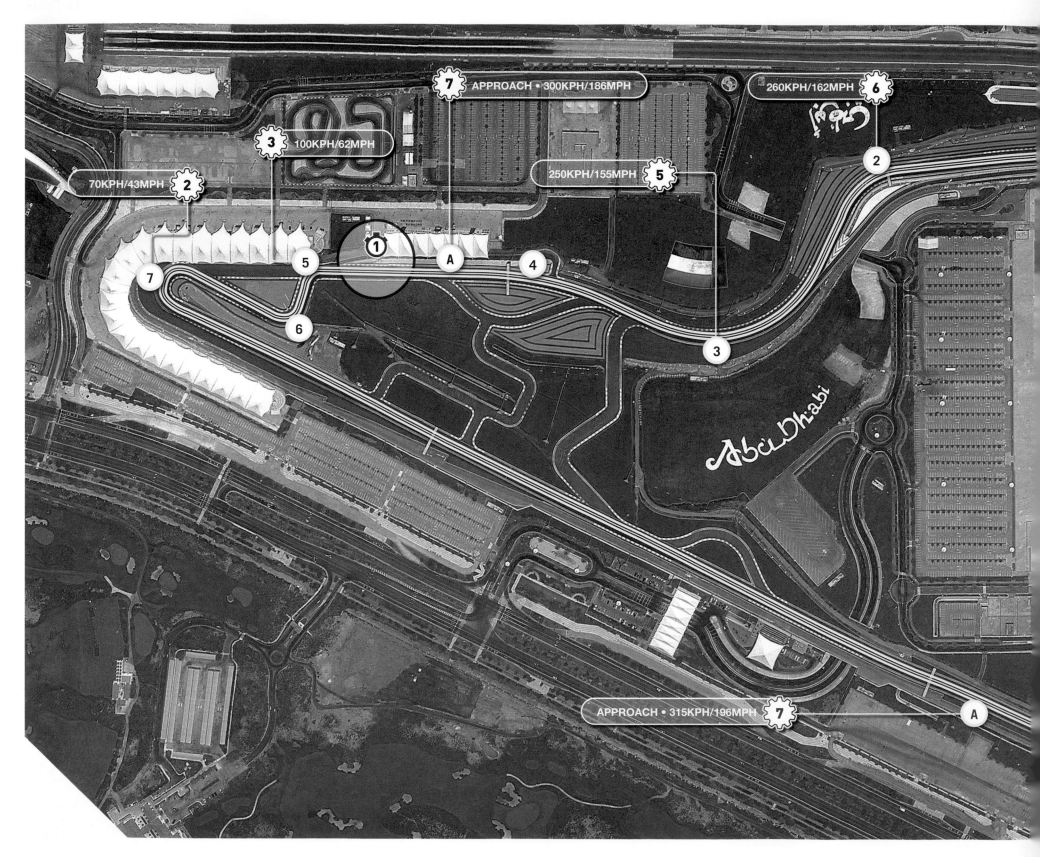

7 APPROACH • 300KPH/186MPH

260KPH/162MPH 6

3 100KPH/62MPH

2

250KPH/155MPH 5

70KPH/43MPH 2

5

1

A

4

7

6

3

Abu Dhabi

APPROACH • 315KPH/196MPH 7

A

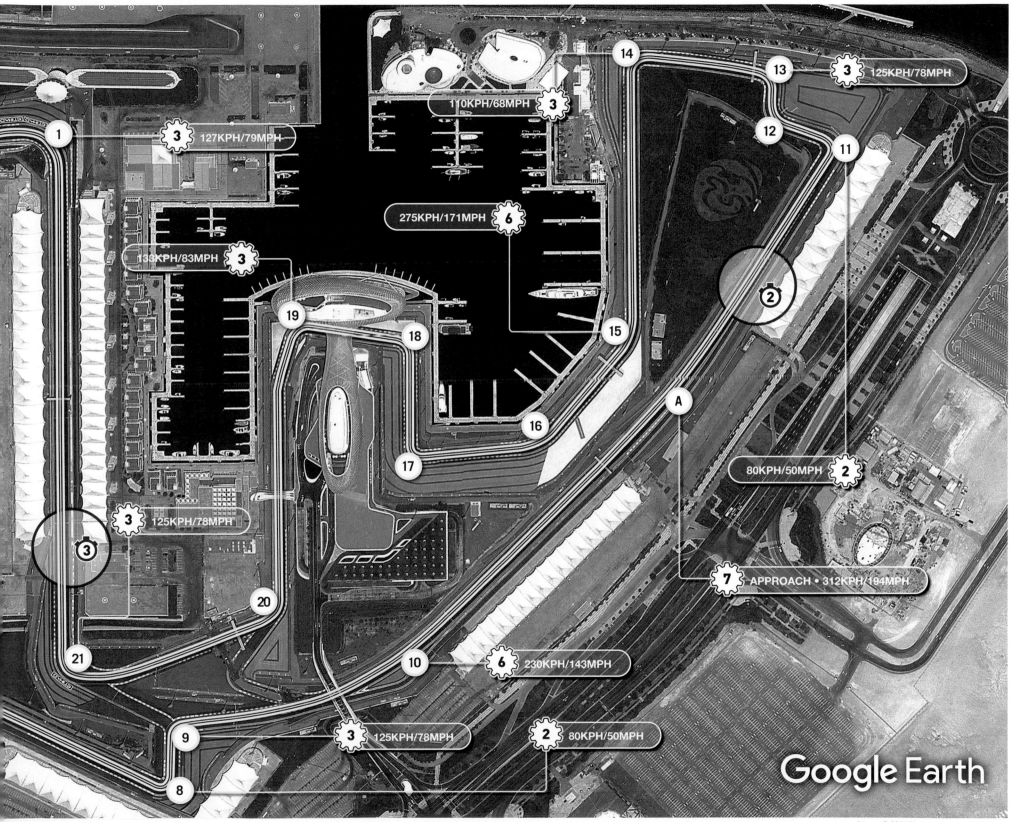

1

3 127KPH/79MPH

3 110KPH/68MPH

14

13

3 125KPH/78MPH

12

11

133KPH/83MPH 3

6 275KPH/171MPH

19

18

15

2

16

17

3 125KPH/78MPH

3

A

80KPH/50MPH 2

7 APPROACH • 312KPH/194MPH

20

10 6 230KPH/143MPH

9

3 125KPH/78MPH

2 80KPH/50MPH

21

8

Google Earth

Image © 2014 DigitalGlobe © Google 2014

Circuit Guide

The Yas Marina circuit is one that offers a challenge for the drivers, its starkly different sectors presenting them with everything from very fast to very slow plus the unusual experience of driving through fading light and then under floodlights.

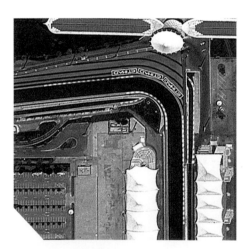

Turn 1 •

Gear: **3**

Speed: **127kph (79mph)**

The flat-out blast from the starting grid to the first corner is one of the shortest the F1 drivers face and it has an unusual feel because it's hemmed in by lofty grandstands on either flank. It can get crowded on arrival at this third-gear 90-degree lefthander, with the potential reward of making a passing move not always outweighing the risk, as Rubens Barrichello discovered in Abu Dhabi's inaugural grand prix in 2009, when he bent one of his Brawn's front wing endplates against Mark Webber's Red Bull.

Turn 5 •

Gear: **3**

Speed: **100kph (62mph)**

After the fast, serpentine sequence of twists through Turns 2, 3 and 4, the drivers have to hit the brakes hard for Turn 5. They might wish to make a passing move into this tight lefthander, but being fast into this corner can compromise the ability to tackle Turn 6 that follows immediately beyond it. To make matters more complicated, the most important part of the corner is making a good exit in order to be in position for the Turn 7 hairpin.

Turn 8 •

Gear: **2**

Speed: **80kph (50mph)**

The sooner a driver can get the power down out of the Turn 7 hairpin, the more speed a car can build down the back straight. If all has gone well, and a slipstream tow has been achieved, then the entry to this tight left is a potential passing point. It's an unusual corner, because the drivers can see little other than a huge grandstand straight ahead of them. Balancing braking and exit speed is critical because it feeds straight into a chicane.

Turn 10 •

Gear: **6**

Speed: **230kph (143mph)**

Accelerating hard out of the righthand second part of the Turn 8/9 chicane, drivers then keep their foot planted on the throttle as the track starts to arc away to the left; they change up to sixth gear, looking to get close enough to the car in front to be able to catch a tow down the remainder of the straight towards Turn 11. With grandstands along the righthand flank, the drivers' view is largely of the hotel and marina complex further around the lap.

Opposite: Jenson Button rockets past the marina as he heads for Turn 15 in his McLaren in 2011. *Above left:* The setting of the sun, as shown here over the pit straight grandstands in 2013, adds to the spectacle.
Above right: The floodlights are on as Lewis Hamilton negotiates the twisting entry to Turn 4 in his Mercedes in 2013.

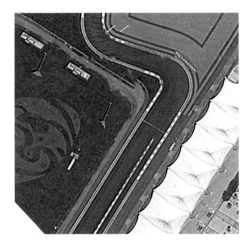

Turn 11 •

Gear: **2**
Speed: **80kph (50mph)**

Not dissimilar to Turn 8 in that it's a tight lefthander at the end of a long straight, Turn 11 differs chiefly in that its grandstand is to the righthand side of the track rather than in front of it, making it feel less imposing to the drivers. Entry to the corner is far from simple: like Turn 8, it feeds directly into another, and drivers looking to pull off an overtaking move must be aware that their work could be undone if they drift wide on exit.

Turn 13 •

Gear: **3**
Speed: **125kph (78mph)**

This sharp lefthand turn out of the third chicane complex feels like the point at which the circuit exits its second sector and enters its third. From here, the sweeping and then fast sectors feed into slower, tighter corners that run around the marina; drivers have to accept that they will be running in line astern because there's little opportunity to pass another car. Acceleration, balance when cutting across the kerbs and precision under braking are now the key for the remainder of the lap.

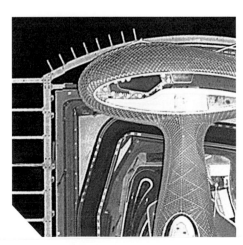

Turn 19 •

Gear: **3**
Speed: **133kph (83mph)**

Three corners from the completion of the lap, this 80-degree lefthander feels to drivers as though it is releasing them into a more open world again because they tackle it seconds after running under the elaborate, architectural span of the Yas Viceroy Hotel. Back into full light, in daylight conditions at least, they are best advised to let their cars run towards the outside of the track on the exit but immediately consider pulling across to the other side, the left, for the approach to the following corner.

Turn 21 •

Gear: **3**
Speed: **125kph (78mph)**

After negotiating quick Turn 20, drivers have to brake and change down to third gear for the final corner of the lap. This is a righthander of around 100 degrees, which is tucked in quite close to the inside of the Turn 8/9 complex at the end of the back straight. Feeding the cars back into view of the fans in the grandstands lining the start/finish straight, this corner is more critical in qualifying than it is in the race because it's not a spot for overtaking.

Sakhir

Countries in the Middle East had long wanted to attract F1 to their shores, and Bahrain won the race to do so. This was in 2004 and they built a new circuit in the desert to do this. It has yet to fill its grandstands and missed its 2011 slot due to political unrest, but it now has the attraction of being a night race.

❝ The layout is tricky and there arc some interesting corners with good sequences that you have to time perfectly in order to get them right. ❞
Juan Pablo Montoya

With considerable backing from the Bahraini royal family, led by Crown Prince Shaikh Salman bin Hamad Al Khalifa, the Bahrain International Circuit was opened on the site of a former camel farm and oasis at Sakhir, roughly 32km (20 miles) to the south of capital city Manama in 2004. Designed by Hermann Tilke, it immediately gave the World Championship a different flavour, offering something far removed from tree-lined Spa-Francorchamps, Montreal's island-based Circuit Gilles Villeneuve, Melbourne's suburban Albert Park or the streets of Monaco.

To give the circuit visual appeal, which isn't easy in this rocky stretch of desert, Tilke decided to split the circuit into two, making the area around the pits and paddock the "oasis" sector denoted by lush green grass verges. Then, as the track moves away from the circuit's hub, it enters its "desert" sector ,where all is as arid as the landscape around it, with a craggy, rocky feel rather than the rolling sand dunes that most people imagine when conjuring the image of a desert. Despite this concept, the circuit's most distinctive feature is the VIP Tower, a 10-storey edifice with a definite Arabic style that stands high above the first and second turns and Turn 10, offering the lucky VIPs fabulous views across the entire circuit. At the opposite end of the pitlane, there's a further nod to local style with a three-storey race control building in the style of a desert pavilion.

The layout of the Bahrain International Circuit has an opening section that bunches the cars together and makes overtaking possible not only on the opening lap. There follows a good length of a straight to a hairpin, before a middle section dotted with sweepers and some tight corners; then it all starts to open out again to end the lap with a good long stretch of top gear motoring. With not much of a backdrop to draw the eye, Tilke added to its interest by using what gradient was available, with Turns 4 and 13 the highest points.

The circuit was admired by the teams on their first visit in 2004 because it exceeded their expectations and the facilities were excellent. What was remarkable too, was the way that the project management team had had to cope with the date of Bahrain's inaugural grand prix being brought forward by six months at F1 supremo Bernie Ecclestone's insistence, cutting their schedule from two years to 18 months – they managed this in style. It was a definite accolade for Bahrain, and the finished project looked like $150m well spent.

Concerns that racing in the desert would be made farcical by sand blowing across the track and catching the drivers out were abated by glue being sprayed onto the verges of the desert section of the track.

In 2010, in a bid to boost the chance for more overtaking, an extra loop of track was added, turning left from the straight after Turn 4 and then swerving right, then tight left before doubling back through three more turns and rejoining the straight further down towards the start of the Turn 5/6/7 sweeper sequence. This wasn't adjudged to be a success, though, as it was too tight and merely reduced the number of times that the cars came past the grandstands without adding any extra overtaking.

One factor that the race organizers must hope is now behind them is the political unrest that hung over this event for several years, which included rioting in the streets and led to the cancellation of its grand prix in 2011. Fortunately, this appears to have calmed down and the teams' fears were allayed as they enjoyed successful races from 2012 to 2014. Yet, even in years when there were no threats of terrorism, the circuit's capacity of 70,000 grandstand seats seemed excessive and they have yet to be filled at any of the grands prix – a problem exacerbated by the grand prix being held on a Sunday, a working day in Islamic countries. Unfortunately for the circuit's management, the arrival of the Abu Dhabi GP in 2009 with its more attractive Yas Marina circuit and all of its tourist attractions have certainly reduced this race's appeal. ■

Opposite: With Nico Rosberg already pulling clear, fifth-placed Felipe Massa heads Mark Webber, Kimi Raikkonen, Jenson Button, Sergio Perez et al out of Turn 10 in 2013.

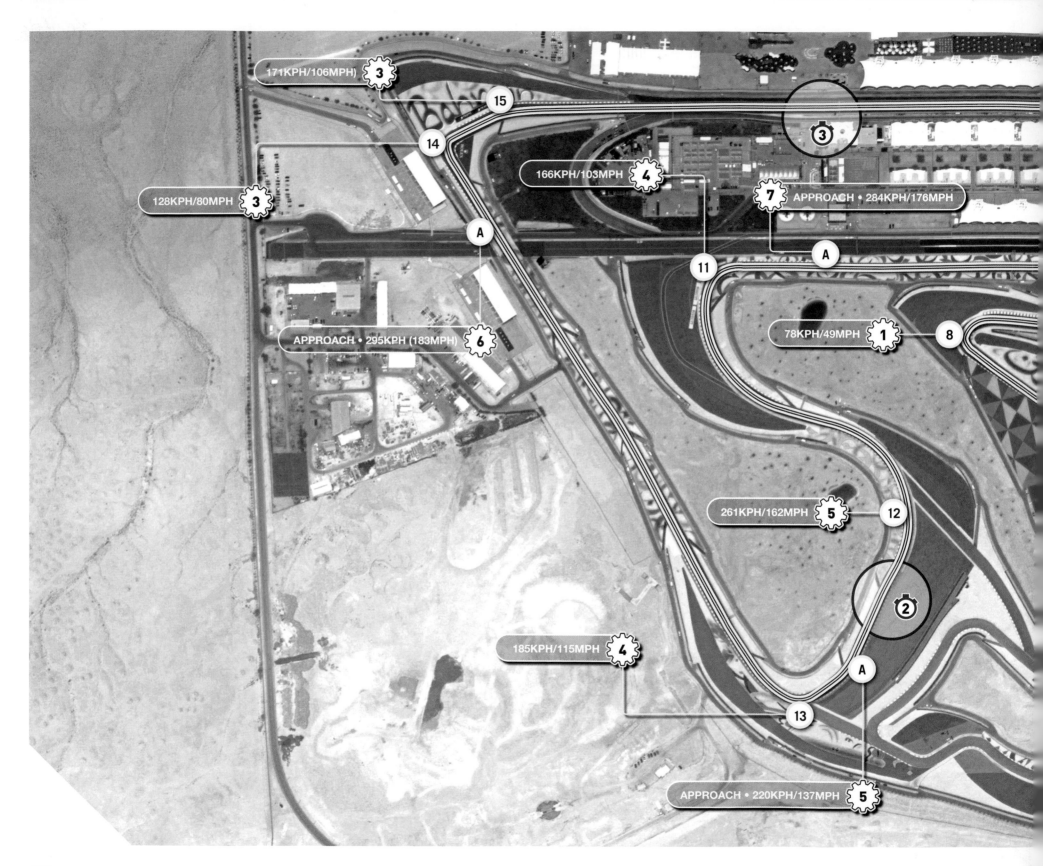

171KPH/106MPH) **3**

15

14

3 ●

128KPH/80MPH **3**

166KPH/103MPH **4**

7 APPROACH • 284KPH/176MPH

A

11

A

APPROACH • 295KPH (183MPH) **6**

78KPH/49MPH **1**   **8**

261KPH/162MPH **5**   **12**

2 ●

185KPH/115MPH **4**

A

13

APPROACH • 220KPH/137MPH **5**

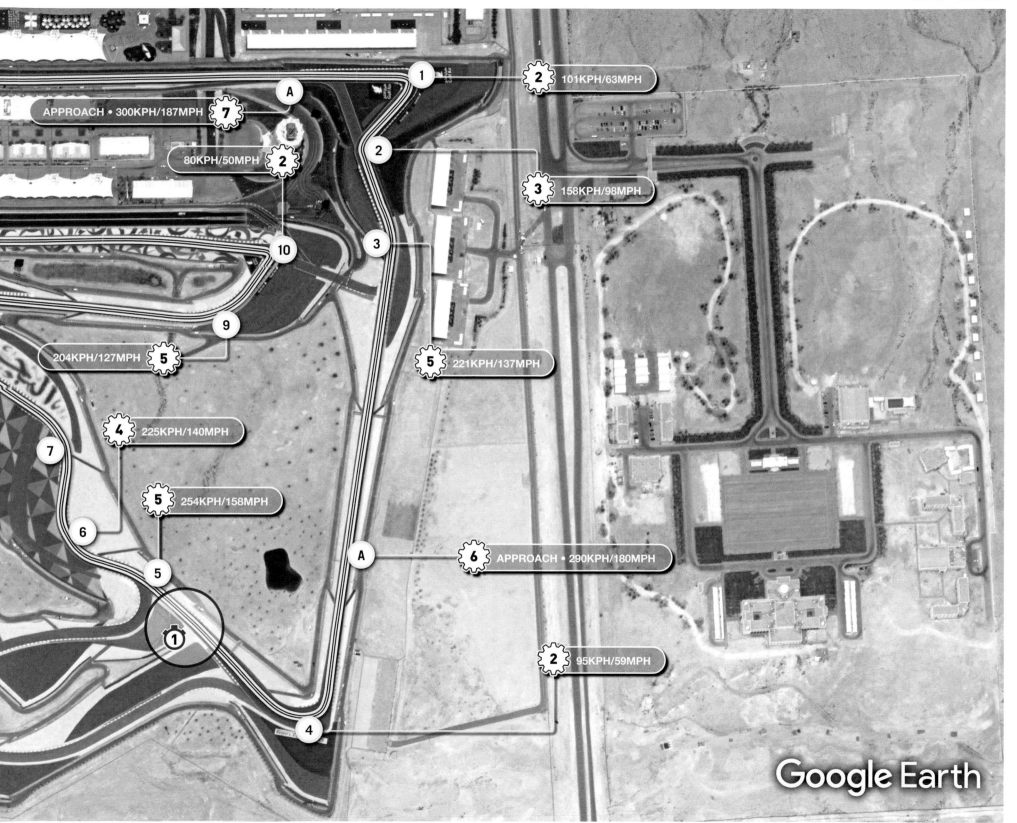

APPROACH • 300KPH/187MPH **7**

A

1

2 101KPH/63MPH

80KPH/50MPH **2**

2

3 158KPH/98MPH

10

3

9

204KPH/127MPH **5**

5 221KPH/137MPH

4 225KPH/140MPH

7

5 254KPH/158MPH

6

5

A **6** APPROACH • 290KPH/180MPH

1

4

2 95KPH/59MPH

Google Earth

Image © 2014 DigitalGlobe © Google 2014

Circuit Guide

Designed to have two different-feeling sectors, the lap of Sakhir is split into oasis and desert: the track in the area around the pits and paddock is the oasis, with grass verges, which contrast with the desert sand and rock to the rear.

Turn 1 ●
Gear: **2**
Speed: **101kph (63mph)**

This is a great opening corner, being a tight right approached down the circuit's longest straight with a wide entry to offer any attacking driver a clear opportunity to overtake. Similar to the first corner at Sepang, but not as acute a corner, it feeds back on itself and directly into Turn 2, and so drivers have to ensure that their bold moment into Turn 1 doesn't push them too far to the outside for them to get back onto line for Turn 2.

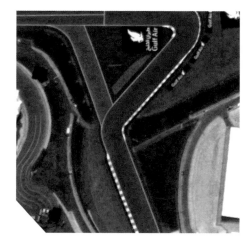

Turn 2 ●
Gear: **3**
Speed: **158kph (98mph)**

Taken one gear higher than the first corner, Turn 2 is where drivers who were able to grab the inside line into the first corner, and thus have the shorter approach, are now on the outside line. They must resist being pushed too wide out of this lefthander; getting edged out onto the kerbs could cause them to lift off the throttle and thus lose vital momentum onto the lap's second straight. Accelerating hard, the right kink of Turn 3 follows almost immediately.

Turn 4 ●
Gear: **2**
Speed: **95kph (59mph)**

Having hit close to 306kph (190mph) on this blast deep into the desert section of the lap, drivers are faced with almost uninterrupted views into the rocky desert beyond. They must focus on identifying their braking point, though, as well as checking for errant sand, as they brake and change down to second gear, ready to double back to the right. Luckily, there's a wide exit and the kerbs are not too vicious, so they don't have to hold it tight as they put the power down.

Turn 5 ●
Gear: **5**
Speed: **254kph (158mph)**

Possibly the most spectacular stretch of circuit as far as the TV cameras are concerned is this trio of downhill sweepers located midway down the long approach to Turn 8. Turn 5 whips cars away to the left, then Turn 6 back to the right and Turn 7 back left again to complete the deviation from the course. Cars can be seen teetering for grip as they negotiate this, with drivers hoping to keep their throttle pedal planted. A failure to carry speed can ruin a qualifying lap.

Opposite: Ferrari's Felipe Massa leads a pack of points-chasers into Turn 13 early in the 2013 Bahrain GP. *Above left:* A few palm trees and an artificial pond don't make an oasis, but this ornamental oasis at least brightens the infield by Turn 12. *Above right:* Fernando Alonso leads fellow frontrunners Nico Rosberg, Paul di Resta, Felipe Massa, Mark Webber and Jenson Button out of Turn 1 into Turn 2 in 2013.

Turn 8 ●

Gear: **1**

Speed: **78kph (49mph)**

Fast approaching the rear of the paddock, this is the point at which the drivers have to arrest their speed again, hauling their cars down to first gear and less than 80kph (50mph) for this ultra-tight right. The ideal attacking line into here is to be fully on the left side of the track in order to turn in from the widest angle and thus be able to carry the greatest amount of speed into the corner. If being attacked, a driver might need to hold a middle line to defend their position.

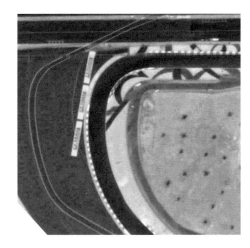

Turn 11 ●

Gear: **4**

Speed: **100kph (103mph)**

This marks the return to the desert section of the circuit, with the lefthander approached along the grass-lined straight behind the paddock. An open corner, it tightens halfway around its arc as the drivers hit the throttle again and the track starts to rise for the gentle climb all the way up the slope to Turn 13. There's a slight camber to help cradle cars through the turn, enabling drivers to really throw their cars into the corner and yet still get around it, with run-off aplenty if they get it wrong.

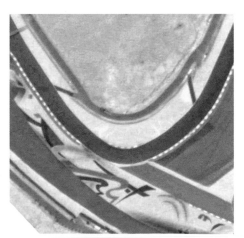

Turn 13 ●

Gear: **4**

Speed: **185kph (115mph)**

Like Turn 4, this is a double-back corner that turns the cars back towards the oasis sector that completes the lap. A curving, slightly uphill approach is followed by a righthander that tightens on itself halfway around. There's plenty of space on the exit to run a little wide if necessary, but the drivers' main concern is getting hard onto the power as soon as possible because the track starts to dip away for the descent that follows down a straight to the final two corners.

Turn 14 ●

Gear: **3**

Speed: **128kph (80mph)**

Turns 14 and 15 are really one corner, with Turn 15 simply being a swerve on the exit of Turn 14. Approached down the lap's second longest straight, it could be seen as a possible passing place, but this works only for a leader coming up on a backmarker; drivers of cars lapping at similar speeds tend to concentrate more on getting the perfect exit so they can be in position to complete the passing move at the end of the start/finish straight into Turn 1 after flashing past the pits.

Shanghai

Built on marshy land to the north of fast-expanding Shanghai, this circuit wows everyone who has visited it since 2004 because of its sheer scale. Everything about the Shanghai International Circuit is huge, except for the crowds who have resolutely not yet taken to F1, perhaps needing a Chinese driver to cheer.

❝ This track has high-speed and low-speed corners, good rhythm, even a bit of a banked corner. The layout is more like the old tracks, just with the walls pushed out. ❞

Jacques Villeneuve

The thing that excited the Formula One circus the most when talks of a possible grand prix in China were first discussed, was the fact that it would offer the teams and their sponsors a way into the gargantuan and fast-expanding Chinese market. F1 management and teams alike dreamed of this gateway to massively enhanced sales in the world's most populous country. It was a no-brainer to make sure that it happened. And so, with Chinese governmental backing, it did, with the Shanghai International Circuit opening in 2004.

Thus, in one fell swoop, China had a world class racing facility, having previously had only minimal contact with motor racing. This had come in several forms – a street circuit in Portuguese enclave Macau since the mid-1950s, then a street circuit in nearby Zhuhai from 1993, followed by China's first permanent racing circuit being built just outside Zhuhai in 1996. This had been built with the hope of landing a grand prix, even making its way onto the provisional World Championship calendar for 1998, but it was then dropped because of "infrastructure problems" and so it remained not fully finished, although operational for lower level racing.

The Chinese then became more focused on its bid for the 2008 Olympic Games, but Shanghai wanted something to counter Beijing's Games

and so the circuit was commissioned in 2001, with a deal clinched the following year for a grand prix from 2004.

Circuit designer Hermann Tilke described this circuit as his "toughest project" because he had to build the circuit and all the associated facilities on land that was "really very swampy, 300 metres [984ft] deep." What he had to do to solve this problem was to sink huge polystyrene blocks 14 metres (46ft) deep to stabilize the ground and then construct all the buildings on concrete piles. In all, 40,000 piles were driven into the ground to increase rigidity for what was to be built on top.

The lap starts with an intriguing uphill righthander that feeds directly into a further right on the crest of the rise; this in turn feeds directly into a sharp left as the track levels out again at the foot of the rise. The turning doesn't stop there, either, as Turn 3 leads straight into Turn 4, where drivers try to get onto the throttle as early as possible for the straight that follows. The circuit then opens up and, after a hairpin at Turn 6, follows a meandering course until it reaches Turn 11, where it starts a sequence of tight twists not dissimilar to Turns 1 to 3, albeit on the level. Then it really opens out with an incredibly long straight down to a hairpin before an open kink leads the cars back on to the start/finish straight.

In addition to the sheer size of the gigantic pit straight grandstand, the feature that marks the circuit out as unique is what is to be found behind the giant paddock. Offering a rare element of national identity among the endless concrete are individual two-storey villas for each of the teams to use as their headquarters while at the grand prix, built in a Chinese style, approached over bridges and surrounded by lakes and gardens.

Since the first Chinese GP, won by Rubens Barrichello for Ferrari in 2004, there have been some great races at the Shanghai International Circuit, with many a change of position into the first corner, into Turn 6 and, mostly, into the hairpin at the end of the back straight. However, it's not a circuit to which the sport has warmed, because it is so large that it dwarfs the people there, making it feel empty. In fact, much of it is empty, with the huge grandstands encircling the Turn 11–13 complex never being used and now being covered in advertising banners to mask this fact. Add the smog that often obscures the sun, and the circuit can feel characterless. ∎

Opposite: The view from the top of the giant grandstand opposite the pits towards Turn 6 is amazing, unless smog sets in.

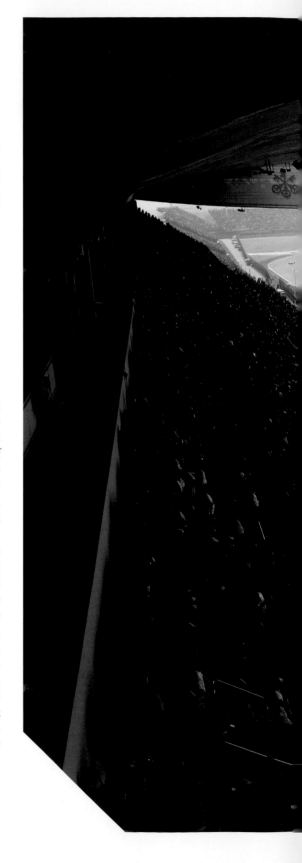

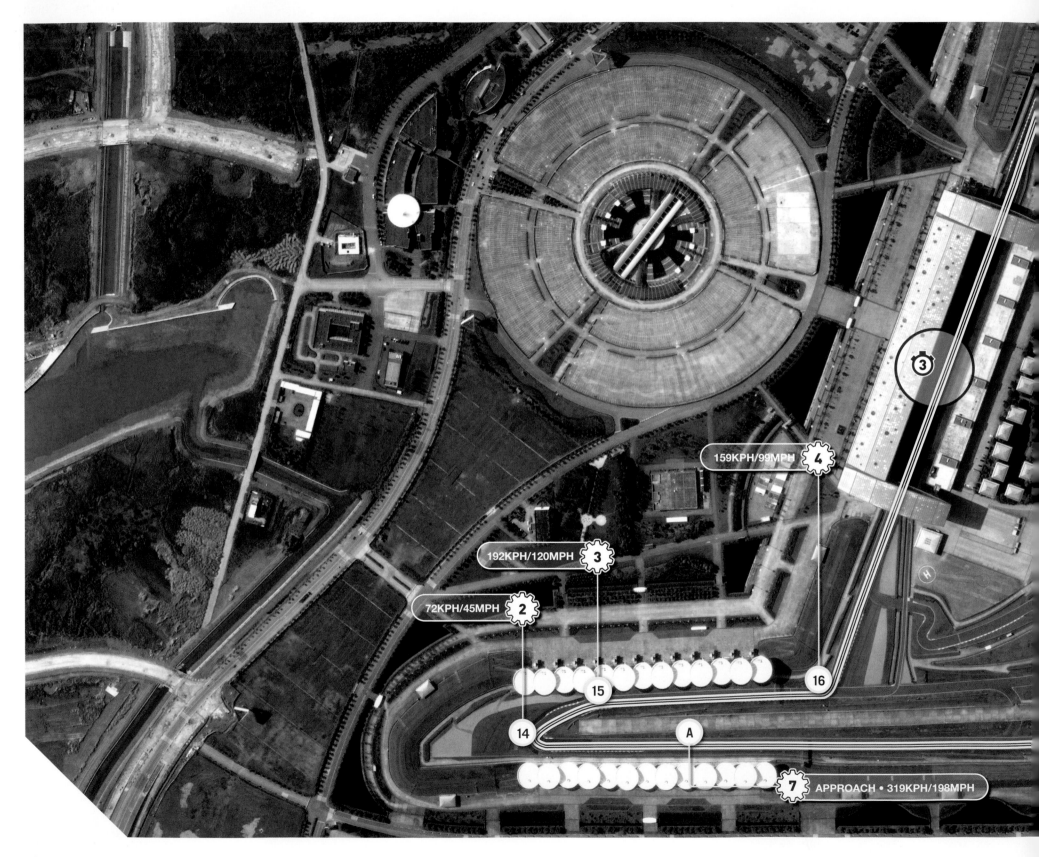

159KPH/99MPH **4**

192KPH/120MPH **3**

72KPH/45MPH **2**

15

16

14

A

7 APPROACH • 319KPH/198MPH

1

4 175KPH/109MPH

6 APPROACH • 298KPH/185MPH

3

2

5

A

2 76KPH/47MPH

4

6

3 110KPH/68MPH

1

2 85KPH/53MPH

A

5 APPROACH • 220KPH/137MPH

7

6 270KPH/168MPH

A

3 108KPH/67MPH

6 APPROACH • 270KPH/168MPH

9

8

12

2 85KPH/53MPH

3 185KPH/115MPH

10

11

2

13

4 187KPH/116MPH

E

EXIT TO TURN • 249KPH/155MPH 5

Circuit Guide

From the seemingly never-straightening first four corners up and over a ridge to the wicked sweepers around the back of the paddock and the wide and incredibly open back straight into a hairpin, this track provides the drivers with a real ride.

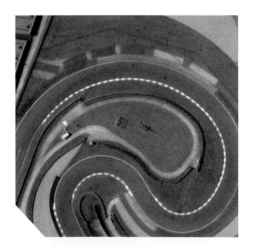

Turn 1 ●
Gear: **4**
Speed: **175kph (109mph)**

The track is broad as the cars pass under the second "wing" over the start/finish straight and arrive in the braking area for the first corner. The view ahead is open across a large concrete apron, but a driver's eyes must be focused on how the track narrows and rises to the right. Dropping from top gear to fourth, drivers have to pick their line according to whether they are attacking or defending, with a line around the outside often proving the best if attacking.

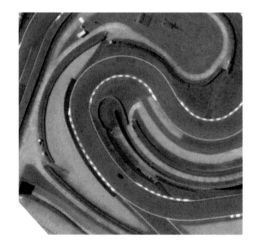

Turn 3 ●
Gear: **2**
Speed: **85kph (53mph)**

Dropping sharply into a compression as the track reaches the level of the start/finish line again, drivers have to change down to second gear and, on the opening lap in particular, be wary of wing-bending attacks from either side because the traffic can become very heavy at this squeeze point. This is the first really sharp corner of the lap and is very physical simply because of the simultaneous change in both direction and gradient. A tight line out of the turn can pay dividends.

Turn 6 ●
Gear: **2**
Speed: **76kph (47mph)**

Drivers arrive at this turning point having built up some decent speed along the kinked straight from Turn 4. Braking from 298kph (185mph), they then have to drop down from sixth gear to second. With low grass banks set back some way on either side, it feels wide open, but the righthander is relatively tight, albeit with its angle relaxing after the apex; drivers use the kerbs on the way out so that they can start getting the power down again as soon as possible.

Turn 7 ●
Gear: **6**
Speed: **270kph (168mph)**

This little considered stretch of the Shanghai circuit at the rear edge of the paddock is actually one of the most exciting, because both the cars and the drivers are really made to work through this pair of sweepers. Drivers don't have time to really appreciate the view of the lofty grandstand ahead of them as they turn in on as smooth an arc as possible through this sixth-gear lefthander, knowing that they must achieve the balance to be on line for Turn 8.

Opposite: The pit entry can be tricky, as Lewis Hamilton discovered in 2007, when he didn't get this far... *Above left:* Braking hard, Sebastian Vettel leads Romain Grosjean and Jenson Button into Turn 14 in 2013.
Above right: The giant main grandstand is in the background as Jean-Eric Vergne negotiates Turn 4 in his Toro Rosso in 2013.

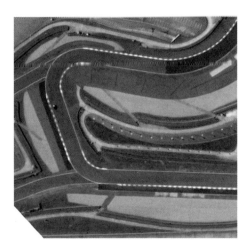

Turn 10 •

Gear: **3**
Speed: **185kph (115mph)**

After decelerating for third gear Turn 9, drivers have to turn left again almost immediately, accelerating as they do so. To take as much speed as they can onto the straight that follows, many cut across the kerbs on the inside then use those on the outside as they head off towards the furthest end of the track. Back in 2005, Juan Pablo Montoya triggered a safety car period when he ran over a drain cover here in his McLaren and dislodged it.

Turn 13 •

Gear: **4**
Speed: **187kph (116mph)**

Passing the giant but empty grandstands encircling this section of the track (which is shaped like the head of a hockey stick), this is the point at which the drivers can get on the throttle again after negotiating the sharp lefthander of Turn 11 followed immediately by a long right. More open in angle than Turn 12, exit speed from this constant radius righthander is vital because it feeds onto the incredibly long back straight. Cars look slower than they are here because of the scale of the place.

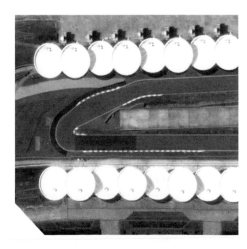

Turn 14 •

Gear: **2**
Speed: **72kph (45mph)**

Few drivers arrive at this righthand hairpin without needing either to attack the car in front or to defend their position from a rival. Having hit more than 322kph (200mph) on a good lap down the back straight, they are offered plenty of space to try their move, because the track is wide here when they start braking as they pass the grandstand on their left. They change down to second or even first gear, hoping that they won't need to use the run-off space ahead of them.

Turn 16 •

Gear: **4**
Speed: **159kph (99mph)**

The final turn is reached through a slight kink and then a gentle rise. With a lofty grandstand on the drivers' left side and open space on their right, drivers are naturally drawn towards the more open side of the track; this is the correct place to be because this is the line they need to tackle this fourth-gear lefthander. The corner will be forever remembered as the place where it went wrong for Lewis Hamilton when he slid into the gravel trap in 2007.

Great Drivers & Great Moments

Victories in China matter a lot to the teams because of the shop window that this race provides their sponsors in this burgeoning economic powerhouse, but the drivers are more than happy to win here too, and there have been some epic scraps since the Shanghai International Circuit's World Championship debut in 2004.

Opposite top: Fernando Alonso flashes past the chequered flag in 2013, with his second Shanghai win putting him into early championship contention.

Opposite bottom left: Rubens Barrichello heads to victory in the first Chinese GP in 2004 after overcoming challenges from Kimi Raikkonen, then Jenson Button.

Opposite bottom right: Lewis Hamilton added Mercedes's third win in China in 2015 when he and team-mate Nico Rosberg appeared to have performance in hand over all of their rivals.

Great Drivers

 Lewis **Hamilton**
Shanghai wins – 3

 Fernando **Alonso**
Shanghai wins – 2

 Kimi **Raikkonen**
Shanghai wins – 1

 Nico **Rosberg**
Shanghai wins – 1

Victory in China in 2008, when it was the penultimate round, set Lewis up for his second title bid as he won with ease ahead of Ferrari's Felipe Massa. It took until 2014, though, for the English driver to win here again when he made it three wins from the first four rounds by leading every lap. His Mercedes team-mate Nico Rosberg was hot on his heels in 2015, with Ferrari's Sebastian Vettel close behind, but the team was accused of sandbagging to hide its performance advantage.

The Chinese GP was the final race of the 2005 World Championship and Fernando triumphed for Renault by 4 seconds from Kimi Raikkonen's McLaren in an event spoiled by a safety car deployment to move a dislodged drain cover. At the time it seemed unlikely that Alonso would have to wait another eight years for his next win here, but he did. Driving for Ferrari in 2013, he won what was likened to high-speed chess as drivers found their tyres going off markedly.

Ferrari claimed its third win in Shanghai in 2007 on F1's fourth visit and the driver at the wheel for this one was Kimi Raikkonen. The race was see-sawing between him and McLaren's Lewis Hamilton as the conditions kept changing with rain blowing in and out, when Hamilton slid into a gravel trap. Ferrari's Finn then motored on untroubled to win easily. Raikkonen headed to the final round in Brazil seven points behind, and an outside title shot but, famously, he won.

Having a World Champion for a father can often make a young driver's life at the track difficult. Not so in the case of Keke's son Nico, because the 1982 World Champion stays in the background, but he had reason to be delighted when everything went Nico's way in the race here in 2012. Nico didn't put a wheel wrong in his Mercedes while others did, allowing him to score his first F1 win at his 111th attempt. This was also Mercedes GP's first F1 victory.

Great Moments

 **2004** Rubens **Barrichello** wins inaugural GP for Ferrari

 2007 Lewis **Hamilton** slides off and blows it

 2010 Jenson **Button** reads the condition right to win

2012 Nico **Rosberg** takes Mercedes' first win

Michael Schumacher was the main man for Ferrari when the teams visited Shanghai. However, it was team-mate Rubens Barrichello who came away with the spoils because the German, who seemed to have relaxed, had an extraordinary weekend. Already World Champion, Schumacher slid off on his qualifying run and ended up 18th, then started from the pits with a new engine but could climb only to 12th, while Barrichello held off Jenson Button's BAR.

McLaren's rookie Lewis Hamilton looked set to claim the drivers' title. He started the race with a 12-point lead over Fernando Alonso and was leading from Ferrari's Kimi Raikkonen, but his rain tyres were going off. McLaren waited to see if more rain would come and Raikkonen went past to lead. Then, when Lewis finally peeled off to change to dry tyres, he slid into the gravel trap at pit entry and was beached there. Thus Raikkonen was able to win for Ferrari and keep the title race open.

Jenson had an inspired 2009 season in which he and Brawn GP stormed to their first and only F1 titles, and the start of the 2010 season with McLaren gave him victory on only his second outing, in Australia. Then, when he came to Shanghai for the fourth round, he won again, followed home by his more highly rated team-mate Lewis Hamilton; Jenson profited from an early-race decision to stay on dry tyres as rain began to fall, before it dried again.

Created from Brawn GP, which had dominated in 2009, this Ross Brawn-led team took time to find its feet again, but its third year as Mercedes GP gave the squad reason to cheer. Its breakthrough came at Shanghai, when Nico Rosberg started from pole and saw off the challenge of team-mate Michael Schumacher, who retired with a loose wheel. Jenson Button looked to have the pace to beat him due to three-stopping his McLaren, but a pitstop blunder allowed Rosberg to stay in front and win.

● Suzuka

Built as long ago as 1962, Suzuka has always been a considerable challenge and few places show a Formula One car being put through its paces to the same extent. It's a magnificent combination of high-speed corners, changing gradient and camber, which really makes the drivers work for their living.

❝ Suzuka's the most beautiful race track along with Nürburgring's Nordschleife and Macau, and it's a dream to drive, but overtaking is harder than it looks. **❞**
Sebastian Vettel

Many of the world's greatest racing circuits are the result of local topography rather than clever design work. Take Spa-Francorchamps or the Nürburgring Nordschleife, both twisting their way around rolling landscape. Suzuka has a foot partly in this camp, because its raw ingredient of an open hillside in Japan was a great starting point, although the circuit was designed for purpose rather than simply taking over public roads as happened at Spa-Francorchamps.

This great circuit was shaped in 1962 at the behest of Honda by John Hugenholtz, the circuit manager who had interpreted the ideas of Sammy Davis, the Le Mans 24 Hours winner, for the creation of fast, flowing Zandvoort in his native Holland in the late 1940s. The result is such a gem that Suzuka is all but unchanged more than 50 years later, and very few circuits of similar vintage can match that.

The basic shape of the layout that was draped over the hillside near the city of Nagoya is a figure of eight, making it one of only a handful of circuits that crosses over itself. Suzuka was intended to be simply a test circuit on which Honda could test its motorbikes and the cars from its new automotive division. However, it was too good to be restricted to this and soon races started to be held, with future Lotus F1 boss Peter Warr winning the Japanese GP for sportscars in 1963. It was a further 24 years before it landed a grand prix date, though.

Not only was its lap an intense challenge, but it also produced some great racing, with the drama kept high by it often being the penultimate or final round of the World Championship. Few will forget the shoot-outs between Ayrton Senna and Alain Prost in 1989 and 1990, when they came into contact each time, helping neither of them. Michael Schumacher's attempts to keep McLaren's Mika Hakkinen from the 1998 drivers' title was incident-filled too, from the moment that he stalled his Ferrari on the starting grid.

What helped to make the racing so exciting is that this circuit, built in the grounds of an amusement park, offers more than a few places at which drivers have a reasonable chance of making a passing move stick. The downhill blast to the fast first turn is the main one of these, but there's also scope to try to overtake into the hairpin, and again at the Casio Triangle right at the end of the lap if a driver has been brave enough to get into a slipstreaming tow down the back straight and through mighty 130R.

In between this trio of points, the track uses the gradient well to make the drivers and their cars really work hard, and the photographers love the opportunities it offers them, with the amusement park's lofty Ferris wheel or monorail providing an unusual backdrop. On a bright day, which is far from guaranteed in the grand prix's traditional autumnal

date, fans in the main grandstand can see all the way past the first corner and on down to the sea. On many an occasion, though, they have been fortunate to see even the far side of the track because, when the rain comes down, it really comes down. This was topped in 2004, though, when a typhoon blew through and came close to forcing the cancellation of the race.

The Japanese fans also give the grand prix a sense of occasion because they are unbelievably passionate in the way that they support their heroes, sitting all day long festooned in face paint, scarves and flags.

Despite being ready to host a grand prix from the outset, it took a quarter of a century before the circuit made its Formula One bow; Japan stayed on F1's sidelines despite Fuji Speedway hosting two grand prix in 1976 and 1977. Then, in 1987, with the Casio Triangle having been inserted a few years earlier to slope the cars' passage through the final corner, it landed its place on the World Championship calendar. That first race was deprived of the main excitement when Nigel Mansell crashed in qualifying and so couldn't race, leaving the way clear for his Williams team-mate Nelson Piquet to take the drivers' crown. ■

Opposite: Felipe Massa (right) and Fernando Alonso guide their Ferraris through the Casio Triangle in 2013, with the funfair in the background.

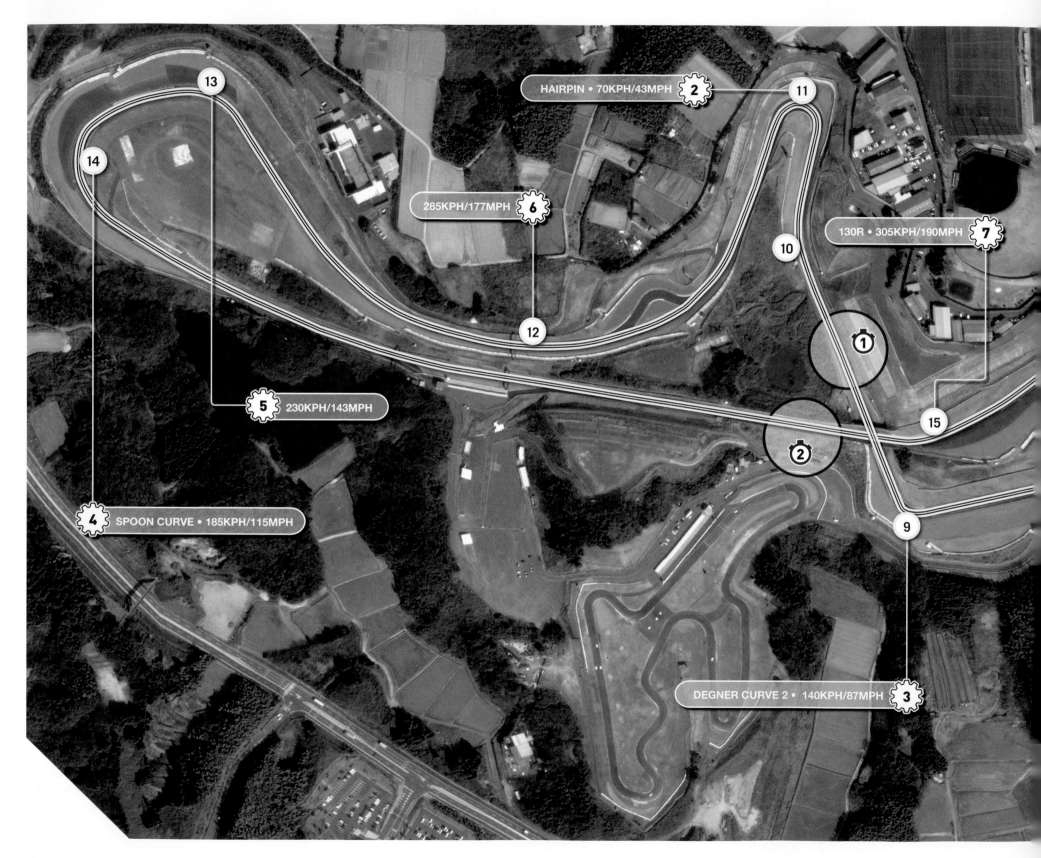

HAIRPIN • 70KPH/43MPH **2**

285KPH/177MPH **6**

130R • 305KPH/190MPH **7**

5 230KPH/143MPH

4 SPOON CURVE • 185KPH/115MPH

DEGNER CURVE 2 • 140KPH/87MPH **3**

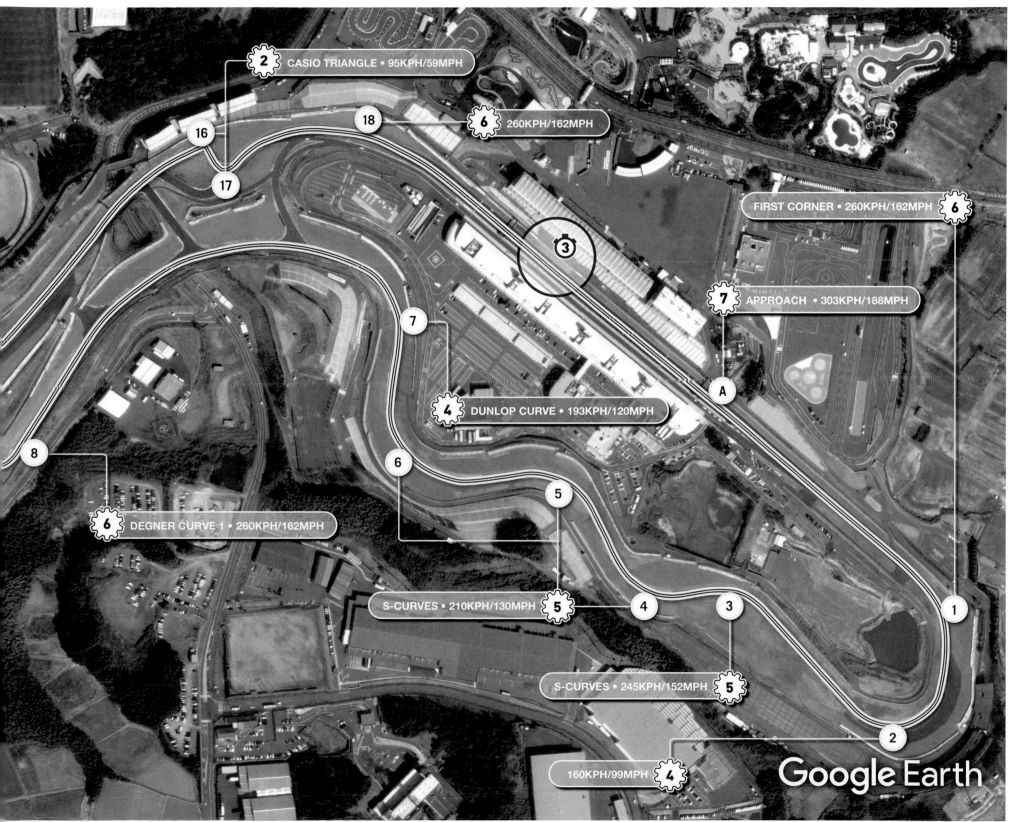

2 CASIO TRIANGLE • 95KPH/59MPH

6 260KPH/162MPH

16

18

17

6 FIRST CORNER • 260KPH/162MPH

3

7 APPROACH • 303KPH/188MPH

7

A

8

4 DUNLOP CURVE • 193KPH/120MPH

6

5

1

6 DEGNER CURVE 1 • 260KPH/162MPH

5 S-CURVES • 210KPH/130MPH

5

4

3

2

5 S-CURVES • 245KPH/152MPH

160KPH/99MPH **4**

Google Earth

Circuit Guide

The S Curves are there to be attacked, the Degners for carrying as much momentum as possible, the Spoon Curve for picking the perfect exit and 130R simply for the brave to hang on through, meaning that every lap is a challenge.

Turn 1 • **First Corner**
Gear: **6**
Speed: **260kph (162mph)**

Approaching this first corner down a gentle slope, drivers are travelling at 314kph (195mph) and the corner appears open, with a wide gravel trap straight ahead for a feeling of safety. A dab of the brakes is all that's required as they carry as much momentum as possible through this gently angled righthander and then attempt to ensure that they remain to the outside for the much tighter second turn, something that isn't always easy in traffic on the opening lap. This is where Senna and Prost collided in 1990.

Turn 3–6 • **S-Curves**
Gear: **5**
Speed: **210kph (130mph)**

130R is perhaps Suzuka's most famous corner, but this uphill sweep of esses is by far its hardest sequence. In fact, many reckon that it's F1's toughest challenge, harder to get right even than Silverstone's Becketts sweepers. The approach looks simple enough, but the first left is followed almost immediately by a right, then a left and then a second right (this tighter than any of the three before it, and steeper too), with speeds dropping with each turn. Any mistake is magnified in each subsequent turn.

Turn 7 • **Dunlop Curve**
Gear: **4**
Speed: **193kph (120mph)**

The drivers are on the lefthand side of the track when they exit the last of the S-Curves, but need to pull directly to the opposite side to be in position to tackle what follows as the slope flattens out behind the top end of the paddock. This is a corner that seems to keep on turning and turning some more, and drivers really have to hang on through here; not surprisingly, many are sometimes afflicted by understeer as they try to get the power down before the exit.

Turn 8 • **Degner Curve 1**
Gear: **6**
Speed: **260kph (162mph)**

There are two Degner Curves and they could not be more different in nature. This first one is approached at great speed in sixth gear as the track dips slightly, with drivers immediately being presented with the more enclosed approach to the second Degner. With the earth bank topped by the return leg of the track looming on the right, drivers have to drop down to third gear to be slow enough to negotiate this tighter right and then get on the power under the bridge.

Opposite: A critical moment at the chicane in 1993 as Ayrton Senna comes up to lap an obstructive Eddie Irvine's Jordan. *Above left:* Romain Grosjean pushes Sebastian Vettel out of the final uphill S-Curve towards Dunlop Curve in 2013. *Above right:* Putting his Mercedes's power down out of Turn 2 in 2013, Lewis Hamilton prepares to attack the S-Curves.

Turn 11 • **Hairpin**
Gear: **2**
Speed: **70kph (43mph)**

After powering their way under the bridge carrying the return leg of the lap, there's a righthand flick and then, suddenly, full view of one of the few obvious places to overtake. This lefthand hairpin is a tight one and drivers have to drop to second gear, taking very different lines in according to whether they're attacking a car ahead or defending from one behind. With a rising exit, drivers can get on the power early and the gradient change helps to cradle the car.

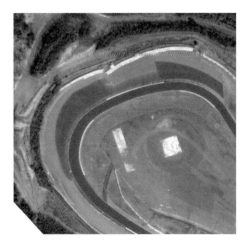

Turn 13/14 • **Spoon Curve**
Gear: **4**
Speed: **105kph (115mph)**

After the incredibly long, sweeping righthand bend that runs up the slope from shortly after the hairpin, and then a longish left that it switches into over the crest of a gentle incline, the drivers reach this, the furthest point of the track. Called Spoon because of its shape, it's a vital corner to get right because it feeds the cars onto the long back straight. With the second part dropping and tightening, a dab on the brakes is required to steady the car before accelerating out.

Turn 15 • **130R**
Gear: **7**
Speed: **305kph (190mph)**

The straight from Spoon Curve is long, with the separate club circuit down the bank to the right. Then, having reached 314kph (195mph), the drivers arrive at what was once the most feared corner. It's described as a flat-out bend, but 130R (so called for its 130-degree radius) is only flat-out for the brave, with most having a slight lift off the throttle. The earth bank on the exit was moved back a few years ago to provide more run-off for any who run wide.

Turn 16/17 • **Casio Triangle**
Gear: **2**
Speed: **95kph (59mph)**

In complete contrast to the blast through 130R, drivers have to hit the brakes and hit them hard for this right/left chicane. As they approach and consider possible passing manoeuvres, the second part of the corner is out of their sight, and it's made all the more difficult by the fact this second part of the sequence is even sharper. Then, as the track falls away on the exit, drivers have to start accelerating hard through the dropping righthander that feeds them onto the start/finish straight.

Great Drivers & Great Moments

Such is the difficulty of this magnificent circuit – the challenge of its mix of corners and the often torrential rain which can hit it – that a win here feels like two at most other circuits, and Suzuka has enjoyed some epic races across the decades.

Great Drivers

Michael **Schumacher**
Suzuka wins – 6

Second in 1994, Michael Schumacher went one better for Benetton in 1995. He then finished second on his first outing here for Ferrari in 1996 before taking a second Suzuka win in 1997, showing his affinity for this circuit. The home fans really respected his skills and, once Ferrari hit form in 2000, there was no stopping him: Michael rattled off further wins in 2001, 2002 and 2004. He was all set for a seventh win in 2006, his last year before quitting for the first time, when his engine failed.

Sebastian **Vettel**
Suzuka wins – 4

Despite having contested just over a third of the grands prix that Michael Schumacher did, Vettel picked up wins in Japan for Red Bull Racing in 2009, 2010, 2012 and 2013 in a run broken only in 2011, when Jenson Button won for McLaren and he was third, 2 seconds adrift. The best of his four wins was in 2012, when he started on pole and led every lap to beat Ferrari's Felipe Massa by 20 seconds, with title rival Fernando Alonso being taken out at the first corner.

Ayrton **Senna**
Suzuka wins – 2

No overseas driver has ever been as celebrated in Japan as Ayrton Senna. Perhaps it was because he scored so many wins around the world for cars powered by Honda engines. Perhaps it was because they saw something of the warrior in him. However, he also earned their appreciation by winning here in 1988 to beat his McLaren team-mate Alain Prost to the title. He would win again at Suzuka in 1993 with a masterful drive in which he saw off Prost's more competitive Williams.

Gerhard **Berger**
Suzuka wins – 2

Gerhard was in his third year of F1 when the World Championship visited Suzuka for the first time in 1987, and he came away with the honour of being the first winner here, as Ferrari hit strong late-season form. He qualified on pole, then won easily ahead of Ayrton Senna's Lotus. Four years later, the Austrian won again, this time for McLaren, when Senna, now his team-mate, moved over to let him by because second place was enough for the Brazilian to retain his world title.

Great Moments

1990 Alain **Prost** meets Ayrton **Senna**

They had clashed at Suzuka in 1989, when racing for McLaren and fighting over who'd become champion, and Alain Prost and Ayrton Senna would fight again in 1990 when in a similar position, but with Prost now with Ferrari. Angered by the FIA's refusal to move pole position away from the dirty side of the track, Senna dropped behind Prost on the run to Turn 1 and ducked up the inside, and they collided. He'd later admit that this was in revenge for being hit by the Frenchman in 1989.

1994 Damon **Hill's** wet weather masterclass

Michael Schumacher held the upper hand in the 1994 title battle when they arrived in Japan, but Damon Hill for Williams wasn't going to give up without a fight. In atrociously wet conditions, he produced a drive that's considered by many as his finest moment. The race was stopped early on as cars aquaplaned off the track, then restarted and Benetton's Schumacher pressured Hill, but he never put a wheel wrong and closed the gap between them to just one point before the Adelaide finale.

1998 Mika **Hakkinen** clinches his first world title

Victory in the penultimate round at the Nürburgring had given McLaren's Mika Hakkinen a four-point lead over Ferrari's Michael Schumacher, so the stage was set for a shoot-out at Suzuka. The German wasted his pole position by stalling at the beginning of the parade lap, forcing him to start from the back. He made strong progress as Hakkinen led, climbing to third, but then hit debris and had a blow-out, forcing him to retire. Thus Hakkinen was able to cruise and collect his first F1 title.

2005 Kimi **Raikkonen's** last lap move

Very few grands prix are decided on the final lap, but this one was – and in spectacular style. Giancarlo Fisichella led for Renault, but Kimi Raikkonen, who had started 17th for McLaren after rain arrived before he could take his qualifying run, finally caught him. Earlier, he had demoted reigning World Champion Michael Schumacher, and he didn't stop there but got into the Italian's tow and simply drove around the outside of him at the first corner to take a famous victory.

Sepang

Circuit architect Hermann Tilke is accused by some race fans of designing bland circuits, but this early work remains one of his best because it offers drivers not just a sinuous lap to get their teeth into, but plenty of space for them to line up and execute overtaking manoeuvres.

" You feel very safe on this circuit, with wide run-off areas and the possibility of overtaking. The only difficult point is to handle the temperature and humidity. **"**

Jean Alesi

Some F1 fans might presume that Malaysia's involvement with motor racing dates back only to 1999, when it hosted a grand prix for the first time, but they are out by several decades if they believe this. Led by expatriates working there, the first motorsport in Malaysia was in the 1960s, using temporary street circuits at Penang and Johore Batu, with many drivers heading down to neighbouring Singapore for races there.

Malaysia's first permanent circuit was built at Johore Batu in 1968. Also known as Selangor after a palace that overlooked it, it gave Malaysian drivers a place to race until 1977, when it was closed after an accident in which six children were hit by a car and killed. Modified and reopened as Shah Alam, it went on to host a round of the World Endurance Championship in 1985. However, conditions were too hot and humid for the comfort of the drivers and the track was considered way too bumpy, which is typical for tracks in the tropics because of the extreme weather to which they are exposed. Worse still, the World Championship event attracted only 3,000 spectators.

It was time for a rethink and, after several false starts as the country's motorsport movers hatched plans for Asia to host its first grand prix beyond Japan, a brand new circuit was built in a tree-fringed depression alongside Kuala Lumpur's international airport in 1999. This was Sepang, and the ample budget used for the programme was clearly money well spent because circuit designer Hermann Tilke produced a design that set new standards. Even a cursory glance at the plans that he had concocted with former F1 racer Marc Surer revealed that this was a circuit designed from scratch to really allow drivers to race. For example, there were two 900m (half-mile) straights into hairpins. Also, to ensure that chasing drivers had a chance to pull off a passing move, the track at the entry to these corners was wide; the value of this has been proved ever since, as it allows drivers to defend and those behind them to attack.

The lap is augmented by some wonderful, sweeping sections where the cars are able to be shown at their most dynamic, with the runs through Turns 5 and 6, then through Turns 12 and 13 of particular merit. Many a circuit can be a challenge to a driver, but this one was designed so that it could be challenging as well as a place where they could actually race each other. No small part in this was the fact that the circuit's management team showed plans to Michael Schumacher and took heed of the suggestions that he made. History relates that it was wise to stick with the design for the opening hairpin and the way it feeds into Turn 2, as Michael had wanted the hairpin tightened, but the reason that it works and provides such great racing is that they retained the width that Tilke had recommended.

One of Sepang's key features is the double-sided grandstand. This gives 50,000 spectators views of the pits and start/finish straight, much of the track from Turn 1 to Turn 6 and also, for those sitting on the reverse face, of the return straight to the final corner as well most of the run of the circuit from Turn 8 to Turn 14. Topped by a huge integral canopy, this provides essential shelter for the fans, not only from the intense sun but the tropical rain that comes quick and heavy when it hits. The drivers simply have to suffer in the heat and humidity.

Rain has played a role in many of the grands prix held at Sepang since its debut in 1999, notably in 2009, but what stands out is how Tilke got it right from the outset: the facilities still look great and the circuit hasn't needed a single amendment since it opened. It's that rare thing, a drivers' circuit where they can race as well, which is fantastic because the Malaysian GP usually follows the opening round in Melbourne and so offers a first chance to see the cars flat-out. ∎

Opposite: Sebastian Vettel powers his Red Bull RB9 down the main straight past Sepang's trademark canopied grandstands in 2013.

270KPH/168MPH **6**

3 LANGKAWI • 110KPH/68MPH

4

1

3

6 GENTING • 260KPH/162MPH

191KPH/119MPH **4**

2 80KPH/50MPH

252KPH/157MPH **6**

6

5

2 72KPH/45MPH

96KPH/60MPH **2**

3

2

1

15

7

APPROACH • 301KPH/187MPH **7**

A

A

7 APPROACH • 300KPH/186MPH

2 SUNWAY LAGOON • 122KPH/76MPH

8

14

9

A

71KPH/44MPH **1**

KLIA • 200KPH/124MPH **4**

10

E

13

12

A

6 APPROACH • 285KPH/177MPH

EXIT • 200KPH/124MPH **4**

A

5 APPROACH • 225KPH/140MPH

2

APPROACH • 255KPH/158MPH **5**

11

KENYIR LAKE • 152KPH/94MPH **3**

Google Earth

Fernando Alonso's Ferrari F138 leads
Mark Webber's Red Bull, Lewis Hamilton's
Mercedes and the rest of the field into
Turn 9, on the opening lap of the 2013
Malaysian grand prix.

Circuit Guide

From the wide straight leading down to the first hairpin via the sweepers midway around the lap to the high-speed sweepers at the back of the circuit, this is a track that has a fabulous flow and, better still, allows for racing with plenty of overtaking.

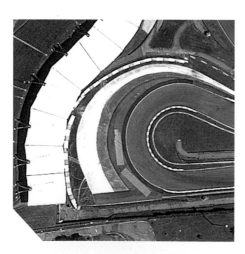

Turn 1 •
Gear: **2**
Speed: **80kph (50mph)**

The track is wide here and feels wider still because the spectator banking is some way back on the drivers' left; the feeling of space is augmented by the grandstand beyond the corner being way back behind an enormous gravel trap. The drivers have to brake heavily down from near on 306kph (190mph) to around 80kph (50mph) in second. As this righthander turns through around 200 degrees before feeding almost straight into Turn 2, drivers choose their line according to traffic around them.

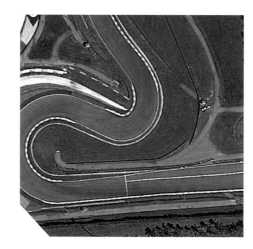

Turn 2 •
Gear: **2**
Speed: **72kph (45mph)**

If a driver gets through Turn 1 without contact on the opening lap, they then have to get on the power quickly before braking hard for even tighter Turn 2. Ideally, they'd attack this from the righthand side of the track, in order to be quicker on the dipping exit, but this isn't always possible if a driver has run wide coming out of Turn 1. On occasion, a driver can make a bold passing move here, like the one produced by McLaren's David Coulthard on Michael Schumacher's Ferrari in 1999.

Turn 4 • **Langkawi**
Gear: **3**
Speed: **110kph (68mph)**

After accelerating all the way from Turn 2 through the arc of Turn 3 and up the gentle slope from there, hitting 290kph (180mph), the drivers have to brake hard because the slope suddenly flicks up before the corner, meaning that they arrive over a crest. Taken in third gear, drivers must try to prevent their cars from understeering as soon as possible on the exit of the corner because the track now opens up into a sweeping run all the way to Turn 9.

Turn 6 • **Genting**
Gear: **6**
Speed: **260kph (162mph)**

The Sepang circuit is really finding its flow by this point, a third of the way around the lap, and this righthand sweep, taken in sixth, is the counterbalance to the lefthand sweep that precedes it. A driver will know for sure whether his car is handling well if it can run through here with a good balance. At this point, the driver will be trying to maintain as much speed as possible for the short straight that follows, and any loss of momentum will cost him.

Opposite: Sebastian Vettel leads the pack into the first corner in 2013, with the 21 other runners jostling for position on a damp track. *Above left:* There's no escaping the country you're in – as shown by Lewis Hamilton flashing past a Malaysian flag in his Mercedes in 2013. *Above right:* Mark Webber arrives at the end of the back straight in his Red Bull in 2013, braking hard to slow for Turn 15.

Turn 9 •

Gear: **1**
Speed: **71kph (44mph)**

The sweeping back section of the circuit is brought to a near halt at this lefthand hairpin, drivers dropping from seventh gear to first. It's possible to make a passing move into here if the driver ahead has clipped a kerb or run wide through the close-together combination of Turns 7 and 8. Yet, there can be contact too, because the entry is wide enough but the hairpin's rising exit is incredibly cramped and traction is not always easy to come by, especially if the circuit is wet.

Turn 12 •

Gear: **6**
Speed: **257kph (160mph)**

After climbing to Turn 11 and accelerating out of the third gear righthander, the track now drops away again gently, with drivers getting a great view of the back of the lofty covered grandstand that runs along most of the start/finish straight. They need to ignore that, though. The sixth-gear lefthander ahead of them needs to be got exactly right to carry vital momentum through it – it takes an esse-like course because the track almost immediately starts turning to the right again.

Turn 14 • **Sunway Lagoon**

Gear: **2**
Speed: **122kph (76mph)**

Heavy braking is required as the drivers arrive at the penultimate corner of the lap at the end of a long and tightening arc from Turn 12 to Turn 13. Changing down to second gear, drivers have to ensure that they don't carry too much speed when they arrive at the apex of this tight right because it's more important to get turned in cleanly and get back onto the throttle so that they can accelerate out down the circuit's second longest straight.

Turn 15 •

Gear: **2**
Speed: **96kph (60mph)**

The cars hit 306kph (190mph) in top gear in the shadow of the giant grandstand and drivers file towards the righthand side of the track as they line up their approach to the final corner. This is a lefthand hairpin that works best with a "wide in, wide out" line, but many an overtaking driver is presented only with the option of trying their passing move down the inside and then trying to sort out their exit, with many moves seeing the passed driver emerge in front again.

Great Drivers & Great Moments

With plenty of space for slipstreaming and overtaking, there have been some classic races at Sepang since its debut in 1999. The often extreme weather here has also played its role in creating the excitement when tropical storms have struck during the grand prix.

Great Drivers

 Michael **Schumacher**
Sepang wins – 3

 Fernando **Alonso**
Sepang wins – 3

 Sebastian **Vettel**
Sepang wins – 3

 Kimi **Raikkonen**
Sepang wins – 2

This seven-time World Champion could have claimed the honour of winning Sepang's inaugural grand prix at the end of 1999, but he handed that instead to his title-chasing Ferrari team-mate Eddie Irvine. As if to prove the point, he triumphed in 2000, when he was chased all the way by McLaren's David Coulthard, then won again in 2001 in a monsoon ahead of team-mate Rubens Barrichello. In 2004, he added a third when he was chased all of the way by Williams racer Juan Pablo Montoya.

Fernando has not only won the Malaysian GP three times but has the distinction of having done so for three teams. His first, with Renault, came in 2005 in a race that he led all the way to win by 25 seconds from Jarno Trulli. Then, having just moved to McLaren, he won again in 2007 after getting ahead of Ferrari's poleman Felipe Massa at the first corner. The Spaniard's most recent victory came in 2012 with Ferrari when he hit the front in the wet and resisted an attack from Sergio Perez.

Having scored his maiden F1 win in 2008, then added four more after moving to Red Bull Racing in 2009, Sebastian got his 2010 campaign off to a good start by winning here in the third of that year's 19 rounds. This gave him the momentum that resulted in his first drivers' title. He won at Sepang again in 2011 as he set off towards title number two, lost out with a puncture in 2012 and then won once more in 2013 as Red Bull again controlled proceedings.

Kimi's second ever grand prix was here in 2001, and it ended in disappointment when his Sauber failed on the opening lap. However, he gave his second season with McLaren some momentum when he won here in 2003. This was his first F1 win and, after failing to land the drivers' title in 2005, he joined Ferrari in 2007 and won here for a second time in 2008 in a race that gave the Italian team a boost after a disastrous showing in Australia.

Great Moments

1999 Ferrari assists Eddie **Irvine**

2001 **Ferrari** falls off then picks the right tyres to win

2009 Jenson **Button** splashes to victory

2012 Sergio **Perez** hounds Fernando **Alonso**

F1's first visit to Sepang was made dramatic by it being the penultimate race of the 1999 season, with McLaren's Mika Hakkinen holding only a two-point lead over Ferrari's Eddie Irvine. After missing six races with a broken leg, Michael Schumacher returned to action to support Irvine and led from pole, but let the Ulsterman go past, then delayed Hakkinen to help Irvine win. The Ferrari one-two was later rescinded because the cars' bargeboards exceeded the limits, but both drivers were reinstated on appeal.

This was the first time the Malaysian GP was held near the start of the season and it slotted in behind Australia and produced the same winner. However, it came the hard way after Michael Schumacher and team-mate Rubens Barrichello spun off on oil at Turn 5 on lap 3. Rain had just started and the safety car was deployed. Opting for intermediates when others went for rain tyres was a masterstroke as they roared up the order and by lap 16 Michael was back in front, where he stayed.

In the opening races of 2009, it seemed that Jenson Button really could walk on water because he won five of the first seven rounds. At Sepang, he really did walk on water: although Nico Rosberg led early on, the way that Button adapted to the rain in his Brawn put him in front and he was still in front when it got too wet to continue. The cars sat on the grid, but there was to be no restart because it got too late and light was fading, thus handing victory to Button.

Every now and again a performance from a young driver stands out. One such drive happened in 2012, when second season F1 racer Sergio Perez came close to winning for Sauber. Lewis Hamilton had led away for McLaren in the wet, but the race had to be stopped until conditions dried out. He led away again, but he overshot his pit and Ferrari's Fernando Alonso took over. Late in the race, Perez caught Alonso, shaped up to pass him, but slid wide and so missed his chance.

Marina Bay

This circuit was like a breath of fresh air when it made its bow in the World Championship in 2008. Not only was it the sort of city-centre circuit that F1 had sought for years, but it had the added attraction of its race being held after nightfall, making F1 look more spectacular than ever.

❝ It's a very physical circuit and so you need to put a lot of work into the car to get a good lap. I'd say it requires double the effort of Monaco. ❞

Lewis Hamilton

With the World Championship swinging its attention towards having an ever-increasing number of grands prix beyond Europe, the plans for what would become the Singapore GP surfaced in 2006, presenting drivers not only with the concept of racing on a street circuit other than Monaco but also of racing after nightfall. These dreams were realized when the Marina Bay Street Circuit was opened in time for the 15th round of the 2008 World Championship.

This was far from the country's first taste of motor racing, though, as there had been racing in Singapore since 1961, when the Orient Year GP for sportscars was run on a temporary circuit. This was laid out on the Upper Thomson Road with a slower, twistier return leg completing the 4.8km (3-mile) lap, and the race was won by Ian Barnwell in an Aston Martin DB3S. The event would become the Malaysian GP, then Singapore gained independence in 1965 and it hosted its own grand prix from 1966. Single-seaters gradually took over and the race was run until 1973, when Vern Schuppan won in an F2 March. Plans to build a permanent circuit in the mid-1980s came to nothing, so it was to be another 35 years until powerful single-seaters raced in Singapore again.

With government backing, a route for a temporary circuit was plotted with the city's most iconic buildings as a backdrop. This was important because the money was being spent not just to appease sports

fans but to market Singapore globally. When F1 fans got their first look at the Marina Bay circuit, the first thing that made it stand out wasn't, in fact, its city centre location. Instead, it was the fact that almost all of the action was run after dark as F1 experienced its first night race. The images were amazing and Singapore looked stunning in the backdrop, a city lit up to emphasize that this was no race tucked away in a rural backwater. This was racing where perhaps a whole new audience could enjoy its thrilling spectacle and sound. Any concerns felt by the drivers beforehand, that they might have trouble in the dark, were dispelled: there were 1,500 lights shining onto the track and the floodlighting for the braking zones and corners in particular was more than good enough for them to pick out their markers.

The setting also afforded some incredible viewing points, with 1982 World Champion Keke Rosberg doing some TV commentary work from high above the circuit on the Singapore Flyer, a giant Ferris wheel.

What marks the circuit out from other street circuits, apart from being used after nightfall, is the fact that it has plenty of long straights rather than the usual twists and turns. Indeed, Kimi Raikkonen set the race's fastest lap for Ferrari at over 172kph (107mph), making it 16kph (10mph) faster on aggregate than Monaco.

As well as its combination of long straights, tight corners, crossing a bridge and handful of fast

bends in its 23-corner lap, the circuit also offered the novel experience of the track running right underneath a giant grandstand between Turns 19 and 20 before feeding back onto Raffles Avenue.

Drivers liked the concept of the race and its location. Some even found racing after dark to be pretty special, but they were unanimous after their first visit that something had to be done about the bumps, especially on the straight down Raffles Boulevard between Turns 5 and 7. What the teams did like, though, was that although the circuit is temporary, the pit buildings are impressive and permanent, ensuring a high standard. The people who loved the Marina Bay circuit the most, though, were the TV camera crews and the photographers, who could combine cars racing, night skies and buildings illuminating the backdrop.

In 2011, it was mooted that the grand prix might relocate to a circuit away from the middle of the city, but this wasn't realized. Other plans discussed included changing Turn 10, with Sebastian Vettel one of a handful of drivers requesting that this tight lefthander be modified to improve its safety because they reckoned its kerbs were too high and the surface too bumpy at this narrow point. ∎

Opposite: F1 cars racing after dark has been a revelation since Singapore joined the world championship. This is Romain Grosjean leading Mark Webber in 2013.

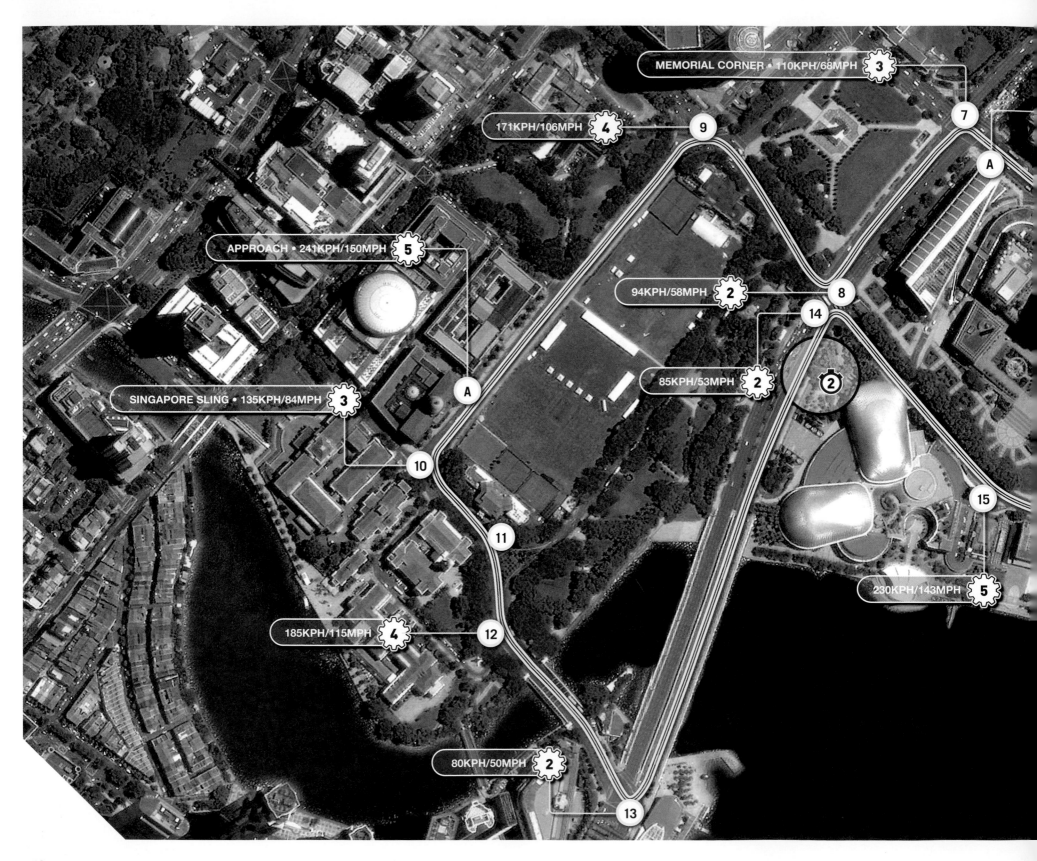

MEMORIAL CORNER • 110KPH/68MPH **3**

171KPH/106MPH **4** 9

7

A

APPROACH • 241KPH/150MPH **5**

94KPH/58MPH **2**

8

14

SINGAPORE SLING • 135KPH/84MPH **3**

85KPH/53MPH **2**

2

A

10

15

11

230KPH/143MPH **5**

185KPH/115MPH **4** 12

80KPH/50MPH **2**

13

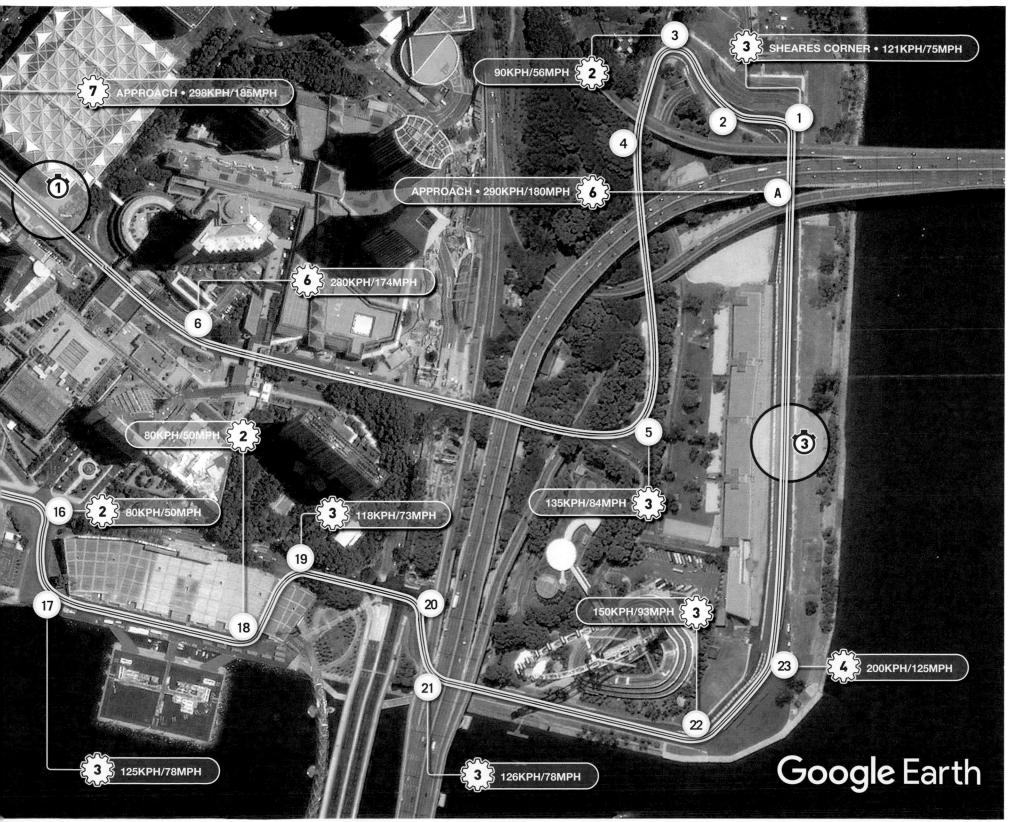

7 APPROACH • 298KPH/185MPH

3

3 SHEARES CORNER • 121KPH/75MPH

90KPH/56MPH 2

2

1

4

1

APPROACH • 290KPH/180MPH 6

A

6 280KPH/174MPH

6

5

3

80KPH/50MPH 2

135KPH/84MPH 3

16

2 80KPH/50MPH

3 118KPH/73MPH

19

17

18

20

150KPH/93MPH 3

21

23 4 200KPH/125MPH

22

3 125KPH/78MPH

3 126KPH/78MPH

Google Earth

Circuit Guide

With concrete barriers lining the route and 90-degree corners more prevalent than open sweepers, this is a circuit on which drivers can't afford to relax for an instant. Throw in the difficulties of racing under floodlights, and it's definitely a test.

Turn 1 • **Sheares Corner**
Gear: **3**
Speed: **121kph (75mph)**

Purpose-built rather than converted from a public road, this part of the track is smoother than the rest, but the first corner is made difficult by being the first part of a three-corner sequence: it feeds directly into Turn 2 and that, in turn, into Turn 3. Passing the pits at 290kph (180mph), drivers have to brake hard under a road bridge for this lefthander and try to stay off the kerbs. On the opening lap, it's extra busy, and drivers are aware that avoiding contact is imperative.

Turn 3 •
Gear: **2**
Speed: **90kph (56mph)**

This is the lap's first slow corner and the drivers have to drop to second gear to slow sufficiently for this tight left onto Republic Boulevard. Getting into position to take the apex isn't always easy after their jousting through the first two corners. If they look up, they have the strange sight of running under the curving flyovers that carry Singapore's main roads as they open up for the blast down to Turn 5 and then all the way on down to Turn 7.

Turn 7 • **Memorial Corner**
Gear: **3**
Speed: **110kph (68mph)**

The kinked straight before this 90-degree lefthander offers a rare chance for the engines to breathe, with drivers topping 298kph (185mph) when they flash past the city views that are revealed as the track runs past Singapore's top hotels and prime shopping malls, before having to drop to third gear in order to turn off Raffles Boulevard and onto the Nicoll Highway. This is where Lewis Hamilton clashed with Mark Webber as he tried to pass the Australian's Red Bull after a safety car restart in 2010.

Turn 10 • **Singapore Sling**
Gear: **3**
Speed: **135kph (84mph)**

The drivers race down St Andrew's Road with City Hall and Singapore's Supreme Court on their right and the Padang playing fields, home to the Singapore Cricket Club, on their left. Then it's time to get hard on the brakes and drop from fifth gear to third as the circuit feels like a typical street circuit again with a left/right/left chicane. Kimi Raikkonen got it wrong here in a late charge in 2008, when he hit the kerbs and fired his Ferrari into the wall.

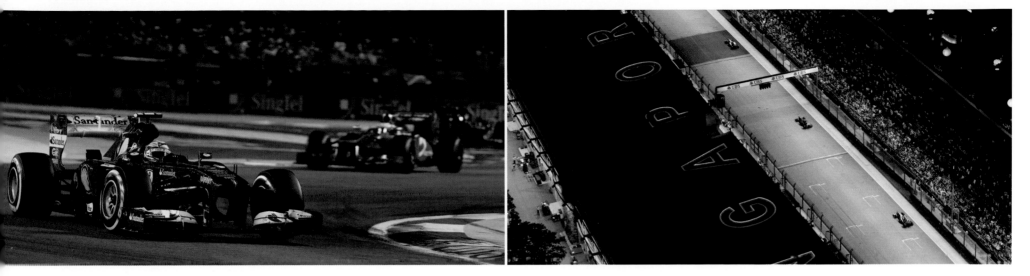

Opposite: The start lights are out and Sebastian Vettel and Nico Rosberg lead the charge down towards the first corner in 2013. ***Above left:*** Felipe Massa leads Jenson Button into tight Turn 3 in 2013. ***Above right:*** There are numerous high vantage points for photographers to capture out-of-the-ordinary shots of F1 cars in action.

Turn 13 •

Gear: **2**
Speed: **80kph (50mph)**

After taking a sinuous route past the old colonial parliament buildings on Connaught Drive and across the century-old, steel-framed Anderson Bridge, drivers have to jink right and then brake heavily for this tight lefthander in front of the Fullerton Hotel. As with so many tight corners, exit speed is everything, especially with the long blast that follows, along which drivers accelerate hard over the much longer and wider Esplanade Bridge, rising over its crest and then dropping towards Turn 14.

Turn 14 •

Gear: **2**
Speed: **05kph (50mph)**

Any aerial view of the circuit shows just how close this righthander, where the drivers turn off Esplanade Drive onto Raffles Avenue by the Esplanade Theatre, comes to Turn 8, where the cars also turn sharp right before starting their circumnavigation of Padang park. They appear to be just metres apart, albeit separated by the barriers that run up the middle of this dual-carriageway. Like at the lap's other tight corners, good traction out of this corner is what a driver will be looking for.

Turn 17 •

Gear: **3**
Speed: **125kph (78mph)**

For the fastest line through the run of six medium-speed corners that start at Turn 16, drivers need to use the kerbs to take the most direct route through this serpentine sequence. Infamously, this lefthander is where Nelson Piquet Jr gyrated his Renault into the wall in 2008 and brought out the safety car that immediately helped team-mate Fernando Alonso, who had just pitted, to move to the front and win. (It was discovered the following year that Piquet Jr had been instructed to crash.)

Turn 22 •

Gear: **3**
Speed: **150kph (93mph)**

Having weaved their way under the grandstand between Turns 19 and 20, the corners open out a little. This penultimate corner is one through which drivers will have no time to admire the Singapore Flyer Ferris wheel to their left. Instead they will be focusing on taking the smoothest line through this left kink and the fourth gear kink that follows straight after it as they accelerate hard towards the start/finish straight and hopefully hit 290kph (180mph) before having to brake for Turn 1.

The view down from the Circuit of the America's observation tower across Turn 17 towards the run of sweeps from Turn 3 to Turn 6.

Chapter 3
The Americas

Buenos Aires

Brazilian drivers hold far more titles than Argentinian ones, but it was Argentina that led the way for South America in the 1950s, with their attack spearheaded by Juan Manuel Fangio and Buenos Aires – then the continent's leading circuit. Its third stint of hosting a grand prix ended after Michael Schumacher won in 1998.

> **"** The track is a little bit Mickey Mouse in terms of layout, but it's good fun to drive on, as the corners are slow, so you can slip and slide. **"**
>
> *Eddie Irvine*

Argentina's first love in motor racing was the Temporada races that roared across the country from town to town, but there were fatalities, including Juan Manuel Fangio's co-driver Daniel Urrutia as well as spectators, and this led to a push for the building of permanent circuits. The most important of these was built in 1951 in Buenos Aires' Parc Almirante Brown on a flat piece of swampy land with the city skyline as a backdrop. Finance came from the government, with a clue to its backer President Perón being given by its name, the Autodromo 17 Octobre, commemorating the date he came to power.

It opened for racing in 1952, the scale of Perón's ambition shown by the fact that it had 12 different circuit layouts, putting it very much ahead of its time. The reason that Perón was happy to spend so much money was that he saw motor racing as a way of building Argentina's reputation abroad. And, in Fangio, he had the perfect ambassador. The sport's organizers took heed and Argentina was granted the opening grand prix of 1953, making it the first country outside Europe to host a round of the World Championship. This inaugural race was spoiled, however, by the death of 15 spectators when Giuseppe Farina crashed his Ferrari into the crowd in avoidance of a spectator who had run across the track. Despite this horrendous start, the European visitors loved the circuit and, especially, the cosmopolitan city. The racing wasn't bad, either, and

the race's January date offered them welcome respite from the European winter. For the tens of thousands of Argentinian fans, matters improved in 1954, when Fangio scored the first of four consecutive wins here, and history was made in 1958, when Stirling Moss scored the first World Championship win for a rear-engined car on a day when Fangio and the others had to pit for fresh tyres while his nimble Cooper made its tyres last the full distance.

When Perón was deposed in 1955, the circuit was renamed as the Autodromo Oscar Alfredo Galvez after the country's leading touring car driver.

The lap started with a long righthander that fed the cars onto a back straight down to high-speed Ascari corner. Next up was a hairpin, an esse and then a looping infield section before a straight down to a hairpin, with the lap ending with a left kink. Known as Circuit No 2, this was used when F1 first visited. When sportscar races were held, a longer layout was used: Circuit No 15. This veered left midway through the first corner and turned it into a right/left sweep before opening out onto a straight over a lake down to a long, double-apex righthander that led onto the back straight. This was fast, open territory where drivers could hit top speed before reaching a tighter, twistier section starting just before Ascari, which included some mid-speed corners and two hairpins to take it out to 5.9km (3.7 miles) in length.

Despite this strong start, Argentina was dropped from the World Championship after 1960 because the organizers were short of money, and F1 didn't go back until 1972, after a trial return for a non-championship race in 1971. This time, it used Circuit No 9, which was like Circuit No 2, except that the run down to the final hairpin close to the landmark arch at the circuit's entrance was truncated. Then, from 1974, the F1 drivers were allowed to cut loose on Circuit No 15, with Jody Scheckter's victory on the Wolf team's first outing in 1977 standing out and Ligier's Jacques Laffite beating pre-season favouites Lotus two years later, sending a similar shockwave through F1. However, as a result of political unrest because of the Falklands War in 1982, the Argentinian GP was dropped again.

The circuit's final spell hosting a grand prix began in 1995 and lasted for four years, with drivers using yet another track derivation, Circuit No 6. This was effectively Circuit No 9 with 0.8km (half a mile) of infield loop added to it. This was done by the track cutting sharp right through the first corner and then following this with a pair of lefts and another righthander before hitting the back straight. ∎

Opposite: Damon Hill powers his Williams away from pole position in 1996, followed by Michael Schumacher, Jean Alesi and Gerhard Berger.

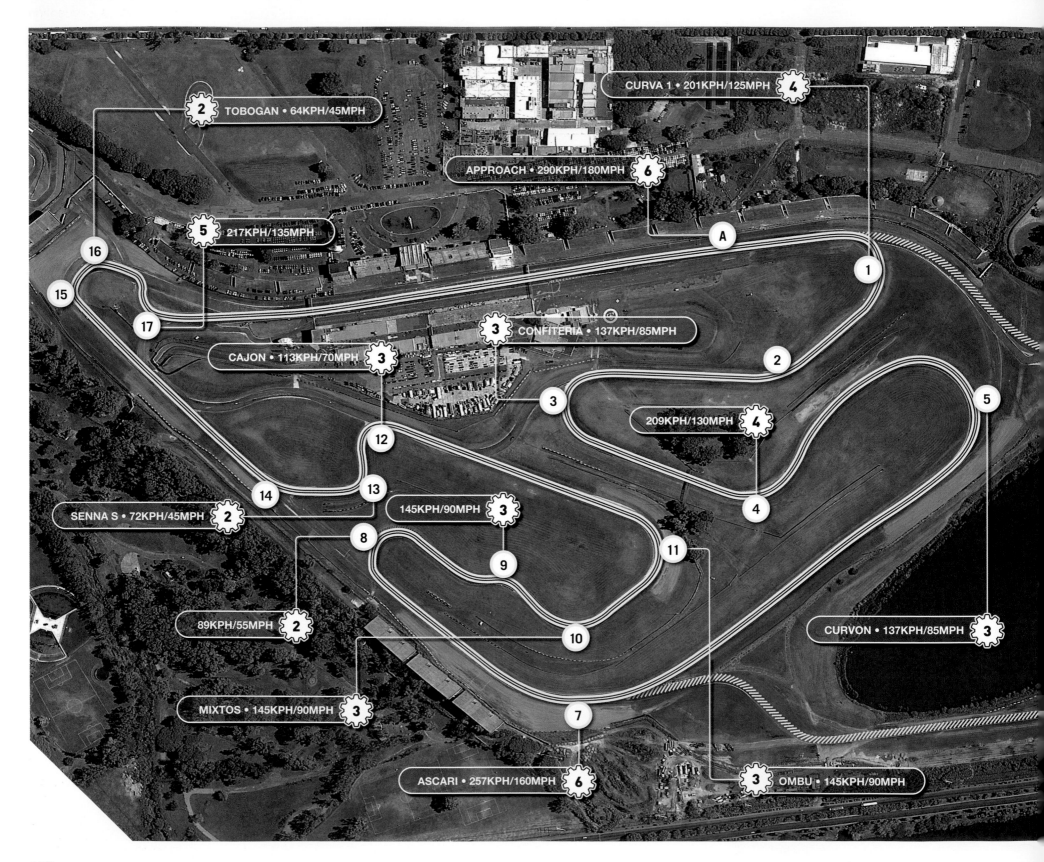

CURVA 1 • 201KPH/125MPH **4**

TOBOGAN • 64KPH/45MPH **2**

APPROACH • 290KPH/180MPH **6**

5 217KPH/135MPH

A

16

15

17

1

3 CONFITERIA • 137KPH/85MPH

CAJON • 113KPH/70MPH **3**

2

3

12

209KPH/130MPH **4**

5

13

14

SENNA S • 72KPH/45MPH **2**

145KPH/90MPH **3**

4

11

8

9

89KPH/55MPH **2**

10

CURVON • 137KPH/85MPH **3**

MIXTOS • 145KPH/90MPH **3**

7

ASCARI • 257KPH/160MPH **6**

3 OMBU • 145KPH/90MPH

Image © 2014 DigitalGlobe © Google 2014

Circuit Guide

Once famed for its long straights, the circuit layout that F1 used for its last four visits in the 1990s was very different, being made up almost entirely of medium-speed corners and hairpins that did little to excite drivers or fans.

Turn 1 • Curva 1
Gear: **4**
Speed: **201kph (125mph)**

Approaching the first corner in fifth gear, drivers have to brake in front of the array of grandstands to their left, then use the broad sweep of the track to turn in to the righthander at 201kph (125mph) in fourth gear. It's a popular spot for overtaking, so drivers have to defend the inside line if under attack, but a wider entry line is preferable, with drivers then usually holding a middle line around the corner so they can cope when it tightens halfway around its arc.

Turn 3 • Confitería
Gear: **3**
Speed: **137kph (85mph)**

After the drivers have accelerated through the kink at Turn 2, and on down the short straight after it, they brake hard for this tight, double-apex lefthander behind the paddock. One of the most spectacular incidents that occurred here came in 1996, when Pedro Diniz's Ligier pulled off on fire. He'd only just rejoined the race following a refuelling stop in which the fuel valve jammed open; fuel ignited on the exhausts after it sloshed out when he braked for the first corner.

Turn 5 • Curvon
Gear: **3**
Speed: **137kph (85mph)**

A real feature of this circuit is long, double-apex corners and this one feeds the drivers onto the back straight, with drivers having to brake hard and drop from fifth gear to third before getting back onto the throttle as early as possible in order to power through the second apex and carry as much speed as they can out of the corner. Embarrassingly for the Jordan team, Ralf Schumacher barged team-mate Giancarlo Fisichella out of second place here in 1997 before finishing third himself.

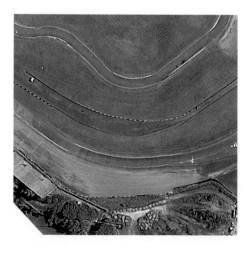

Turn 7 • Ascari
Gear: **6**
Speed: **257kph (160mph)**

The entry to this high-speed corner used to be made extra tricky by a bump right on the apex where the loop of the longer Circuit 15 rejoined the grand prix circuit, and it would make cars go light at this critical point. A further problem was the lack of kerb on the exit, meaning that anyone running wide could be in for a scary run across the grass beyond. So, for two reasons, the lines through here were limited and caution had to be employed.

Opposite: Francois Cevert accelerates his Tyrrell 006 through the final corner onto the start/finish straight, with the landmark arch down by the main entrance. *Above left:* The same corner, Turn 17, seen from the opposite direction, with the pit buildings in the background. *Above right:* Ralf Schumacher turns his Jordan into Turn 3 in 1997 after accelerating up the slope from Turn 1.

Turn 8 •
Gear: **2**
Speed: **89kph (55mph)**

Having accelerated out of Ascari, the drivers then have to scrub speed quickly for the tightest hairpin of the lap, dropping from fourth gear to second. If superior momentum has been achieved through Ascari, this is a possible overtaking point. Providing no rivals are attacking from behind, drivers turn in from the extreme left to take the widest line through this tight right, aware that the most important part of the corner is getting the power down early to build speed for the esses that follow.

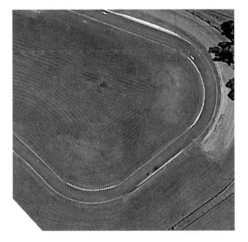

Turn 9/10 • **Mixtos & Ombu**
Gear: **3**
Speed: **145kph (90mph)**

This quick pair of corners, turning left and then right, is no place for overtaking because drivers try to straightline the corners as much as possible, using the kerbs to do so. Coming so soon after tight Turn 8, the drivers are accelerating hard here, but hold on to third gear rather than changing up to fourth because the esses are followed almost immediately by the first of a pair of medium-speed lefthanders, where taking the wrong line into the first can have ramifications into the second.

Turn 14 • **Senna S**
Gear: **2**
Speed: **72kph (45mph)**

Much tighter than the esses that went before it – Viborita – this left/right combination introduced in 1995 for F1's return really slows the flow down: the opening lefthander tightens partway around before the track veers off to the right. It was here that Luca Badoer rolled his Forti Corse without injury in 1996 after clashing with Pedro Diniz when the Ligier driver tried to lap him. There's then a right kink leading onto a short straight down to the second hairpin.

Turn 16 • **Tobogan**
Gear: **2**
Speed: **64kph (45mph)**

The penultimate corner is a righthand hairpin with drivers thankful that at least the second part of the corner is less extreme than the first. It is possible to overtake on the way in, but drivers are aware that good exit speed is more important. Accelerating hard out of here, the drivers then keep fully on the power as they flick left onto the start/finish straight. James Hunt spun his Hesketh out of the lead here in 1975 and had to make do with second place.

Great Drivers & Great Moments

The Argentinian fans had to wait only until the second Argentinian GP for a home win, thanks to Juan Manuel Fangio. Sadly, compatriot Carlos Reutemann wasn't able to match this when he carried their hopes through the 1970s into the 1980s.

Great Drivers

 Juan Manuel **Fangio**
Buenos Aires wins – 4

Argentina's government believed so much in Juan Manuel Fangio's remarkable talents that it financed his forays to Europe in 1948, understanding see how his successes would boost the country's image abroad. Having retired from its inaugural grand prix in 1953, Fangio then didn't put a wheel wrong, winning the race for the next four years. In 1956, though, his Lancia-Ferrari had its fuel pump fail, so team-mate Luigi Musso was ordered to pit and Fangio then took over his car and raced to victory.

 Emerson **Fittipaldi**
Buenos Aires wins – 2

Perhaps as revenge for Argentinian ace Carlos Reutemann winning the first Brazilian GP, Brazilian ace Emerson Fittipaldi made successful cross-border raids in the other direction to win the season-opening races in 1973 and 1975. He won the first of these for Lotus after getting past Jackie Stewart when his Tyrrell hit tyre problems. Two years later, now with McLaren, Emmo did it again, this time getting past first Reutemann and then overhauling James Hunt's Hesketh.

 Damon **Hill**
Buenos Aires wins – 2

In being first to the chequered flag in both 1995 and 1996, Damon Hill managed to win a grand prix that his father Graham never did. The first of these came in an event that marked F1's first visit to Argentina since 1981. Damon had to wait while his Williams team-mate David Coulthard led away, then Benetton's Michael Schumacher had a spell in front before he took over for good. The following year, he won again, leading all the way from pole position.

 Denny **Hulme**
Buenos Aires wins – 1

The dogged Kiwi's victory was down to determination combined with the failure of his rivals' machinery. Ronnie Peterson led away, but his Lotus was passed on lap 3 by local hero Carlos Reutemann's Brabham. Peterson then slowed with a brake problem, yet there was to be no home win, as Reutemann's air scoop broke loose with a few laps to go, his engine lost power and McLaren's Hulme motored past for his eighth and final grand prix win before retiring at the end of the year.

Great Moments

1954 Juan Manuel **Fangio** sends the crowd wild

The opening round of the 1954 World Championship was a great one for Argentina's F1 fans because Juan Manuel Fangio came out on top of the first race for the new 2.5-litre F1. His works Maserati was the only non-Ferrari on the front row of the gird, and he had no answer to the pace of Giuseppe Farina's in particular. Yet he stayed close to them and finally made progress when rain fell mid-race, using his wet weather skill to keep his car straight while his rivals went spinning.

1958 Stirling **Moss** scores first rear-engined win

The opening race of 1958 has a place in F1 history because it was the first grand prix won by a rear-engined car. The man who achieved this was Stirling Moss after running non-stop in his Rob Walker Racing Cooper on a day when his rivals all had to change tyres. Mike Hawthorn led off for Ferrari, then Juan Manuel Fangio took over in his Maserati. However, this developed a misfire and Ferrari's Luigi Musso backed off, thinking Moss was going to have to pit, which he didn't.

1980 Alan **Jones** lays out his stall for a Williams year

Alan Jones ended the 1979 season in style for Williams. In 1980, he hit the ground running and qualified on pole here for the opening round. He led away, but a plastic bag covered one of his radiators and he had to pit for it to be removed, falling to fourth. From there, he picked his way past Gilles Villeneuve, Nelson Piquet and Jacques Laffite to beat Piquet by 24.6 seconds. It was a sign of things to come: Jones raced on to the drivers' title.

1998 Michael **Schumacher** muscles his way through

This was the third round of the season and McLaren had dominated the first two races and then looked set to do the same, but Ferrari's Michael Schumacher had other ideas. He passed Mika Hakkinen early on, then barged David Coulthard out of the lead. The German opted for a two-stop strategy, so his car was lighter than Hakkinen's and this helped him pull clear, make his extra pitstop and still come home first. Coulthard's recovery from sixth was thwarted when he clashed with Jacques Villeneuve's Williams.

Interlagos

This circuit may be rough around the edges, in need of investment to bring it up to contemporary standards, but it remains one of the sport's great venues, with its dipping and swerving lap made all the more exciting by the passion of the crowd and the bonus that it often hosts the championship decider.

❝ Interlagos has some great corners such as the Curva do Laranja and there are real overtaking opportunities into the Senna S at the start of the lap and under-braking for Descida do Lago. **❞**

Rubens Barrichello

Brazilians seem always to have loved motor racing: plans made for this neighbourhood of São Paolo as long ago as 1920 by British engineer Louis Romero included a circuit along with the houses in a "satellite city". It was at this point that the name Interlagos, meaning "between the lakes", was suggested by a Frenchman who said it reminded him of Interlaken in Switzerland. The land was then found to be unsuitable for housing, so the plot lay empty.

Nothing happened for years, until São Paulo hosted a street race in 1936. This had a disastrous outcome, though, as French racer Hellé Nice crashed and killed six spectators, although she escaped with her life. This certainly sped up the process of building a permanent circuit. The Sanson construction company decided in 1938 to buy a sloping site that formed a natural bowl on the outskirts of the city and Brazil's first purpose-built racing circuit was ready for racing in 1940. It has been a much-loved facility ever since, where spectators are able to enjoy some of the world's most panoramic views over a circuit. Throw in their effervescent passion for F1, and Interlagos is a riotous place to go racing. Undoubtedly, its facilities are tired by contemporary standards, and team personnel have been held up at gunpoint while stuck in traffic jams outside the circuit gates, but the fact that it's currently F1's only

South American venue means that the country that produced Ayrton Senna will remain a key part of the World Championship until somewhere more modern comes along.

Unusually, the lap runs in an anti-clockwise direction, and the first corner is an immediate test for whether the less used muscles on the right side of the drivers' necks can cope with a rapid change of direction. The circuit then drops away and pours the drivers down the face of the slope to Descida do Lago before turning left and coming back up the slope again to Ferradura. The stretch that follows has the cars rising and falling across the slope, with next to no chance of overtaking. Instead, drivers get as close as they can to the car in front and focus on getting the best possible exit from Juncao so that they can accelerate harder and faster than the car they're chasing up the arcing stretch of track past the pits from there.

This 4.3km (2.7-mile) lap is entertaining for drivers and fans alike, but it's a shadow of its original self because the circuit that was used until 1979 was just a fraction under 8km (5 miles) long; all of this additional length came from an extra loop that headed straight on at the first corner, then ran deeper into the valley around a lake before coming back up the slope and then dipping down and

rising again to meet the current circuit at Ferradura.

Neighbouring Argentina had hosted a World Championship round in Buenos Aires since 1953, but Brazil had to wait until 20 years after that. Interlagos held a non-championship race in 1972, won by Carlos Reutemann, and this showed that the circuit could cope with F1, so it became the home of the Brazilian GP from 1973, when Emerson Fittipaldi gave the fans a hometown winner. The race then transferred to Rio de Janiero's Jacarepagua circuit, after a trial race there in 1978, and it wasn't until 1990 that Interlagos got it back for good, using the current circuit layout for the first time to bring the cars past the grandstands more often.

The circuit's full name is the Autodromo José Carlos Pace after the popular Brazilian Brabham driver who won here in 1975 but was killed in a light plane crash two years later, although it continues to be known universally as Interlagos.

São Paulo is often hit by rain and the torrents that run across the track have been known to affect the outcome of more than one race. There's never anything predictable about Interlagos. ∎

Opposite: The sprawling suburbs of Sao Paulo are the backdrop as Felipe Massa descends towards Pinheirinho in his final outing for Ferrari in 2013.

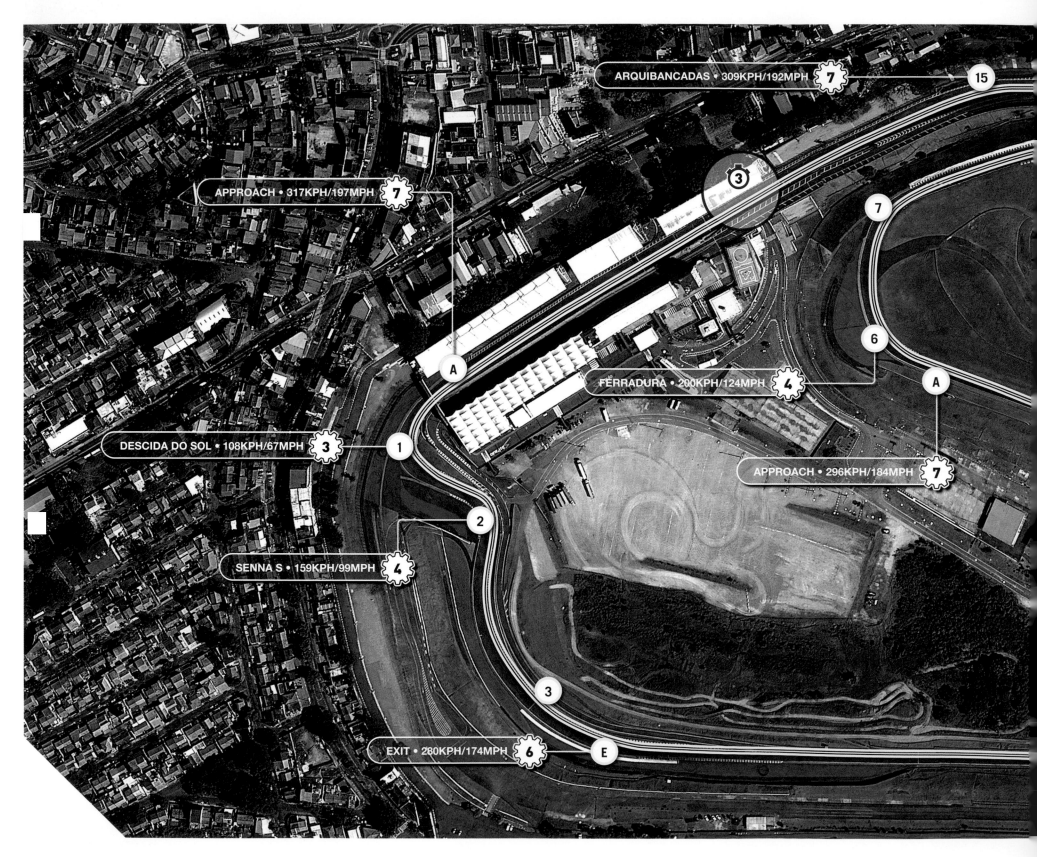

ARQUIBANCADAS • 309KPH/192MPH **7** **15**

APPROACH • 317KPH/197MPH **7**

3

7

A

6

FERRADURA • 200KPH/124MPH **4**

A

DESCIDA DO SOL • 108KPH/67MPH **3** **1**

APPROACH • 296KPH/184MPH **7**

2

SENNA S • 159KPH/99MPH **4**

3

EXIT • 280KPH/174MPH **6** **E**

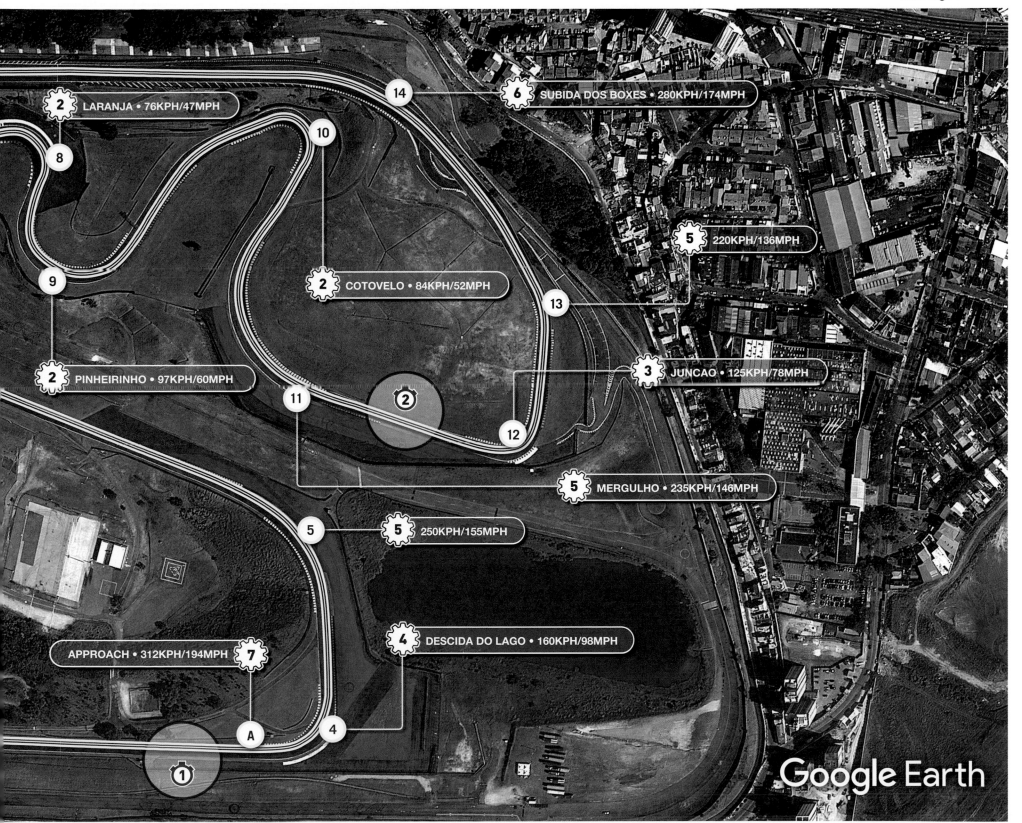

LARANJA • 76KPH/47MPH

SUBIDA DOS BOXES • 280KPH/174MPH

5 220KPH/136MPH

COTOVELO • 84KPH/52MPH

PINHEIRINHO • 97KPH/60MPH

JUNCAO • 125KPH/78MPH

MERGULHO • 235KPH/146MPH

5 250KPH/155MPH

DESCIDA DO LAGO • 160KPH/98MPH

APPROACH • 312KPH/194MPH

Circuit Guide

From the blind entry to the first corner through the compression at Senna S, then the drop out of Laranja and the need to make the perfect exit from Juncao, a lap of Interlagos is something very special.

Turn 1 • Descida do Sol
Gear: **3**
Speed: **108kph (67mph)**

The approach to this corner is scary enough for the drivers because they are enclosed by high walls on either side as they run flat-out up the rising and curving start/finish straight. The turn is blind on entry, hidden by the end of the pitwall, and the corner requires heavy braking from 322kph (200mph) in top gear to third. The track drops away sharply to the left and drivers must try to avoid running too wide onto the grass bank beyond, because Turn 2 follows immediately.

Turn 2 • Senna S
Gear: **4**
Speed: **159kph (99mph)**

If a driver can hold a tight exit line from Descida do Sol, they will be well placed for the Senna S that follows straight after it. With the track dropping into a compression, the drivers need to take the widest line they can manage because the track swings right. They want to be hard on the power once their car is settled because this corner then feeds via an arcing lefthander onto the lap's second longest straight, down the hill to Descida do Lago.

Turn 4 • Descida do Lago
Gear: **4**
Speed: **160kph (98mph)**

This is a definite overtaking point because the track is broad as they arrive, the drivers often looking to pull out of another's slipstream to make a move into this fast lefthander. Braking from almost 322kph (200mph), they have to change down to fourth gear. It can go wrong, though, as shown in 1994, when Jos Verstappen's Benetton was pitched off on the approach, then veered back into the path of Eddie Irvine, who then clipped Martin Brundle and Eric Bernard after Verstappen was sent rolling.

Turn 6 • Ferradura
Gear: **4**
Speed: **200kph (124mph)**

From the lowest point on the hillside at Descida do Lago, the drivers power through open Turn 5, then on up the hill to this, the first of three righthand corners that make up a sweep over a crest before the track drops down again. With a view largely of the earth bank behind the corner, drivers have to drop to fourth gear and find a balance for their car through this and the next corner before having to brake and drop to second for the final part of the complex.

Opposite: Vitaly Petrov keeps his Caterham at the head of the midfield pack on the climb from Pinheirinho to Cotovelo on lap 1 in 2012. *Above left:* Rain strikes often and Fernando Alonso is shown kicking up spray on the pit straight in 2012. *Above right:* The first corner is always fraught on the opening lap, so Lewis Hamilton is best placed by leading into the blind lefthander in 2012.

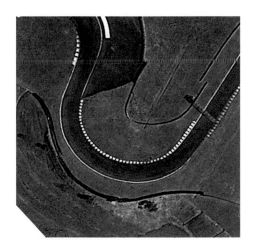

Turn 9 • **Pinheirinho**

Gear: **2**

Speed: **97kph (60mph)**

With the circuit now taking a serpentine course across the face of the hillside, Pinheirinho is the first bend of the passage with a downhill entry, and it's a long lefthander that simply turns the cars around and sends them up the slope again. Traction is quite difficult here and drivers risk losing momentum if they try to get onto the power too soon for the short, kinked straight that leads them to the following corner. There's no scope for overtaking here.

Turn 10 • **Cotovelo**

Gear: **2**

Speed: **84kph (52mph)**

This is the slowest point on the circuit, a tight righthand hairpin. The first part of the corner looks relatively open as the drivers come up the climbing approach, but then it reaches an apex and tightens noticeably, and requires drivers to drop to second gear or even first. The drivers accelerate hard down the slope and on through the long lefthander that follows, taken in fifth gear with a feathered throttle because a lack of traction can be a problem.

Turn 12 • **Junção**

Gear: **3**

Speed: **125kph (78mph)**

Junção is the one that drivers consider to be the most important corner of the lap. The reason that this innocuous third-gear lefthander is so vital is that it leads onto the start of the start/finish straight. The sooner that a driver can get his braking done, get the car balanced and start accelerating, the better, for this advantage will then be carried all the way to the first corner and a quick exit will give a driver a chance to pick up a slipstreaming tow.

Turn 14 • **Subida dos Boxes**

Gear: **6**

Speed: **280kph (174mph)**

Most drivers don't really consider this to be a corner, but rather the second of three kinked points in the run from Junção to the first corner, Descida do Sol. However, it was here that Lewis Hamilton moved into the fifth place that he needed to become World Champion in 2008, when he had just blasted his McLaren past Timo Glock, who was struggling in a dry-tyred Toyota on a wet track on the final lap. In doing so, he pipped Ferrari's Felipe Massa to the title in the most dramatic fashion.

Great Drivers & Great Moments

Some circuits deliver wins that can seem straightforward, yet there is almost always a twist at Interlagos, whether through contact, mechanical failure or, most often, through the arrival of rain. So, any driver who has won here can take special satisfaction in his work.

Great Drivers

Michael **Schumacher**
Interlagos wins – 4

Michael scored his first Interlagos win in 1994 with Benetton, opening his campaign with victory by a full lap over Damon Hill after passing Ayrton Senna, who later spun out. He won again here in 1995 after Hill led but retired and he was chased home by David Coulthard in the other Williams. Michael then doubled this tally after moving to Ferrari by winning in 2000 after Mika Hakkinen's McLaren failed and again in 2002 by a nose from his brother Ralf's Williams.

Emerson **Fittipaldi**
Interlagos wins – 2

Emerson was a driver who was almost brought up at the circuit, with his father being a radio commentator, so it's fitting that he should win the first grand prix held here. Racing for Lotus in 1973, he moved past pole-sitting team-mate Ronnie Peterson and led every lap to win easily. He then won again in 1974 for McLaren after passing Peterson, before finishing second behind compatriot Carlos Pace's Brabham in 1975. He then finished fourth for the family team in 1977 before the race moved to Jacarepaguá.

Juan Pablo **Montoya**
Interlagos wins – 2

This Colombian hard-charger was denied in 2002 when he clashed with Michael Schumacher's Ferrari on the opening lap. However, after crashing out in the wet 2003 race, he then won at Interlagos in 2004 for Williams in a race that featured an incredibly close battle with McLaren's Kimi Raikkonen. Juan Pablo won again in 2005 after changing teams to join McLaren and again pipping Raikkonen who was, this time, his team-mate, with newly crowned World Champion Fernando Alonso third.

Felipe **Massa**
Interlagos wins – 2

When he had made it to F1, Felipe said the only time he'd worked at Interlagos before was as a pizza delivery boy… So, imagine his delight in 2006 when he scored his second win to round out his first year with Ferrari. This was Brazil's first home win since Ayrton Senna in 1993. He scored a second win in the dramatic 1998 finale when it looked as though this would land him the title, only for Lewis Hamilton to gain the place he needed on the last lap.

Great Moments

1991 Ayrton **Senna** finally wins at home

Ayrton was the pre-eminent driver of his age, but his record in Brazil was one of frustration, with second place his best result in six visits to Jacarepaguá. After placing third on F1's return to Interlagos in 1990, he achieved his longed-for home win in 1991, when he not only resisted the challenge of Williams drivers Nigel Mansell and Riccardo Patrese but managed a gearbox problem through the closing laps. The crowd went wild, but Ayrton was so exhausted he had to be lifted from the car.

2003 Giancarlo **Fisichella** comes out on top

Through the history of the World Championship, there have been a handful of races where not everyone present has been sure of the identity of the winner. The 2003 Brazilian GP was one such race. Run in wet conditions, the race was red-flagged after Fernando Alonso had a huge crash. Kimi Raikkonen was adjudged to have won the restarted race for McLaren, but so confused were the timekeepers that it took several days before it could be confirmed that Giancarlo Fisichella had won for Jordan.

2007 Kimi **Raikkonen** pips McLaren's men

Denied in 2003, Raikkonen would win in Brazil after all four years later. He was the underdog in a three-way title battle with McLaren's Fernando Alonso and Lewis Hamilton, but they hit problems, with Hamilton's gearbox dropping into neutral for an agonizing 30 seconds and then excessive tyre wear forcing him to make an extra pitstop, and the Finn was able to work his way to the front for Ferrari, to be followed to the finish faithfully by team-mate Felipe Massa as he took the title by a point.

2008 Lewis **Hamilton** wins his second shoot-out

For the second year in a row, Interlagos hosted a last round title shoot-out. As in 2007, this involved Lewis Hamilton and it appeared as though he'd been pipped at the last by Ferrari's Felipe Massa after losing ground with poor tyre strategy and having to watch the Brazilian win the race and, apparently, the title. But the Toyotas were still on regular tyres as rain fell ever more heavily and so Lewis was able to pass Timo Glock on the climb to the finish line and deny Massa.

Montreal

This is a circuit on which it's hard to overtake, the cars take a physical battering and the pit and paddock facilities are cramped, yet the Circuit Gilles Villeneuve was a hit from its introduction in the late 1970s and remains popular today because it has a great atmosphere and everyone loves visiting Montreal.

> **"** The track has a great history and it's like a street circuit, as it's quite bumpy. It's like a go-kart track too, as we have to take the kerbs to achieve a quick lap. **"**
> *Lewis Hamilton*

By the mid-1970s, as the push for improved driver safety was gaining momentum, it became clear that Mosport Park's days of hosting the Canadian GP were numbered. The picturesque circuit in the wooded hills of Ontario had hosted a Canadian GP for sportscars from 1961, with F1 taking over the slot in 1967. However, few upgrades had been done and the lack of run-off was starting to spook the drivers, something that was emphasized by Ian Ashley, who suffered leg injuries when he crashed his Hesketh in practice in 1977.

So, for 1978, the Canadian GP had a new home, in Montreal, financed by Labatt's brewery. Not only did this take racing to the people rather than expecting them to drive 72km (45 miles) from the closest city, which was Toronto in Mosport Park's case, but it offered an exciting circuit with brand new facilities and the city's skyline as an attractive backdrop.

Built on the Ile de Notre Dame in the St Lawrence River, but connected to the city centre by both road bridges and metro line, the site was certainly easy to get to. The island is narrow, though, so finding a route for the circuit took some planning; it has to weave its way around the futuristic pavilions left there after Expo World Fair in 1967, a large casino, and the rowing lake used when Montreal hosted the Olympic Games in 1976. The result is a long,

thin circuit that runs down one side of the rowing lake, extends at its southern point to the edge of the river before it doubles back and threads through a wooded section on its run to the hairpin. The overall feeling is of alternating between sections that seem fairly cramped for the drivers and those where it seems very cramped, as there are concrete walls and trees close in on either side of the track, with the blast from the hairpin to the pits the only truly open stretch. Yet, there's scope for plenty of flat-out motoring. Combine this with the heavy braking required at several points around the lap, and it's easy to understand why it's so punishing on both cars and drivers.

Ferrari's Gilles Villeneuve was Canada's new racing hero in 1978, so the timing of the opening of this circuit in his native Quebec could not have been better. When he then rewarded the home fans with victory first time out, it was the dream start for the race organizers and why they immediately renamed the track as the Circuit Gilles Villeneuve. His death in 1982 hit the Canadian fans hard, especially because there was no rising Canadian star to take his place. Almost a quarter of a century later, though, they finally had another reason to wave their Canadian and Quebecois flags as they came out in their thousands to support Gilles' son

Jacques, but sadly he never managed to land them the win that they craved.

Perhaps the greatest draw of all for the circuit is that it's located just a short ride from downtown Montreal, making it an enormously fun and cosmopolitan place to stay for teams, drivers and fans alike, also giving the television crews considerably more chance to put F1 into context than they get at a circuit deep in the countryside such as Silverstone or Hockenheim.

Due to the width restrictions around the wall-lined route of the circuit, there have been many race-ending accidents since the circuit's debut in 1978. The worst of all, though, came in 1982, when Didier Pironi stalled his Ferrari and Riccardo Paletti was unable to avoid slamming his Osella into the back of it. The Italian rookie would die later in hospital.

One of the greatest developments in Montreal's history of hosting the grand prix came in 1982, when its race date was brought forward to early summer. Thus, the risk of cold snaps was eliminated, although rain remains an occasional threat. ∎

Opposite: Montreal has always produced a big crowd. Here, they get to see Romain Grosjean run wide at L'Epingle behind Mark Webber and Giedo van der Garde in 2013.

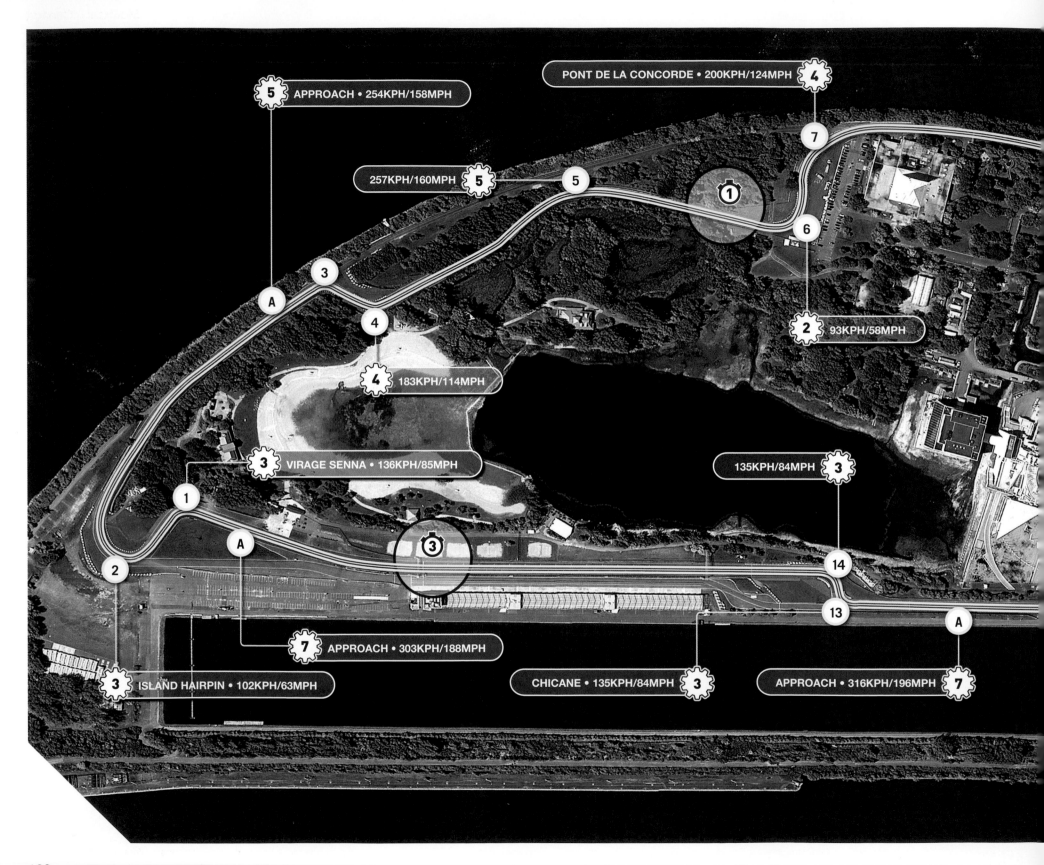

PONT DE LA CONCORDE • 200KPH/124MPH **4**

5 APPROACH • 254KPH/158MPH

257KPH/160MPH **5**

2 93KPH/58MPH

4 183KPH/114MPH

3 VIRAGE SENNA • 136KPH/85MPH

135KPH/84MPH **3**

7 APPROACH • 303KPH/188MPH

3 ISLAND HAIRPIN • 102KPH/63MPH

CHICANE • 135KPH/84MPH **3**

APPROACH • 316KPH/196MPH **7**

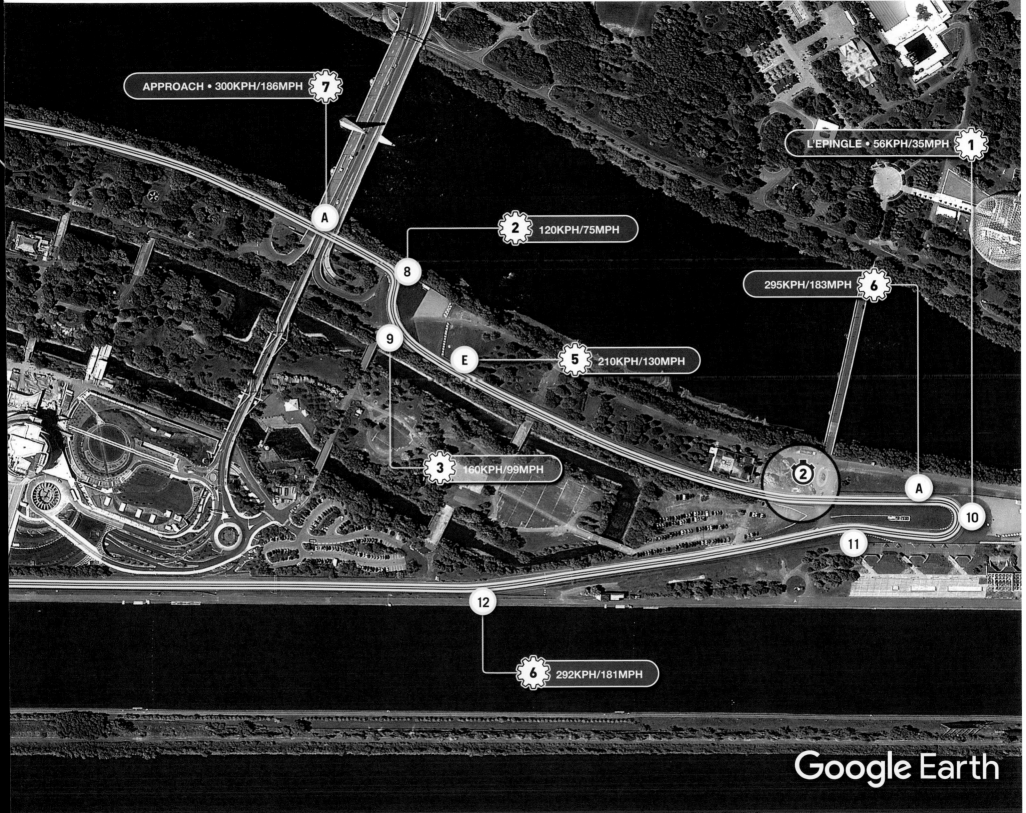

APPROACH • 300KPH/186MPH **7**

L'EPINGLE • 56KPH/35MPH **1**

A

2 120KPH/75MPH

8

295KPH/183MPH **6**

9

E   **5** 210KPH/130MPH

3 160KPH/99MPH

②

A

10

11

12

6 292KPH/181MPH

Google Earth

Circuit Guide

Built on an island and hemmed in by trees and a lake, this strip of a track feels alternately enclosed, tight and twisty, and open and flat-out for the return leg. It's a car-breaker, working the cars' engines and brakes harder than most.

Turn 1 • Virage Senna
Gear: **3**
Speed: **136kph (85mph)**

The drivers arrive through a right kink, then almost immediately have to hit the brakes hard for the first corner. They have to halve their speed from almost 306kph (190mph). On lap 1, fortunately, they arrive at a slightly reduced velocity after their standing start, which is fortunate because the cars inevitably bunch for this tight left, and Benetton's Alexander Wurz was famously sent rolling here in 1998, when Jean Alesi's Sauber cut across its path. This doesn't stop drivers trying moves on lap 1, though.

Turn 2 • Island Hairpin
Gear: **3**
Speed: **102kph (63mph)**

Any driver who has run wide coming out of the first corner will have to pay the price when they get to this corner into which it immediately feeds. Arriving at the feet of the people in the grandstand here, they will then find themselves running out of room to get around this wide righthand hairpin, because the ideal entry line is from the left side of the track, not the right. Inevitably, this is also the scene of many a first lap collision as drivers jostle for position.

Turn 4 •
Gear: **4**
Speed: **183kph (114mph)**

The drivers have just relaxed into accelerating hard along this stretch of track from the Island Hairpin with a bank of trees on their right and distant views across the river to the city on their left when they have to slow again as this chicane comes suddenly into view. Dropping down the gearbox, they have to flick right, then left and the exit is critical because there's a wall right on the edge of the track with which drivers make contact if they get it wrong.

Turn 6 •
Gear: **2**
Speed: **93kph (58mph)**

This back section of the circuit offers pretty much only one line through its constant twists, the drivers feeling channelled by the concrete walls that line either flank of the track. At Turn 6, though, they enjoy the "luxury" of having a grass verge ahead of them, as they turn hard left into the first part of a wider-spaced chicane. This is where Sebastian Vettel slid wide in his Red Bull in 2011 and Jenson Button powered past for a famous win for McLaren.

Opposite: Force India's Adrian Sutil leads a train of cars through the sweeper past the pits and enters third-gear Virage Senna in 2013. *Above left:* Nico Rosberg leads Mark Webber and Fernando Alonso at the 2013 Canadian Grand Prix. *Above right:* Nico Rosberg resists the challenge of Red Bull's Mark Webber out of Island Hairpin early in the 2013 Canadian GP.

Turn 7 • **Pont de la Concorde**
Gear: **4**
Speed: **200kph (124mph)**

A less extreme corner than the one before it, Pont de la Concorde is where the drivers have to get through the corner and then get hard back on to the power; good exit speed from this third gear righthander is vital because the track starts to open out from here and the run to the hairpin is an appreciable one. As elsewhere, the walls aren't far from the racing line and it was here that Olivier Panis crashed his Ligier in 1997, breaking his legs.

Turn 9 • **Pont des Iles**
Gear: **3**
Speed: **160kph (99mph)**

The third chicane of the back section, this right/left flick presents the drivers with an extra challenge as they brake hard and shave more than 130kph (80mph) off their speed. They drop to second gear because the track is bumpy here – a legacy of Montreal's long, freezing winters – and this can upset the cars. The second part of the chicane is less tight and drivers enjoy having rare run-off to their right as they power out onto the short straight to the hairpin.

Turn 10 • **L'Epingle**
Gear: **1**
Speed: **56kph (35mph)**

With a grass verge on either side and a rare feeling of space – the drivers can see the return leg as they approach this ultra-tight righthander – drivers have to focus on the fact that this is one of only a handful of places at which it is possible to overtake. Many prefer, though, not to risk a move into here but to concentrate on exiting the hairpin right on the tail of the car ahead so that they can line up a passing manoeuvre down the circuit's main straight that follows.

Turn 14 • **Chicane**
Gear: **3**
Speed: **135kph (84mph)**

The straight runs alongside the 1976 Olympic rowing lake and drivers are finally able to hit top speed and stay there for more than a few seconds, catching a tow down towards this right/left flick onto the start/finish straight and plot their move. The lefthand exit isn't visible until the drivers are turning into the first part of the chicane and drivers are advised to stay off the kerbs on the exit; many have run over them and then clattered the wall beyond.

Great Drivers & Great Moments

On a circuit that is notorious for being a car-breaker thanks to its flat-out blasts and frequent heavy braking, a modicum of mechanical sympathy can pay dividends, and Michael Schumacher clearly found the right formula because he won here seven times. Collisions or glancing the walls have scuppered others.

Opposite top: Canadian hero Gilles Villeneuve couldn't have picked a better place to score his first F1 win on Montreal's debut as the closing race of 1978.

Opposite bottom left: Jean Alesi also scored his breakthrough win in Montreal, triumphing for Ferrari in 1995 after Michael Schumacher hit trouble.

Opposite bottom right: Lewis Hamilton absolutely loves racing in Montreal, as he took his first win here in 2007, then added his fourth for Mercedes in 2015.

Great Drivers

Michael **Schumacher**
Montreal wins – 7

Schumacher's career really lifted off in 1994 and he won here in dominant fashion for Benetton. With the exception of his eight wins at Magny-Cours, Montreal proved to be one of his most successful stamping grounds (equal only to Imola), for Michael would win here in 1997 after joining Ferrari, then again in 1998, 2000, 2002, 2003 and 2004. The highlight among these was the one in 2004, when he managed to get to the front from sixth on the grid.

Lewis **Hamilton**
Montreal wins – 4

Lewis scored his F1 breakthrough here in 2007, setting up his first title challenge with McLaren. Three years later, he led home team-mate Jenson Button for a McLaren one-two after a mid-race challenge from Ferrari's Fernando Alonso. In his last campaign before joining Mercedes, Lewis won in Canada again in 2012 by making a two-stop strategy work. His most recent win, in 2015, came on a day when he started from pole and his team-mate Nico Rosberg just didn't have the pace to usurp him.

Nelson **Piquet**
Montreal wins – 3

Once Nelson got BMW turbo power for his Brabham, the wins in Montreal began to flow. The first came in 1982, when he had to work his way to the front. Two years later, he didn't even have to pass anybody because he started on pole and led from lights to flag. Nelson would have to wait until 1991 for his next Montreal victory, when he was racing for Benetton. Nigel Mansell had been set to win for Williams until he stalled at L'Epingle on the final lap.

Ayrton **Senna**
Montreal wins – 2

Hampered by a turbo problem when well placed in 1985, Ayrton only started winning in Montreal three years later in his first season with McLaren, 1988. He qualified on pole and had to sit behind team-mate Alain Prost for 19 laps until he found a way past. He led in 1989 until his engine blew with three laps to go, but had more luck in 1990, when he was beaten to the finish by team-mate Gerhard Berger before the Austrian dropped to fourth with a 1-minute jump-start penalty.

Great Moments

1978 Gilles **Villeneuve** gives circuit dream debut

The timing of Gilles' arrival in F1 couldn't have been better for the people behind this circuit because he had had an increasingly good first full season for Ferrari. Montreal's first race was the season-closer and, having qualified third, he could only watch as Lotus stand-in Jean-Pierre Jarier stormed off into the lead. He passed his team-mate Jody Scheckter for second place, but Jarier was 30 seconds in the lead. Then the Frenchman pulled off the circuit with no brakes and so Gilles was able to delight the local fans.

1995 Jean **Alesi** sheds tears of joy for his first win

There have been few more emotional drivers than Jean. So, you can imagine the tears of joy that he shed in 1995 when he approached the chequered flag in front for the very first time. He was in his fifth year with Ferrari and looked to finish this race second behind Michael Schumacher but, with 11 laps to go, the Benetton called at the pits with a gearbox problem. This left Jean way out front and he duly won by half a minute from the two Jordans.

2008 Robert **Kubica** makes his breakthrough

Sauber had never won a grand prix. Working in partnership with BMW in 2008, it appeared to have a car good enough to score points but not to win. Then came Montreal and the team not only won but took a one-two finish. Robert Kubica benefited when leader Lewis Hamilton hit Kimi Raikkonen's Ferrari that was stationary at pit exit during a safety car period. Early race leader Nick Heidfeld had a great chance to win in the other Sauber, but Kubica's two-stop strategy proved superior.

2011 Jenson **Button** hunts down Sebastian Vettel

This race had the ending of a Hollywood movie. Sebastian Vettel led away on a wet track, McLaren's Jenson Button and Lewis Hamilton clashed, Button was given a drivethrough penalty, then the race was stopped because of standing water. Fernando Alonso and Button collided after the restart and Button got a puncture. The safety car came out and then Button passed car after car, finally catching Vettel, who cracked under the pressure halfway around the final lap for Button to take a famous win.

Circuit _{of} _{the} Americas

The United States of America has been a tough market for Formula One to crack, and its spasmodic passage around the country doesn't make for good reading. However, with the construction of this magnificent circuit outside Austin in Texas, it finally has a circuit admired by people the world over.

> **" The track is tricky and very challenging, and mixed too, with high-speed and low-speed corners. Possibly the best place for overtaking is at the end of the DRS zone into Turn 12. "**
>
> *Sebastian Vettel*

When the teams turned up at the brand new Circuit of the Americas in November 2012, with its lofty grandstands, plunging slopes and sweeping esses, they knew immediately that the USA had finally produced a worthy home for its grand prix for the first time since Watkins Glen took over the honours of hosting the race from Riverside in 1961. For here was a giant among road circuits, a track that had been designed and built without compromise, a track that has world class facilities and, best of all, a layout that is blessed with considerable gradient change that tests the drivers and shows the cars at their best.

The most experienced F1 racer of all time, Rubens Barrichello, was immediately excited by the prospect of the new circuit, telling *F1 Racing*, "Hills make it more interesting. Look at the best corners at Spa: Eau Rouge is steep uphill and Pouhon is downhill. The slopes require increased commitment in the cockpit."

The anti-clockwise layout was filled with corners echoing the best of the best from the leading circuits around the world, with some sequences proving an intense challenge for the drivers, which is just how it should be when a designer has been afforded a clean sheet plus the benefit of a plot with 40.5m (133ft) of gradient. After decades of F1 losing ground in the USA, Hermann Tilke and his

team had to get it right to entice the fans back and the Circuit of the Americas has done just that.

The first thing that strikes anyone about the Circuit of the Americas is its rise and fall. The second thing is the sheer variety of corners, from long straights into tight corners, to a testing run of esses and corners where a driver can really carry some speed, offering American fans a real opportunity to see F1 cars at their best. Furthermore, with so much gradient built into the lap, spectators are treated to panoramic views of much of the track.

The circuit's location in Texas works in its favour too, as the race can be held in autumn, when the F1 season is coming to a climax, without fear of the chill and rain that used to hit Watkins Glen in upstate New York even when its race was held a whole month earlier. Not only is Austin a city looking to boost its global image, but it truly wants the race rather than putting up with it – as Phoenix seemed to do when hosting the US GP between 1989 and 1991 – and it embraces the race, making it part of a festival of events. Having the drivers wear Stetsons on the podium adds a welcome American flavour too.

The teams and drivers like the buzz of the city too. Perhaps best of all, the circuit's proximity to the border brings with it a large influx of Mexican F1 fans, adding an international flavour to proceedings.

With plans for the re-establishment of the Mexican GP in the pipeline, the excitement of a three-race sweep starting here, then going to Mexico City and on for a finale in Brazil makes great sense.

Yet, it would be remiss to fail to point out that the circuit had a bumpy ride through construction, with original front man Tavo Hellmund being eased aside and the race, fleetingly, having its original championship slot taken away from it. The thought of this opportunity being missed was almost too much for American F1 fans to bear, so there was relief when all was settled and construction was able to start again and continue to completion.

The United States really needed to have an F1 circuit of its own, to show American fans that not all racing needs to be held on a banked oval, and so the Circuit of the Americas has taken its place at the head of the country's road racing tree above Road Atlanta, Road America and Mid-Ohio and looks set to be the race's home for years to come, much to the relief of the FIA that has been pushing so hard for the grand prix to establish a permanent base. ∎

Opposite: Red Bull Racing's Sebastian Vettel leads Romain Grosjean, Lewis Hamilton and the pack down the hill into Turn 2 on the opening lap in 2013.

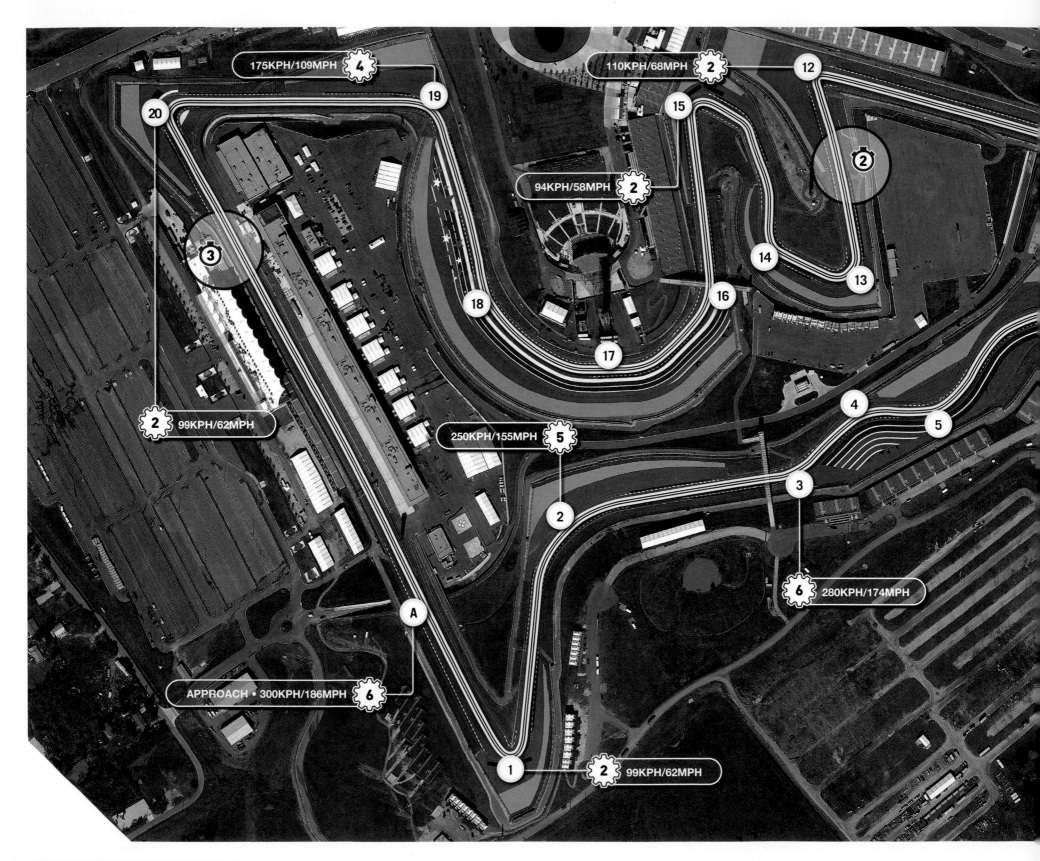

175KPH/109MPH 4

110KPH/68MPH 2 12

19

15

20

94KPH/58MPH 2

2

3

14

13

16

18

17

2 99KPH/62MPH

4

5

250KPH/155MPH 5

3

2

6 280KPH/174MPH

A

APPROACH • 300KPH/186MPH 6

1 2 99KPH/62MPH

190

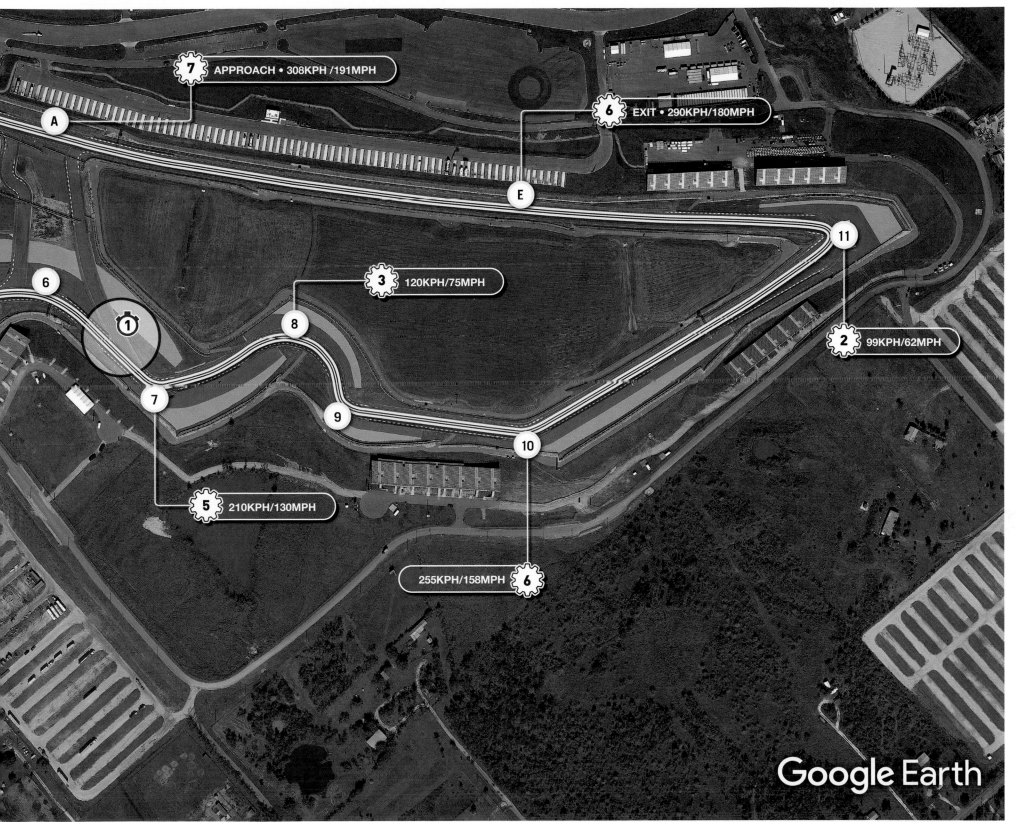

7 APPROACH • 308KPH /191MPH

6 EXIT • 290KPH/180MPH

A

E

3 120KPH/75MPH

11

6

8

1

2 99KPH/62MPH

7

9

10

5 210KPH/130MPH

255KPH/158MPH **6**

Google Earth

Circuit Guide

Hermann Tilke gave the Circuit of the Americas a wonderful flow to its lap. He used the rolling terrain to include corners not dissimilar to the very best turns from the best of Formula One's outstanding circuits around the world.

Turn 1 •

Gear: **2**
Speed: **99kph (62mph)**

Approached by one of the steepest climbs tackled in F1, matched only by Eau Rouge at Spa-Francorchamps and the climb to the first corner at the Red Bull Ring, this lefthander is reached at the crest of the hill, with the track flattening out where the drivers are braking hardest. There is plenty of track width to allow different entry lines, but a driver's work isn't completed on turn-in, because the exit is then made tricky by the way that the track drops away.

Turn 2 •

Gear: **5**
Speed: **250kph (155mph)**

Having accelerated down the descent from the first corner, the drivers get a fantastic view of the distinctive viewing tower and the return leg from Turn 12 to Turn 19 in the distance as they accelerate hard and plunge down the slope past grandstands and hospitality balconies; but they must focus immediately on pulling across from the righthand side of the track to the left so that they can sweep down through the fifth-gear righthand kink at Turn 2.

Turn 3 •

Gear: **6**
Speed: **280kph (174mph)**

This is the start of one of the greatest stretches of track in F1, offering rapid changes of direction as experienced only through Becketts at Silverstone and the S Curves at Suzuka. Turn 3 makes the first of a run of four corners in esse formation. The most impressive thing for people watching here is the fact that the drivers take these in sixth gear, at around 280kph (175mph), and the way the cars stick to the track is testament to the downforce they generate.

Turn 7 •

Gear: **5**
Speed: **210kph (130mph)**

After the shortest of straights, Turn 7 is sharper than the four-corner esses that preceded it and so requires drivers to drop down a gear from sixth to fifth. The cars are still travelling at 210kph (130mph), though, as they start this second run of, admittedly slower, esses before the track drops away out of Turn 10. Precision continues to be everything here where drivers are free to concentrate on their lines because there's no chance of either passing or being passed.

Opposite: Lewis Hamilton's Mercedes W04 leads Mark Webber's Red Bull RB9 Renault out and away from Turn 1 in their battle over third place in 2013. ***Above left:*** Fernando Alonso guides his Ferrari through those sweepers in 2013, with the tower in the background. ***Above right:*** The drivers are shown off to the crowds in the main grandstand before the start in 2013.

Turn 11 •

Gear: **2**

Speed: **99kph (62mph)**

The furthest point of the lap from the paddock is this lefthand hairpin. The drivers arrive at the foot of the slope down from Turn 10 in sixth gear, and this is a definite overtaking opportunity because they have to brake heavily and drop to second gear. As with so many hairpins, especially those where passing is possible on the entry, the exit line can be compromised by others, but a driver arriving alone will turn in from the right and get straight back onto the throttle.

Turn 12 •

Gear: **2**

Speed: **110kph (68mph)**

This tight lefthander is a definite overtaking point, as proved by Mark Webber in 2013, when he pulled off a great passing move on Lewis Hamilton's Mercedes after using the slipstreaming tow that he had been able to harness through the DRS zone down the lengthy straight from Turn 11. Having to trim around 200kph (124mph) from their approach speed means that braking is heavy here, and it's made all the more exciting when drivers' tyres are worn late in the race.

Turn 19 •

Gear: **4**

Speed: **175kph (109mph)**

At the end of the slower section that began at Turn 12, this fast lefthander is approached down a gentle incline behind the paddock, and traction is made hard to come by because the corner has a dipping exit. The sheer diversity of corners around this 20-corner lap shows how the race engineers have to work every bit as hard as the drivers in order to be able to send them out with a car that is set up to manage every type of corner.

Turn 20 •

Gear: **2**

Speed: **99kph (62mph)**

The final corner of the lap is a slow lefthander that is reached just after the cars have negotiated the lowest point of the circuit on the blast from Turn 19, rising up again before the corner. From here, exit speed is everything as strong acceleration onto the start/finish straight can then be carried all the way up the hill towards Turn 1, perhaps enabling a driver to get a tow and thus put them into a position to try a passing move on a car ahead of them.

⬛ Indianapolis

Known around the world as the home of the Indy 500, the Indianapolis Motor Speedway hosted thc United States GP on a specially created circuit using a loop through the infield from 2000 to 2007 and drew huge crowds.

> ❝ It's not a track that flows, which makes it quite difficult.
> The first sector is the only part that has a good feel to it,
> the rest is a bit stop and go. ❞
> *Juan Pablo Montoya*

The Indianapolis Motor Speedway is one of a handful of sporting arenas that is famed outside its own sport. Its legendary status has been acquired through hosting the Indianapolis 500 since 1911, a race that was once the pinnacle of American motorsport and so drew the eyes of the nation. It's a race of faded glory now, and the 4km (2.5-mile) speed oval draws a larger TV audience to watch its annual race for the NASCAR Sprint Cup, the Brickyard 400, an event that it added to its calendar in 1994.

Record books show that the Indianapolis Motor Speedway hosted the United States GP for the first time in 2000, yet this strictly wasn't the first time that it welcomed a round of the World Championship; an anomaly in the rules meant that the Indianapolis 500 was part of the championship each year from 1950 to 1960, but this is discounted because not one F1 team made the journey. Ironically, no sooner had the Indy 500 been dropped from counting towards the World Championship than the F1 constructors started entering cars there, drawn by the huge winner's purse, with Jim Clark being denied victory for Lotus in 1963 before he won there two years later.

The US GP struggled to find a home when its experiment of racing around the streets of Phoenix failed after 1991, and it was decided that this home of American racing would be the best place to revive the race. By taking it to the Indianapolis Motor Speedway, not only did it go to a circuit that existed, with the huge grandstands and infrastructure required already in place, but it went somewhere recognized by fans of other sorts or motor racing who might learn to love F1. The F1 visitors wouldn't race on the oval, though, but on a special circuit made for the occasion that would display the F1 cars' performance characteristics better. The grand prix would be held in early summer, dovetailing nicely with the Canadian GP held a week earlier to help with logistics.

This special track was a combination of the famed banked oval, albeit used in reverse, clockwise direction and a 12-corner loop through the infield. Towered over by the soaring grandstand on their left and the giant control tower and vertiginous scoreboard on their right, the drivers knew that they were somewhere very different as they headed off down the ultra-wide start/finish straight to the first corner. At this point, they turned right and dropped onto the level and started a twisting passage around the grass infield inside the oval's fourth turn before doubling back along a secondary straight alongside the circuit's central access road. More twists followed, around the back of the circuit museum before drivers had to start accelerating as soon as they could out of Turn 11 so that they could power onto the lap's only banked corner, the oval's first turn. With the lap record standing at 214kph (133mph) by the time F1 left after 2006, it was just over 161kph (100mph) slower than the fastest lap achieved on the oval by the Indycar racers; to many American eyes this did F1 no favours as it continued to try to crack the US market where big figures count.

The welcome the F1 teams received when they turned up in 2000 was impressive, though, with 200,000 fans present on race day. Michael Schumacher won on that occasion for Ferrari after surviving contact with McLaren's David Coulthard. Schumacher would win four more times and it would have been five but for a botched attempt to record a dead-heat in 2002, when team-mate Rubens Barrichello was credited with the win by 0.011 seconds. However, the race received a huge loss of momentum after its farcical running in 2005, when the teams using Michelin tyres elected not to race because of the possibility of blow-outs in Turn 13 after this befell Ralf Schumacher in practice. This left just six Bridgestone runners and the crowd showed its disapproval that Ferrari's Michael Schumacher and Barrichello were left with no competition.

After one more visit, F1's time in Indianapolis was done, and it would take six years for F1 to find a far more suitable home at the Circuit of the Americas.

Opposite: The sheer size of the grandstands is shown by this shot of the main straight.

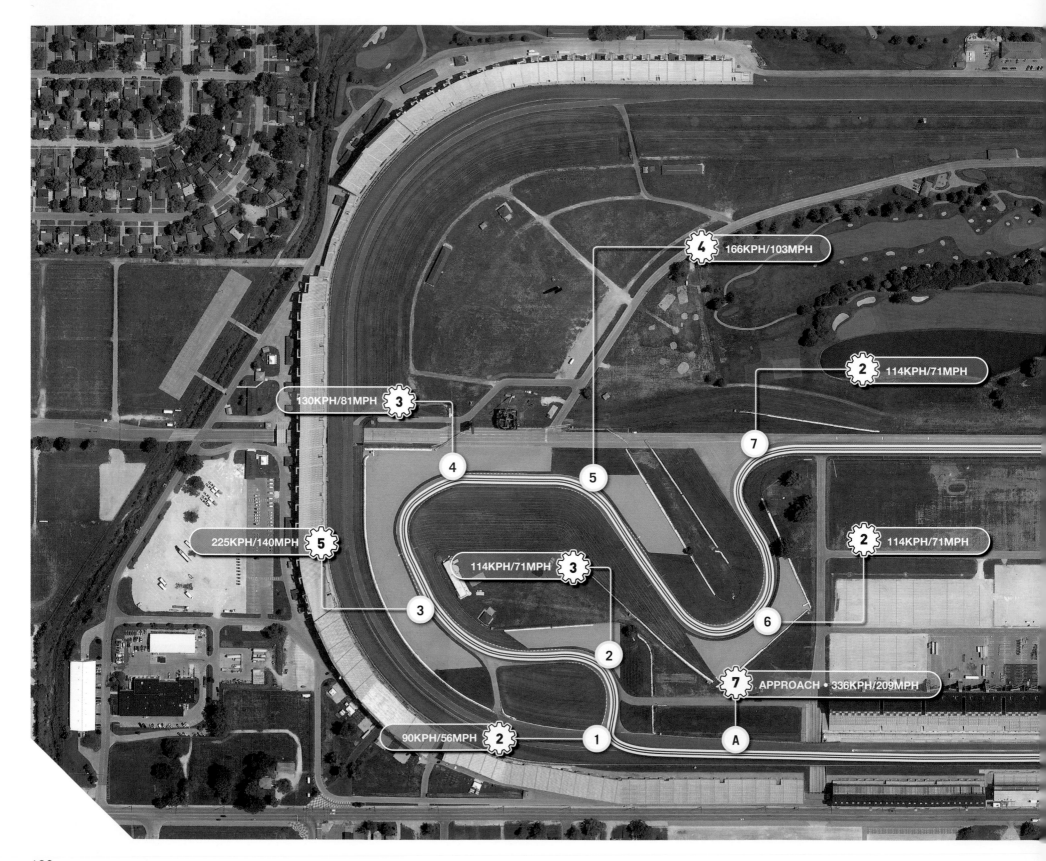

4 166KPH/103MPH

2 114KPH/71MPH

130KPH/81MPH **3**

4

5

7

225KPH/140MPH **5**

2 114KPH/71MPH

114KPH/71MPH **3**

3

6

2

7 APPROACH • 336KPH/209MPH

90KPH/56MPH **2**

1

A

Circuit Guide

While drivers racing on the world famous speed oval have to turn left four times per lap, the F1 racers using the combined oval/infield circuit have a considerably busier time around their 13-turn lap, with a mixture of all corner types.

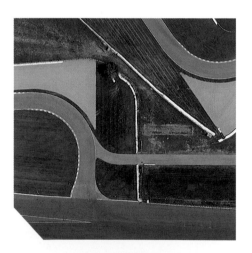

Turn 1 •

Gear: **2**
Speed: **90kph (56mph)**

In the eight grands prix held on this hybrid circuit, this first corner seldom failed to provide entertainment, not just on the opening lap but throughout the race as the lap's main overtaking place. From flat-out in top gear, at 322kph (200mph), drivers have to brake hard and drop to second gear as they peel off the regular oval. The track drops away a little into this 90-degree right and drivers able to approach from the right of the main straight are best placed for a quicker exit.

Turn 2 •

Gear: **3**
Speed: **114kph (71mph)**

The first turn is followed immediately by this lefthand corner and drivers need to get a balance for their car after turning into the corner before flooring the throttle and accelerating across the apex onto the short straight then right flick that follow. In 2006, seven cars were taken out here after Juan Pablo Montoya hit the rear of his McLaren team-mate Kimi Raikkonen's car before clipping Jenson Button, whose Honda then tipped over Nick Heidfeld's BMW Sauber.

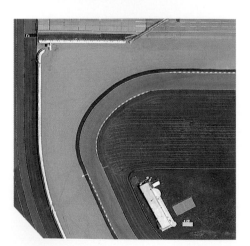

Turn 4 •

Gear: **3**
Speed: **130kph (81mph)**

Having just hit 225kph (140mph) in fifth gear, the early part of the speedway's infield loop reverts to form with this third gear righthander that even tightens towards its exit, slowing the cars further. There's then time for a short burst of throttle application before the drivers have to slow their cars once more for a fifth corner, another righthander. The main grandstands now appear to be far away from the action and equally the speed far away from what's achieved on the oval.

Turn 6 •

Gear: **2**
Speed: **114kph (71mph)**

With the flow still slow, the drivers reach a double-apex lefthander and have to drop to second again. Then, having swept to the righthand side of the track on the exit, drivers need to pull their cars across to the other side so that they can take the widest entry line for the following corner. Every fraction of momentum that can be carried through this second-gear corner is vital because the loop finally gets a straight, running alongside the central access road, the Hulman Boulevard.

Opposite: Felipe Massa leads Nick Heidfeld's BMW Sauber, Heikki Kovalainen's Renault and his Ferrari team-mate Kimi Raikkonen through Turn 2 in 2007. *Above left:* Mika Hakkinen threads his way through the infield on his way to winning the 2001 United States GP for McLaren. *Above right:* Lewis Hamilton leads McLaren team-mate Fernando Alonso through banked Turn 13 in 2007 en route to his second F1 win.

Turn 8 •

Gear: **3**
Speed: **121kph (75mph)**

With cars hitting 298kph (185mph) down the back straight, this is the first corner since Turn 1 to require heavy braking from an appreciable speed. Dropping down three gears to third, drivers must be aware of any drivers looking to dive up their inside in a passing manoeuvre. If there's none, they can stay to the right to take the racing line into this open lefthander. As the corners come thick and fast on the infield, drivers will immediately have to reposition their cars to the left side.

Turn 11 •

Gear: **3**
Speed: **130kph (80mph)**

Turns 9 and 10 have been turned from hairpins to more open corners since F1 last visited, and after Turn 10 drivers immediately have to start focusing on building as much speed as they can to carry onto the banking. This means accelerating hard behind the circuit museum before negotiating this third-gear righthander. Like so many corners through Indianapolis's infield section, it is double-apex in format, with a gentler second part as the drivers aim towards the oval circuit's Turn 2 grandstand.

Turn 12 •

Gear: **5**
Speed: **251kph (156mph)**

A good exit speed from the righthander at Turn 11 is imperative for a driver to carry the maximum speed that he can achieve onto the banked section of the circuit. Turn 12 is taken in fifth gear under full-bore acceleration and the drivers are fleetingly faced with the towering main grandstands directly ahead of them as they hit the banking, before their eyes swing around to the right as they turn onto it. Of course, entry speed will determine terminal velocity.

Turn 13 •

Gear: **6**
Speed: **306kph (190mph)**

The last corner of the lap is the only one in which drivers really ride the banking as it was intended, albeit in the opposite direction to normal. Building speed as they do so, they ought to be hitting 306kph (190mph) at the point at which the corner fades onto the straight, and they flash across the start/finish line famously marked out by the band of bricks. Ralf Schumacher crashed into the outer wall here in both 2004 and 2005, fortunately without serious injury.

🏁Mexico City

Mexico has been in love with Formula One since the early 1960s, when the Rodriguez brothers broke onto the scene. Its grand prix has come and gone since, and Mexico City is now set for its third spell in the World Championship with this high-speed circuit modified to meet contemporary standards.

> ❮❮ I don't think we should be coming here until the track is resurfaced and the run-off areas improved. We go to street circuits with a better surface than we have here. ❯❯
>
> *Ayrton Senna*

Mexico used to be famous for its crazy road race, the Carrera Panamericana. However, it wanted circuit racing too and so this circuit was built in 1962 in the Magdalena Mixhuca area of the capital city. The timing was perfect, as this corresponded with its greatest racing hopes, the Rodriguez brothers, starting to make a splash.

The younger of the Rodriguez brothers, Ricardo, was a Ferrari driver by the age of 19 and he alone filled the grandstands for the first Mexican GP in 1962. This was a non-championship event and Ferrari declined to come, so he was entered in a Rob Walker Racing Lotus. Tragically, he crashed to his death in practice at the slightly banked Peraltada sweeper that concludes the lap.

This was a blow, but the event gained World Championship status for 1963, by which time Ricardo's older brother Pedro had reached F1. Jim Clark won that first one for Lotus and would win again in 1967. It was held as the final round each year from 1964, and there was often extra drama, none more so than in 1964 when BRM's Graham Hill arrived in the championship lead, five points clear of Ferrari's John Surtees. Surtees's team-mate Lorenzo Bandini ran into Hill and damaged his exhausts. Clark now looked set to take victory and title, but an oil leak slowed him and his engine seized on the final lap, allowing Surtees through to grab the crown.

In 1970, 200,000 spectators turned up hoping that local hero Rodriguez could win for BRM. Climbing over the barriers they sat on the grass verges right alongside the track. Despite Rodriguez and Jackie Stewart pleading with them to withdraw, they refused and the race had to go ahead like that. Fortunately, no driver crashed into them as Jacky Ickx motored to victory for Ferrari, but the World Championship decided that enough was enough and would stay away until 1986.

When F1 returned, drivers said that they liked the track, although the bumps that dotted its length were less welcome. The trickiest point, or the one that presented the greatest potential consequences, was the Peraltada, a corner taken flat in fifth gear by those who dared. Naturally, Ayrton Senna was one such driver and he came unstuck at this fearsome righthander in 1991 when he hit the bump towards the exit, lost control and inverted his McLaren in practice. A year later, Senna was caught out by the bumps again, this time going off at the Eses.

Bumps aside, the other main factor that the engineers always had to consider was the thinner air because of the track's altitude of 7350 feet (2,240m) – comfortably the highest elevation out of all the circuits. This meant that the engines struggled to suck in enough oxygen to work efficiently, although turbocharged engines didn't fare as badly.

Gerhard Berger had every reason to like the place, though, as he won on F1's return in 1986, marking not only his but Benetton's first win too.

A decade after F1's last visit in 1992, won by Nigel Mansell for Williams, top level racing returned in 2002 when the ChampCar series headed south of the border, with the Peraltada neutered by the track being fed instead through a baseball stadium that had been built inside the old banked corner. Then, in 2007, the A1GP series made the first of two visits.

For F1's return in 2015, the track has been extended from 4.421km to 4.580km, the extra length being added with a twisting section through the baseball stadium, bisecting the grandstands there before rejoining the old layout halfway around the Peraltada. The main grandstand has been replaced with a new one offering space for hospitality suites and 33 new pit garages. There's also a new control tower by pit entry. Larger temporary grandstands have been erected at the first corner complex, and also at Horquilla, helping to boost the number of grandstand seats to 120,000, with capacity for 30,000 more fans around the circuit perimeter. ■

Opposite: It's Williams in front on Formula One's last but one visit, in 1992, with Nigel Mansell (5) leading the way from Riccardo Patrese as Ferrari's Ivan Capelli crashes in the background.

5 177KPH/110MPH

2 97KPH/60MPH

2 110KPH/68MPH

241KPH/150MPH 6

97KPH/60MPH 3

257KPH/160MPH 6

121KPH/75MPH 3

129KPH/80MPH 3

249KPH/155MPH 6

17

13

16 15 14

12

11

10

9

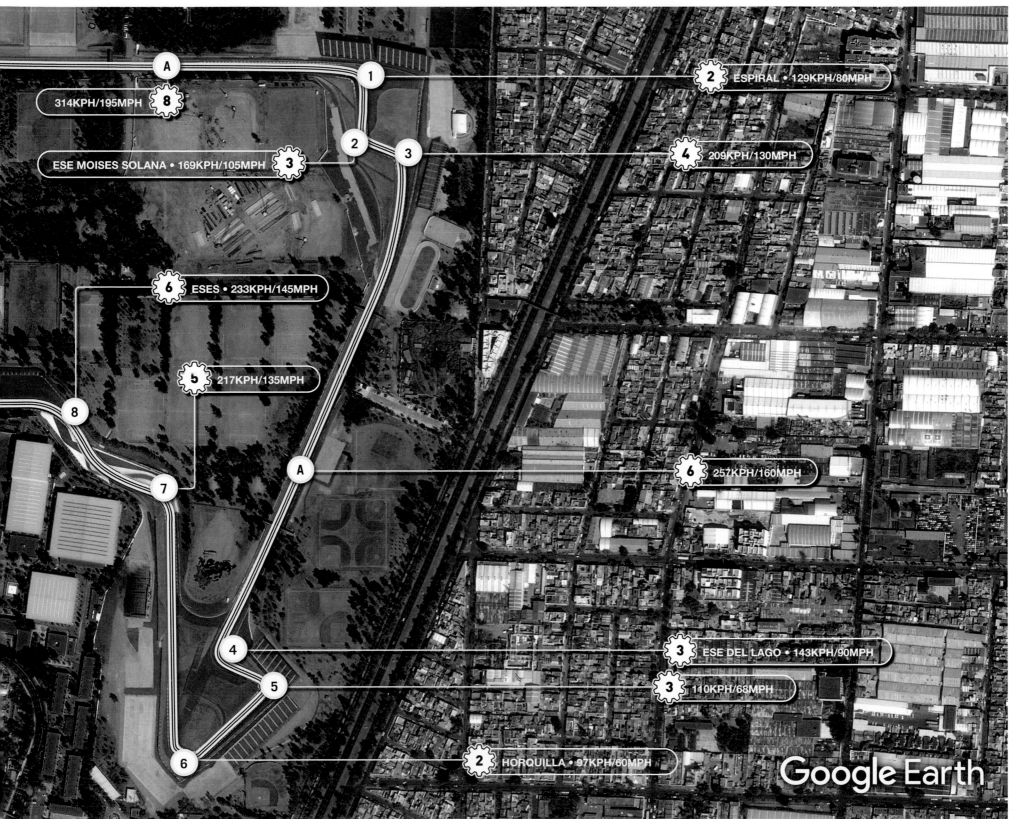

Image © DigitalGlobe © Google 2015

Circuit Guide

Set in parkland, this 4.580 kilometre circuit mixes the high-speed with the sinuous and throws in a stadium section to enhance the drivers' feeling of being in an arena. Hopefully, the bumps for which it became synonymous, will have been flattened.

Turn 1 • Espiral
Gear: **2**
Speed: **129kph (80mph)**

The tree-lined run from the starting grid to the first corner seems to go on and on. It's wide, too, but then it suddenly seems to tighten on the drivers who brake hard and drop down from top gear to perhaps as low as second gear for this 90-degree righthander. Not only is exit speed crucial here, but track position too because it feeds directly into a set of esses, so a passing move not completed out of Turn 1 has every chance of being so by Turn 2.

Turn 2 • Ese Moises Solana
Gear: **3**
Speed: **169kph (105mph)**

The trees are now far from the sides of the track and everything feels more open for the drivers as they position their cars not just for this lefthander but for the righthander that follows directly after it. Unusually for the Autodromo Hermanos Rodriguez, there is a decent amount of run-off here, so drivers are enticed into attempting passing moves, but any loss of momentum out of Turn 3 as a consequence of going off line then costs them down the straight that follows.

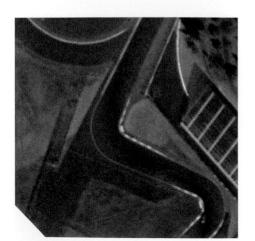

Turn 4 • Ese del Lago
Gear: **3**
Speed: **143kph (90mph)**

Having accelerated past a running track, tennis courts and a park, and under two spectator bridges, the drivers see the grandstands surrounding Horquilla ahead of them, but their course veers to the left first. This requires a drop to third gear and then, almost immediately, drivers must slow further for the even tighter righthander that follows. At the turn-in point there is a sense of space, before a shorter track layout turns right to feed into the famous esses.

Turn 6 • Horquilla
Gear: **2**
Speed: **97kph (60mph)**

This is the furthest point from the pits and has been given an increased identity of its own by increasing the capacity of the grandstands. There will be plenty for fans to see as they can watch the action all the way from Ese del Lago to Turn 7. Immediately in front of them, though, the drivers have to brake hard for a pair of tight righthanders, the second of which is slightly more open, then accelerate up a slight incline towards the esses that run from Turn 7 all the way to Turn 13.

Opposite: Jack Brabham is chased through the Eses by Lotus' Mike Spence in 1964, with the mountains that ring Mexico City as a backdrop. *Above left:* This great shot shows the bewinged cars of 1968 as they run through Ese del Lago on the run to Horquilla. *Above right:* Jacky Ickx leads the way for Ferrari in 1970 followed by Tyrrell's Jackie Stewart and his team-mate Clay Regazzoni, with the crowd overflowing onto the surrounding grass verges

Turn 8 • Eses
Gear: **6**
Speed: **233kph (145mph)**

By this midpoint of the esses, a driver will know clearly whether their car is handling well or not, as the track continues almost relentlessly through a sinuous passage of five twists, going left, right, left, right, left. Making life slightly easier for them, the track is inclined gently towards the apex of each bend to "cup" their cars as the drivers continue to accelerate as hard as they dare. It's a fearsome stretch of track, so drivers will be comforted by the run-off area on either side having been increased.

Turn 11 • Eses
Gear: **6**
Speed: **257kph (160mph)**

The key to this fifth and final swerve through this lengthy run of esses that started back at Turn 8 is for a driver to have their car fully balanced through the right swerve at Turn 10 so that they can skim the apex where the circuit turns left in Turn 11. The short straight that follows down to Turn 12 has the drivers hard on the power as they accelerate past the point where the autodrome's oval circuit feeds onto what would be its back straight.

Turn 12 • Recta del Ovalo
Gear: **3**
Speed: **129kph (80mph)**

When F1 last visited the circuit in 1992, the drivers would have been flat-out at this point, gritting their teeth for the challenge of their sweep into the lap's most daunting corner, the Peraltada. However, it has long been considered too dangerous, with too many bumps and too little run-off. So, the drivers now have to focus instead on braking hard and dropping to third gear for the 90-degree right here which takes them into the baseball stadium, giving them an immediate change of pace and change of feel.

Turn 17 • Peraltada
Gear: **5**
Speed: **177kph (110mph)**

The last corner of the lap is certainly not what it once was. Instead of being taken one gear down from top, as in the 1990s, it's now a much slower bend, through which drivers are hard on the power as they continue accelerating out of the penultimate corner. Every fraction of speed that can be squeezed out by the drivers planting their throttle as they burst from the shade of the grandstand into the full sun of the pit straight is then magnified all the way down the straight.

Melbourne's daytime road traffic seems oblivious to Red Bull's Mark Webber leading Lewis Hamilton in the 2010 Australian Grand Prix.

Chapter 4
Australia

Adelaide

Australia is a country with a rich motor racing pedigree and it had long deserved a grand prix before it finally joined the World Championship in 1985. Adelaide's end-of-season race on its city centre circuit proved to be an instant hit.

> **❝**You sit on the starting grid with fighters roaring overhead and the crowds cheering and you really can't help but be drawn into Adelaide's very special event.**❞**
>
> *Damon Hill*

For a country that takes on and beats the best at various sports, not having a round of the World Championship was galling to its motorsport fans. There was a lively and well-supported national racing scene and there had been an Australian GP since 1928, but this had been a national event held for and largely won by Australian drivers. Run to Formula 5000 regulations in the 1970s, it updated itself to Formula Pacific in the 1980s, but the grids were poor and international interest limited. Yet, with the decision to build a circuit in Adelaide, the nation that had given Formula One three-time World Champion Jack Brabham and, more recently, 1980 champion Alan Jones, was finally granted a seat at motor racing's top table.

Australia's first World Championship round was the final race of the 1985 campaign, and Adelaide landed the right to host this. Having risen from the seed of an idea planted by local businessman Bill O'Gorman, which was then supported by state premier John Bannon, this was something of a coup, as the capital of the state of South Australia had long felt overlooked, with Sydney and Melbourne attracting international recognition for their sights and sporting events. The circuit was laid out in the city's Victoria Park. It was centred on the horse racing course there, and the temporary circuit crossed its layout twice going to and coming back from the section where the F1 cars used the streets

on the perimeter of the park, from Wakefield Street to Dequetteville Terrace.

As soon as the teams and drivers saw it for the first time, they loved it, as there was space for their equipment, a great flow to the lap and a relaxed feel to proceedings: The weather wasn't bad, either. Better still, Adelaide is a small enough city to embrace an event like a grand prix and treated F1's visit as the key ingredient in its annual "Streets Ahead" festival. With the race being the last one of the year, the teams were also more than happy to party once the chequered flag had fallen, with top level concerts adding to the festival feel.

The inaugural grand prix in 1985 was won by Keke Rosberg after a great battle with Ayrton Senna. He had dropped back after the Brazilian damaged his Lotus's front wing against the Finn's Williams before retiring with engine failure. Niki Lauda also led in his final grand prix but wasn't destined to make the finish either, as his McLaren developed a brake problem and he clipped a wall. The following year's race was more famous, though, as its outcome and the championship's, was decided by an incident that is still considered one of F1's iconic moments. Nigel Mansell was in control, all set to become World Champion for the first time when he had a tyre blow at full speed at the end of Dequetteville Terrace, and he did well to wrestle his Williams to a halt in the escape road.

Rain isn't something that one tends to associate with Australia, but it proved a particular problem at Adelaide in the two events that it hit, in 1989 and 1991, as drainage from the circuit was inadequate. This was shown in 1989, when Martin Brundle had spun his Brabham in practice and was immediately hit by Senna, who had been completely unsighted by the hanging spray.

For all the memories of sunshine and rain, plus some great racing, many think of Mika Hakkinen when they think of Adelaide because the Finn had a huge accident in qualifying in 1995 and was fortunate that rapid attention from F1 doctor Prof Watkins kept him alive. That year's race also sticks in the mind, because David Coulthard led but crashed on pit entry, leaving his Williams team-mate Damon Hill free to win, with second-placed Olivier Panis's Ligier fully two laps behind.

However, the party came to an end when Melbourne grabbed the race from them in 1996 and although Adelaide's street circuit continues to be used, its last international event was when the American Le Mans Series hosted a race that started on 31 December 2000 and carried on to New Year's Day 2001. ∎

Opposite: Racing in Adelaide was invariably conducted in a colourful, party atmosphere. This is Ferrari's Gerhard Berger in 1994.

2 RUNDLE ROAD • 129KPH/80MPH

10

5 MALTHOUSE CORNER • 209KPH/130MPH

9

2 EAST TERRACE • 121KPH/75MPH

FLINDERS STREET • 121KPH/75MPH **2**

7

8

APPROACH • 241KPH/150MPH **5**

HUTT STREET • 177KPH/110MPH **4**

5

6

A

WAKEFIELD CORNER • 121KPH/75MPH **2** **4**

1 DEQUETTEVILLE HAIRPIN • 80KPH/50MPH

6 APPROACH • 310KPH/193MPH

3 177KPH/110MPH

5 209KPH/130MPH

5 APPROACH • 225KPH/140MPH

3 SENNA CHICANE • 177KPH/110MPH

2 FOSTER'S CORNER • 97KPH/60MPH

Google Earth

Circuit Guide

This is a circuit of two halves, with its series of 90-degree bends on street junctions contrasting totally with the flat-out blasts and sweeps that follow. It will forever be remembered, though, for Nigel Mansell's blow-out and dive up the escape road.

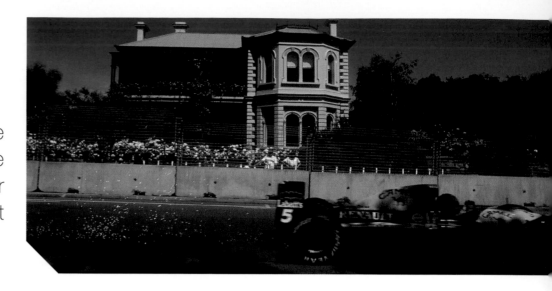

Turn 1–3 • Senna Chicane
Gear: **3**
Speed: **177kph (110mph)**

Starting in the middle of the city's Victoria Park, the circuit certainly doesn't have the feel of the street circuit it becomes and the tree-lined opening esse bend offers a fine flow through its left/right/left sequence. Usually negotiated side-by-side on the opening lap of the race, the key is not so much about achieving optimum exit speed onto the short straight beyond it but simply to avoid any wing-bending contact. Getting to the front on the first lap can be key to making an escape.

Turn 4 • Wakefield Corner
Gear: **2**
Speed: **121kph (75mph)**

The whole feel of the circuit has changed by the time that the drivers reach this, the first of three consecutive 90-degree bends as the lap ventures out of Victoria Park. The park is still on the drivers' right, but there are now shops and houses on their left. Naturally, the drivers' aim is to brake as late as possible for this righthander, but it is very bumpy on the approach, making getting this just right and not sliding onwards extremely difficult.

Turn 5 • East Terrace
Gear: **2**
Speed: **121kph (75mph)**

Finding a flow through the three 90-degree corners is hard and any driver who has failed to pull across to the righthand side of the circuit after rounding Wakefield Corner will struggle to negotiate this lefthander because the straight between them is only short. Going in off line scrubs off what little momentum the drivers have. This was where Michael Schumacher damaged his Benetton when leading in 1994, doing so just out of sight of Damon Hill, who was chasing hard in his Williams.

Turn 6 • Flinders Street
Gear: **2**
Speed: **121kph (75mph)**

The last of the run of 90-degree bends is much the same as the pair that preceded it, with the blast up Flinders Street from East Terrace another short one. Grip is hard to find and the walls surrounding the circuit are there to damage the cars of those who try to go into the corner too fast and get it wrong. This is where Michael Schumacher controversially turned across on Damon Hill in 1994 and settled the outcome of the drivers' title.

Opposite: The circuit's downtown setting is abundantly clear as Nigel Mansell flashes past in his Williams in 1992 *Above left:* The moment of truth approaches at Turn 6 in the 1994 finale as Michael Schumacher is about to swerve his damaged Benetton across into Damon Hill's Williams. *Above right:* Street racing ace Ayrton Senna picks the fastest line through Turn 9 to claim pole for McLaren in 1991.

Turn 7/8 • **Hutt Street**
Gear: **4**
Speed: **177kph (110mph)**

At last, a chance for the drivers to take a corner at speed after the run of 90-degree bends. This left/right sweeper is taken in fourth gear and drivers are naturally keen to start building a flow as the circuit opens out again. However, this corner is made difficult by the camber being adverse. With a concrete wall there to greet them should they get it wrong, it is what Mike Hakkinen once described as a "confidence corner". There's then a short straight to yet another 90-degree bend.

Turn 10 • **Malthouse Corner**
Gear: **5**
Speed: **200kph (130mph)**

The circuit opens up after Turn 9 and this fast right kink leads on to the only appreciable straight of the lap, so it's vital for a driver to get a clean run through this fifth gear corner. However, the kerbs are high on the inside and Mika Hakkinen was fortunate to survive a huge impact here in qualifying in 1995, when his McLaren suffered a rear tyre deflation, vaulted the inside kerbs and hit the outside wall hard. An emergency tracheotomy saved his life.

Turn 11 • **Dequetteville Hairpin**
Gear: **1**
Speed: **80kph (50mph)**

The savage change from flat-out in top gear to heavy braking and dropping down the gearbox to first is required for this righthand hairpin. It offers undoubtedly the main opportunity for overtaking if a driver has worked a tow down the straight. Nigel Mansell, though, discovered in 1986 that it's impossible to turn in to the corner if one of your rear tyres has exploded. He was forced to wrestle his Williams to a halt, along with his world title hopes.

Turn 15 • **Foster's Corner**
Gear: **2**
Speed: **97kph (60mph)**

After a tight left and a sweeping esse behind the paddock, the drivers reach the final corner of the lap. It's another hairpin, but it's way less extreme than the Dequetteville Hairpin and can be taken a gear higher. The bumpy nature of the circuit both on the way in and the way out make braking and acceleration difficult as drivers try to get themselves into a good position to make an attacking run past the pits towards the sweepers that open the lap.

Melbourne

Racing in Melbourne has proved a hit since the Australian GP was moved there in 1996, with the city proving a fun place to be and the grandstands and spectator banking filled to capacity on each of the meetings' three days.

> **"**I love Melbourne, but not only the track, as the atmosphere around the grand prix is fantastic and all the people here enjoy the whole weekend. **"**
>
> *Fernando Alonso*

Adelaide was distraught when its deal to host the Australian GP came to a close at the end of 1995 and the race was moved to Melbourne's Albert Park, and even pushed to host a second Australian race under the convenience title of the Pacific GP. This never happened and Melbourne has been Australia's home of F1 ever since, with its sports-mad citizens having New South Wales premier Jeff Kennett to thank for this.

Kennett negotiated a deal with Bernie Ecclestone and the site he chose for the temporary circuit was in Albert Park, a municipal park to the south of the city centre. Albert Park had hosted racing before, hosting the Australian GP on a temporary layout around the park's lake in 1953 and 1956, when it was a non-championship event largely for driver from Australia and New Zealand. The winner of the second of these, though, was a young British driver by the name of Stirling Moss in a works Maserati, who also won the Tourist Trophy sportscar race at the same event. Local opposition then led to its closure and eventually to the opening of two circuits on the outskirts of Melbourne, at Calder and Sandown Park.

There was strong opposition from a handful of locals, who felt that putting a grand prix circuit in Albert Park again would be environmentally unsound and would lead to the despoiling of the park. Consequently, considerable steps were taken to minimize its impact, with the organizers agreeing to dredge the lake and upgrade the somewhat rundown park's sports facilities as recompense.

The lap they laid out is a mixture of slow and medium-speed corners as it runs in a clockwise direction around the lake in the middle of the park, with the only truly fast corners being Turns 11 and 12, where the circuit swerves left and then right on the far side of the lake. Otherwise, there are a predominance of medium-speed corners, yet the lap still has a good flow. Furthermore, the fans enjoy excellent viewing from grandstands and hospitality decks that line much of the route. Those who choose to sit in the stands overlooking the first three corners are almost invariably treated to some extremely close racing, peppered with incident on the opening lap.

Australians are accustomed to an extremely high level of sporting event, so the grand prix programme is more packed here than anywhere else to keep them entertained, with almost continuous support races whenever the F1 cars are not on track through the three days. In turn, the teams enjoy the city's high quality of hotels and restaurants, while they also appreciate the ease of access to the circuit, because thousands of fans eschew arriving by car and come in by tram, thus reducing the car parking queues that can be such a hassle at other venues.

The city's inaugural World Championship event kicked off the 1996 World Championship, just four months after F1 left Adelaide for good, and was won by Damon Hill for Williams. He was beaten to pole position by team mate Jacques Villeneuve, and after Martin Brundle had an aerial shunt in his Jordan and necessitated a restart, Hill and Villeneuve traded the lead until debutant Villeneuve was told to slow because his Renault engine was blowing out oil. Having let Hill by, he slowed his pace and yet was still able to finish second. The way that Melburnians supported the event, packing out the grandstands, showed that they loved F1's visit every bit as much as their neighbours in Adelaide had. Since that first race, Melbourne's grand prix boss Ron Walker has driven the event forward, made it very much a key part of the World Championship, as a vibrant place to open the season, with capacity crowds helping to show F1 in its rudest health.

Well attended, with the added twist of being the first time each year that the fans get to see how the new cars compare with each other, Melbourne's grand prix is now very much part of the establishment. It's one of Melbourne's sporting crown jewels, along with its hosting of the Australian Open tennis tournament, Test matches at The Melbourne Cricket Ground and the best-attended Australian Rules Football matches. ∎

Opposite: Nico Rosberg runs flat-out around the far side of Albert Park's lake in his Mercedes in 2013, with the city centre as his backdrop.

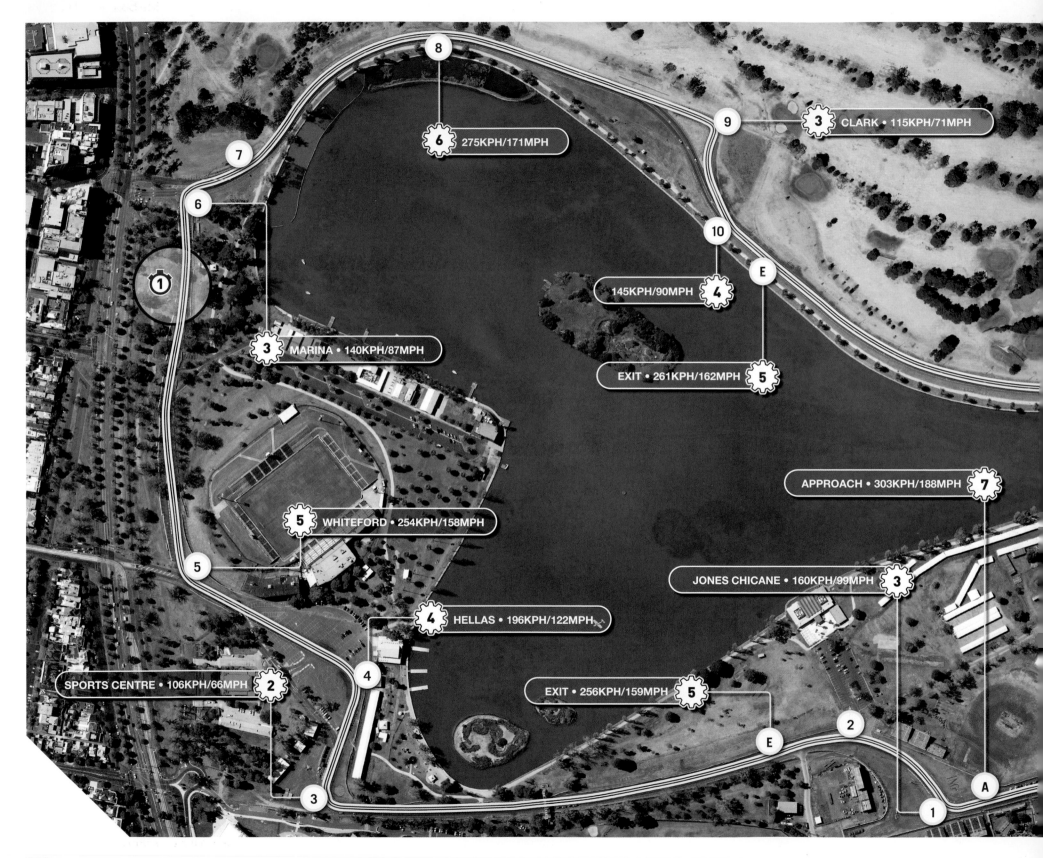

8 275KPH/171MPH

9 **3** CLARK • 115KPH/71MPH

6

7

6

10

E

145KPH/90MPH **4**

1

3 MARINA • 140KPH/87MPH

EXIT • 261KPH/162MPH **5**

APPROACH • 303KPH/188MPH **7**

5 WHITEFORD • 254KPH/158MPH

5

JONES CHICANE • 160KPH/99MPH **3**

4 HELLAS • 196KPH/122MPH

SPORTS CENTRE • 106KPH/66MPH **2**

EXIT • 256KPH/159MPH **5**

4

E

2

3

1

A

ASCARI • 143KPH/89MPH ③

WAITE • 248KPH/154MPH ⑤

12

A

13

APPROACH • 282KPH/175MPH ⑥

11

②

⑤ 226KPH/140MPH

② SENNA • 89KPH/55MPH

15

14

STEWART • 166KPH/103MPH ③

16

MELBOURNE

③

PROST • 180KPH/112MPH ④

Google Earth

Image © 2014 Sinclair Knight Merz & Furgo © Google 2014

Circuit Guide

This has always been a difficult circuit for teams to launch their new cars on at the start of the season, because it's a real mixture, with every type of corner except for any really high-speed ones.

Turn 1 • **Jones Chicane**
Gear: **3**
Speed: **160kph (99mph)**

This opening corner has been the scene of more clashes between cars than almost any other used by F1. The nature of the corner, as it folds back through 90 degrees to channel the cars to the right and almost straight into Turn 2, explains why many an opening lap move goes wrong here, with drivers lured to make rash passing moves by the feeling of space. Famously, Ralf Schumacher got it wrong here in 2002, when his Williams was launched off Rubens Barrichello's Ferrari.

Turn 3 • **Sports Centre**
Gear: **2**
Speed: **106kph (66mph)**

The drivers must feel as though the walls are closing in on them as they exit Turn 2 and the track becomes flanked by walls and the trees behind as they accelerate down the straight to Turn 3. Martin Brundle will certainly recall the bunching that can happen as the cars brake heavily for this 100-degree righthander, because his Jordan clipped another car in the braking zone in 1996 and flew straight on into the mercifully large run-off area that opens outahead of them.

Turn 5 • **Whiteford**
Gear: **5**
Speed: **254kph (158mph)**

After fleetingly enjoying the feeling of space through Turn 4 as it feeds the cars to their left through the car parking area of the Lakeside Stadium, the track immediately narrows down again as it enters its second run funnelled between temporary concrete walls. This right flick is fast, taken in fifth gear, and drivers tend to ride over the inside kerb here as they attempt to take the straightest line onto the short straight that follows.

Turn 6 • **Marina**
Gear: **3**
Speed: **140kph (87mph)**

Running in the shade of the trees that line either flank of the approach to this corner alongside Albert Road, with drivers arriving at 290kph (180mph), Turn 6 requires heavy braking because it's a second-gear corner with an exit that needs to be taken with accuracy. The track then immediately starts to swerve to the left again as the drivers advance to the "lakeside" section of the lap. Many drivers have attempted to go in too fast here and slid off into the vast gravel trap.

Opposite: Sebastian Vettel leads the field through Turn 4 on the opening lap in 2013, but victory would be taken by Lotus's Kimi Raikkonen. *Above left:* Spectators line almost the full length of the circuit. Here, they watch Williams's Pastor Maldonado brake hard for Turn 13. *Above right:* Fernando Alonso leads Adrian Sutil as they accelerate through Turn 2.

Turn 9 • Clark
Gear: **3**
Speed: **115kph (71mph)**

Just as the drivers start to get into a flow through the sweeping corners around the far side of Albert Park's lake, they're hauled back by this tight righthander. If taken right, riding the kerbs a little but not too much, this is a simple chicane. If got wrong, it can waste momentum, so exerting a little caution here is wise because good exit speed is vital for a driver to attain the highest speed their car can manage for a blast that will take them all the way to Turn 13.

Turn 12 • Waite
Gear: **5**
Speed: **248kph (154mph)**

Taken in fifth gear, drivers gain sight of this sweeper only after they have come around the sloping spectator banking that blocks their view until they're hitting the apex at high-speed Turn 11. They have to balance their cars as they fleetingly get a view of the tall buildings on Queens Road and haul their cars to the right through what is effectively a very rapid chicane. There's a great feeling of space again because there are wide grass verges on either side of the track.

Turn 13 • Ascari
Gear: **3**
Speed: **143kph (89mph)**

The high-speed lakeside section of the lap comes to an end here as the track tightens up again at this near 90-degree righthander that turns around the end of the lake. The flow reverts more to how it was through the first few corners of the lap, with a run of similar corners to follow. The track dips under the shade of the trees again on its exit and, providing a driver has resisted any attack into Turn 13, they should stay ahead for the rest of the lap.

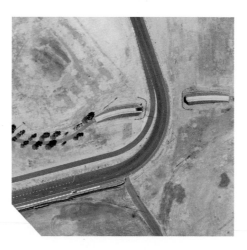

Turn 16 • Prost
Gear: **4**
Speed: **180kph (112mph)**

After tight Turn 15, this final corner looks rather simpler to negotiate, but there's not a lot of space on the outside of the righthander and the desire to carry as much speed as possible out of this corner to perhaps build towards a passing move into Turn 1 has led to drivers running wide over the kerbs. The most famous of these incidents came when Michael Schumacher did just that in 2003 before hitting the outside wall with his Ferrari and spinning across the track.

Great Drivers & Great Moments

As Melbourne has, more often than not, hosted the opening round of the season, the pack has been shuffled, so the world's eyes are always fixed on Albert Park to see who will be the first to lay down a marker for the season ahead.

Opposite top: Mika Hakkinen leads McLaren team-mate David Coulthard down to the first corner in 1998, and this would have ramifications after the Finn mistakenly called at the pits.

Opposite bottom left: Giancarlo Fisichella got his 2005 campaign off to a winning start thanks to clever race tactics by Renault.

Opposite bottom right: Jenson Button looked out of a drive for 2009, when Honda Racing folded, then bounced back to win the opener with Brawn GP.

Great Drivers

 Michael **Schumacher**
Melbourne wins – 4

By Michael Schumacher's lofty standards, four wins from his 14 outings in Melbourne was a poor haul. However, his victories were all important because they marked the start of a campaign, setting the tone for the rest of the year. The first of these was lucky; the McLarens led but broke down in 2000. After that, he was trailed home by David Coulthard in 2001, then won as he pleased after his rivals were caught up in a first corner shunt in 2002 and dominated in 2004.

 Jenson **Button**
Melbourne wins – 3

The collapse of Honda Racing left Jenson without a drive for 2009. Fortunately, not only was it resurrected as Brawn GP, but its car was the class of the field, allowing him to win the season's opening race in Australia then win five more to become a dominant champion. Following on from that incredible year, many thought that his move to McLaren for 2010 would see him playing second fiddle to Lewis Hamilton, but Jenson came here for the second round and won to confirm his credentials.

 David **Coulthard**
Melbourne wins – 2

In becoming the second winner in Melbourne, in 1997 at the start of his second year with McLaren, David was able to put behind him the embarrassment of crashing into the pitwall at the final race in Adelaide in 1995. He was helped by three factors: Eddie Irvine taking favourite Jacques Villeneuve out at the first corner, Heinz-Harald Frentzen's Williams hitting brake problems, and by pitting just once. The Scot would win again in 2003, rising from 11th to win a race of changing fortunes.

 Kimi **Raikkonen**
Melbourne wins – 4

This flying Finn achieved a dream start to his first spell at Ferrari when he won in 2007 after starting from pole. He controlled the race from the front, beating Fernando Alonso's McLaren easily. Then, having returned from his years away in rallying in 2012, Kimi marked the start of his second year back with Lotus by winning in 2013. This was a surprise because everyone thought that a Red Bull would win, but Kimi worked his way forward from seventh through better tyre preservation than his rivals.

Great Moments

1996 **Williams** duo fight for glory on Melbourne's debut

Albert Park's first race of the modern era, in 1996, nearly produced a shock result. It wouldn't have been shocking because a Williams won; this had been the team to beat for years. It would have shocked because the driver at the wheel of the Williams set for victory was Jacques Villeneuve, who was making his F1 debut. Unfortunately for him, his engine started losing oil and so the team told him to let team-mate Damon Hill past. Villeneuve was still able to finish, in second.

1998 David **Coulthard** lets Mika Hakkinen through to win

The outcome of 1998's opening race remains one of the oddest in F1 history. It was clear from the start of practice that McLaren had the best car. Mika Hakkinen and David Coulthard duly filled the front row and raced away untroubled but, midway through the race, Hakkinen thought he'd been called to the pits. He hadn't, so this detour dropped him behind Coulthard. Then, late in the race, the Scot let him past, honouring a pre-race agreement that whichever led into the first corner would win.

2005 Giancarlo **Fisichella** makes a winning return

Giancarlo's return to the team he'd raced for when it was Benetton kicked off in the best way possible when he grabbed pole for the first race of 2005 after benefiting from rain that arrived before his leading rivals had made their runs. Giancarlo then started his Renault with a heavy fuel load and this enabled him to run a long opening stint and it set him up for victory, although the drive of the day came from team-mate Fernando Alonso who rose from 13th to third.

2009 Jenson **Button** gives Brawn its first win

The collapse of Honda Racing and the subsequent reinvention of the team as Brawn GP left few expecting this midfield team to shine, but it very much did just that at the opening race of 2009. Helped by its use of double diffusers, the team's BGP 001s were the class of the field and Jenson Button not only qualified on pole ahead of team-mate Rubens Barrichello but then led every lap to lead home an extraordinary one-two finish for the team ahead of Jarno Trulli's Toyota.

Index

Left: The sun goes down on the Yas Marina Circuit, Abu Dhabi, in November 2013.

Credits

The publishers would like to thank the following sources for their kind permission to reproduce the pictures in this book.

All Formula One Grand Prix Action Photography: © LAT Photographic

Special thanks to Zoë Schafer, Kevin Wood and Tim Clarke at LAT for their expert knowledge and assistance researching the photography for this project.

Every effort has been made to acknowledge correctly and contact the source and/ or copyright holder of each picture and Carlton Books Limited apologizes for any unintentional errors or omissions that will be corrected in future editions of this book.

Bibliography

From Brands Hatch to Indianapolis, Tommaso Tommasi, Hamlyn, 0 600 33557 7
Grand Prix Battlegrounds, Christopher Hilton, Haynes Publishing, 978 1 84425 694 5
The International Motor Racing Guide, Peter Higham, David Bull, 1 893618 20 X
The World Atlas of Motor Racing, Joe Saward, Hamlyn, 0 600 564053
World Motor Racing Circuits, Peter Higham & Bruce Jones, Andre Deutsch, 0 233 99619 2
Plus articles from *Autosport*, *F1 Racing* and *Motor Sport* magazines